Seas and Inland Journeys

Seas and Inland Journeys

LANDSCAPE AND CONSCIOUSNESS
FROM WORDSWORTH TO ROETHKE

James Applewhite

The University of Georgia Press   *Athens*

© 1985 by the University of Georgia Press
Athens, Georgia 30602

Designed by Dariel Mayer
Set in Mergenthaler Linotron 202 Palatino
The paper in this book meets the guidelines for permanence
and durability of the Committee on Production Guidelines
for Book Longevity of the Council on Library Resources.

Printed in the United States of America
90 89 88 87 86 85   6 5 4 3 2 1

Library of Congress Cataloging in Publication Data

Applewhite, James.
  Seas and inland journeys.

  Includes index.
  1. English poetry—19th century—History and
criticism. 2. Landscape in literature. 3. American
poetry—20th century—History and criticism. I. Title.
PR585.L27A67 1985   821'.9'0936   85-1165
ISBN 0-8203-0795-5 (alk. paper)

CONTENTS

PREFACE

The presence of typical Romantic structures and transactions in Modernist and late Modernist poetry (juxtapositions of observer/landscape, house/nature, ship/sea images, with significant interaction between contrasted halves) demonstrates how Romantic themes continue in some sense to be our own. The Romantic legacy, insufficiently acknowledged by earlier Modernist writers and critics, has continued to exert an influence quite at variance with the ostensible rejection of certain attitudes, sources, and structures by the poets who shaped the aesthetic premises of our own time. In many Romantic and Modernist poems, landscape or nature is a symbol for the unconscious, in contrast to the poet's rational ego. This contrast is artistically fruitful so long as it does not harden into rigid opposition. Interaction between the more conscious and the less conscious areas of the total psyche is projected not only into a dialectical imagery but also into narrative patterns I call *rituals of resuscitation*. The incompletion or failure of this conscious/unconscious interaction, beginning in Romanticism, becomes increasingly characteristic of postromantic work. The more explicit acknowledgment of psychological concerns and crises by the late Modernist poet Theodore Roethke provides a suggestive parallel to earlier poets who were his forebears and sources.

The insights presented here are those of a practicing poet who has had a closer relation than that of many recent poets to scholarship in the fields of Romantic and Modernist poetry. My arguments take their particular shape from a career marked, for example, by my hearing a lecture on Carl Jung by the novelist Caroline Gordon while an undergraduate in the 1950s, by association a bit later with that poetic admirer of Wordsworth, Randall Jarrell, and with the great Modernist poet-critic Allen Tate—and, above all, by my assimilation of the peculiarly southern neoromanticism represented in the Poe-Faulkner tradition in fiction.

No poet can entirely account for his sources, and yet, by breathing the air of a time, a poet necessarily reflects that time in his work. In this study I assert certain insights into Romantic and Modernist poetry and the relationship between them—insights that seem to me highly relevant to our contemporary attempt at aesthetic self-definition. I apologize in advance that the literarily biographical aspects of this study were, given my format, not more acknowledgeable, and that the totality of information and influences behind a given perception was not always present to my awareness. I am a poet using scholarship to support positions that have arisen, finally, from my own experience of the creative process. I hope this book may be read as a new attempt to evaluate and understand the relation of major Romantic texts to major texts of the twentieth century, from the perspective of the creative act and those unconscious sources it must utilize. More than anything else, this book represents my struggle to understand and characterize those poets and poems that have most deeply influenced my own approach to writing—an approach that must inevitably be, in many respects, characteristic of the age.

ABBREVIATIONS

Auto.: W. B. Yeats, *The Autobiography of W. B. Yeats* (New York: Macmillan, 1953).

C.W.: *The Collected Works of C. G. Jung*, trans. R. F. C. Hull, 18 vols. (Princeton, N.J.: Princeton University Press, 1953–68). Cited by volume and paragraph: e.g., *C.W.* 9, par. 525.

E.&I.: W. B. Yeats, *Essays and Introductions* (New York: Macmillan, 1961).

Myth.: W. B. Yeats, *Mythologies* (New York: Macmillan, 1959).

Poems of S.T.C.: *The Poems of Samuel Taylor Coleridge*, edited by E. H. Coleridge, 2 vols. (Oxford: Clarendon, 1960).

Poems of W.B.Y.: *The Collected Poems of W. B. Yeats* (New York: Macmillan, 1956).

Prel.: *The Prelude 1799, 1805, 1850*, ed. Jonathan Wordsworth, M. H. Abrams, and Stephen Gill (New York: W. W. Norton, 1979).

P.W.: *The Poetical Works of William Wordsworth*, ed. Ernest de Selincourt and Helen Darbishire, 5 vols. (Oxford: Clarendon, 1940–49).

INTRODUCTION

A veiled or explicit meditation on origins is central to critical debate, especially in the case of the Romantics. English poets from Wordsworth to Keats (and beyond) appear to have projected the experience of psychic origination into the topographical structures we characterize, in their mimetic function, as landscapes. Mythologies of origin attach to and surround these individuating foot journeys, climbs, and adventures on water that were the objective occasions of memorable poems. The Western myth of cosmos created out of chaos, with a fall somehow necessarily annexed, provides a context within which the interaction of poetic consciousness with a landscape it experiences as its antecedent, its fertilizing source, its "beginning-in-unconsciousness," may be perceived in an aspect of psychological encounter. This study suggests, among other things, that the referentiality of a Romantic text is often self-referentiality, for the buried self of the poet may take over landscape as expressive image. Thus, the movement beyond mimesis treated by Abrams's *The Mirror and the Lamp* implies landscape painting as a kind of weather of the spirit rather than the portrait's social face, musical mood (and mode) through quality of sound rather than through the more formal satisfaction of conventions, and the connotative moans and hums of vowels and consonants rather than the denotations of intellectual persuasion, in poems whose content was increasingly feeling.[1]

In this investigation of the subjective experience of landscape as recorded in poems, we will assume the literate reader's knowledge of that fundamental distinction between *conscious* and *unconscious*, as posited by psychoanalysis—now a commonplace of our age. Our readings, though generally psychological, will not be psychoanalytic; we will always avoid merely translating or reducing the poem into the terms of another discipline. Whatever significant tensions between consciousness and landscape (or tower and water, or ship and sea) we analyze will always be elements of the text, and terminology will arise from the text and its historical situation. Psychological signatures or significations (in Riffaterre's sense, as opposed to the "meaning" of mimesis) will be read as a function of tensions between areas of the poem's topography.[2] Although far removed in attitude from the skepticism of deconstruction, this consideration of the major metaphoric structures utilized by the Romantics and their recent successors operates in most respects within the premises established by Derrida himself. The dismantling of theologies, mythologies, metaphysics leads inevitably back to the poetic psyche as source of reference. Beneath the dazzling surface of the Derridian texts, one recognizes a neo-Freudian basis of terminology and approach.

Our topographical paradigm representing consciousness and its origins, with the related mythology of creation and fall, is very much within the "logocentric" pattern that Derrida deconstructs in *Of Grammatology*. Some meditation on the method and strategies of his readings, especially in respect to accounts of contact between primitive and civilized peoples, and of the beginnings of language, are therefore in order. The initial identification which he wishes to expose, present even in Saussure, is that between the sinful, fallen body and writing itself, as opposed to the recoverable purity of breath, speech, logos. Writing, he argues, has been seen as a kind of original sin of language, from which the linguist must try to extract an original and natural relationship between speech and inscription, subject and object. Derrida then chooses for analysis texts by Levi-Strauss concerning the first contact with writing on the part of a preliterate tribe, and Rousseau's *Essay on the Origin of Languages*.[3]

He wishes us to see the mythic thrusts behind these supposedly literal attempts at anthropological and historical explanation. The leader of the Nambikwara imitates the anthropologist's writing with traced lines of his own and pretends to read from this list, thus allying himself with the knowledge of civilization and enhancing his power. The anthropologist sees a mythological pattern, making a "more or less overt reference to the idea of a fall into evil from the innocence of the word." Rousseau proposes a distinction analogous to the primitive/cultured boundary traced by Levi-Strauss: a contrast between northern languages, associated with a harsh, consonantal clarity of articulation, and southern languages, associated with the vowel-rich affective power of their song-like origin. Rousseau sees the human race itself as "born in warm lands," and the speech of these peoples (kept by warmth closer to the primal condition) as still "song, a language of pure accentuation."[4]

We are to see the fallacy of such imagined beginnings in a "warm South," or natural innocence. Derrida distrusts our habitual contrasts of nature/culture, north/south, before/after (the time before writing, or northern articulation, seems "timeless"). As a philosopher of language, he is bound to the proposition that from "the moment that there is meaning there are nothing but signs." If consciousness is identical with language, and if linguistic signifiers are accorded their significations by the "differences" between other signifiers, then language/consciousness can never step outside its own self-enclosed system to contemplate an origin prior to words. Among his more obscure passages are those that attempt to approach the question of origins from within the system of language. "The [linguistic] trace is not only the disappearance of origin—within the discourse that we sustain and according to the path that we follow it means that the origin did not even disappear, that it was never constituted except reciprocally by a nonorigin, the trace, which thus becomes the origin of the origin." The beginning of culture, of society itself, is in Derrida's terms a similar, ungraspable paradox. "This *birth of society* is therefore not a passage, it is a point, a pure, fictive and unstable, ungraspable limit. One crosses it in attaining it. Beginning, it begins to decay. The South passes into its own North."[5]

But though Derrida wishes to show the self-contradiction inherent in any idea that a purer beginning (like Eden) could have preceded this linguistic consciousness we experience as fallen, the mythic dimensions of these texts are precisely what we find most interesting. The deconstruction of Rousseau's rather charming Genesis story does not dislodge its suasion as account of "milk-tongue" creation (Donald Hall) from preconscious sources. Words are a record in part after the event. They existed once in a rich mix of emotion, association, subliminal suggestion in many directions at once, the possibilities moved toward more exciting because open, unexplored. As the nightingale sings, the poet feels drawn out of self toward a "warm South" associated with wine and thus with the entire Provençal landscape of dance, song, and intuitive fullness of existence. But "Fled is that music": when the poet wakes to this realization—that the nightingale identified with the south of affective, vowel-laden utterance (like the south of Rousseau) has ceased its song—then the poet's own music of difference, of problematic waking and sleep, must follow. It is enabled to follow by the first song, but that is then unavailable except as recollection and fading vision. The second song is finite, all we have, and still a reminiscence. Memory is important in Romantic poetry as the conscious mind's retention of the vision it has "already" lost, and "now" begins to sing of—elegiacally. The fall of both consciousness and language—perhaps of consciousness in language—occurs in/after the moment of conception, which has experienced itself as prior to sequence, or time.

Romantic inspiration occurs as the unconscious has opened: "The hiding-places of man's power / Open; I would approach them, but they close" (Wordsworth, *Prel.* 12:279–80). For Shelley, "the mind in creation is as a fading coal" ("A Defence of Poetry"). But as thought-image becomes language, the first point of the conception is "always already" moving beyond recovery and contemplation. Derrida's famous phrase is thus an indication (and a screen blocking our view) of that state prior to the deferring differences of language. Yet these very marks of "differance" distinguish sills or thresholds across which transactions have occurred. The windows so central to Keats's lyrics mark a distinction between the poet in his limiting/enabling condition of consciousness/language, and the landscape visions they open upon. These "magic casements" are the rectangles that impose order on "perilous seas." They are representative of those structures through which the poet sees his landscape of origin, in part by defining his distance and difference from it.

There is a typological resemblance among those texts that attract Derrida's critical energies. Whether those by Levi-Strauss and Rousseau in *Of Grammatology,* or by Freud in *Writing and Difference,* the accounts he dismantles resemble or echo not only our central Western myth of creation and fall but also the Romantic narrative of consciousness itself in its self-perception on waking. The prior sleep is preliterate tribal society, or a mythic south, or the unconscious—parallel to Milton's Eden born of chaos, and the Romantics' nature. Such "base-superstructure" models work as schemes for tracing the mind's response to experience; many poetic texts testify to this fact. In effect, there is agreement on the necessary terms of opposition: nature/culture, affective inflection/articulation, Paradise/history, landscape/consciousness. The difference is in the valuation of, and emphasis on, the areas of investigation. Deconstruction seems to refuse credence to the term *before.* But it may be that the human mind cannot function in an epistemological mode without some myth of origin or first cause. Cosmology must have its Genesis or Big Bang. The world we know demands some turtle upon whose back it can rest, even though that reptilian "supreme fiction" may require whole bestiaries below it.

The question as Derrida poses it is really whether any meditation on origins is possible. Somewhat as in the ontological argument for the existence of God, we have suggested that this meditation is possible because it everywhere exists. It exists in the many forms of the myth of creation and fall, and that myth in a sense implies a structure. Chaos/Eden is the beginning point providing the condition for succeeding sequence (time). It is the sea of no limit, no form, upon whose surface or shore must appear the ship or tower (or Caspar David Friedrich's lonely monk) representing consciousness' self-definition. This source of not-yet-being is precondition for being/becoming; it provides the measureless making measure possible (as well as necessary and interesting). It is the infinite dark *down* from or within which a finite light dawns upward.

The poem defining itself within the blank landscape of the

poet's brain incites a parallel fascination with accounts of creation. The poet has had a direct experience of a source of writing prior to articulated language. This "unexpected supply" (Frost) seems a darkness, a chaos, precisely because it is prior to utterance. The Wordsworthian walker over the landscape, muttering to himself the poem as it forms, already embodies the shape of what he will signify. The image of the psychic boat moving on the water is another such structure with the impact of a meaning. It is a graphic representation of that activity by the mind that takes place in the writing of the poem. The creation poem acknowledges its act of ordination, and the major Romantic landscapes are covert creation poems. The voyage to order is never complete, remains continually provisional. But *images* of successful navigation are embodied as poems: measured, order-assertive arrangements fixed within the flux of discourse. Elegies elegize, among other things, their own fall into the fixity (and limitation) of one language-order. But they console that melancholy by the seemingly endless multiplication of relationships within their finitude of elements. So creation poems construct themselves in the human cosmos of language and internalize a surrogate chaos-principle: the circular illogic of repetition, variation, echo, subliminal suggestion. Their habitual union of structure and landscape, boat and water, is a metaphor to take seriously. In it consciousness self-represents its capacity to symbolize with "fixities and definites" (Coleridge, *Biographia Literaria*, 13), while implying an endless context of psyche, history, language, stretching out of sight to either side and below like the surface of the earth.

With the cooperative, attentive steerage of a helmsman, observer and participant (Coleridge imaged a charioteer with loosely held reins, *Biographia Literaria*, 14), the poem's little ship, like Lawrence's self voyaging back from near oblivion ("The Ship of Death"), tacks into articulation, into definition. Critics argue the text, stressing it to reveal its unconsciousnesses at variance with stated purpose, its blindnesses cohabiting with insight. And these marks are there, legacies of the chaos before literate closure. They are part of the ambiguity that continues resonance, permits fluctuating combinations and permutations between the finite verbal signs. The most comprehensive metaphor creating and containing the class of these deviances toward the left hand, these slips of lip and tongue toward uncountenanced suggestion, is the underworld that originates and receives. A related form is the sea. That ancestral echo-chamber, the underground ocean in "Kubla Khan," is completest of these mother lodes representing the affective unconsciousness prior to the articulations of consciousness/language. The souths of Rousseau and Keats move downward toward this source of speech/song.

For those who have never accompanied Coleridge or Tennyson or Baudelaire or Rimbaud on the voyage, the waves are difficult to characterize. The characters of typography seem relics, artifacts, tossed up by this snot-green, "scrotumtightening" sea. This green animal below Buck Mulligan's tower is our best image of that fecundating preconscious flux wherein counters (images, words) are lined loosely, like buoys, to their referents in reality, and there let float and move musically, into nonutilitarian combinations. The sea is the source of play, the residuum of cradle babble, the reminiscence of oral eroticism. It induces the chips that mark language's debt to reality to play their own game, to behave for the sake of blue next to green, rather than for the sake of a meaning. We will be interested in the ways this sea, like the artist's self-portrait, obtrudes its image into the pictures it has helped to paint.

Art is the outcome (and image) of a psychic activity whose unity and modes of transaction are in some sense prior to language. One must immediately make the other half of this argument. The artistic psyche tends to specialize in its chosen language. The initial psychic inclination enters into a symbiosis with aesthetic conventions and historical precedent, so that imagination and the possibilities of a medium act and react on one another. Poets create the blank verse drama, then that form helps create a grander poetry. This story, in fact, resembles the evolution of human intelligence. Increased brain size makes language possible, then the development of language helps increase the brain's size and power. Yet for all the centrality of language, it cannot be seen as an autonomous, self-perpetuating activity outside the domain of consciousness. It does not write itself. The musicality or painterly vision of poets and the literary inclinations of composers suggest that the impulse toward aesthetically rewarding form is an inclination of certain psyches, which may be manifested in alternative mediums or languages.

This study assumes, then, the existence of artistic psyche, with its analogy to the "primary process" (Freud) behind dreaming. It takes poets at their word and explores the psychic image-structures they have created, especially in poems that tend self-reflexively to comment on the creative act. A dualistic imagery of evolution into consciousness from preconscious sources becomes inevitably apparent, and associates itself with creation myth, especially in the work of those Romantic poets who were the first to make poetry conscious of itself in the peculiarly modern fashion.

Using the analogy of psychoanalysis rather than its technical terminology, we will unfold, not the unconscious signification or content of central works, but their dual conscious/unconscious structure. Our concern will be not with words per se, with writing in the sense of Derrida, but rather with visual/spatial models not identifiable with specific verbal formulations, and recognizable through analogies between related figures. Yet language as a system of "differance" provides a satisfactory context for such discussion. The poem insofar as it produces a verbal replica of the preconscious origin is "always already" in the realm of signification. From words of the unconscious landscape as a portion of the signifier, contrasting words of the observer (or conscious dome of pleasure) distinguish themselves. Thus, there is an investigatable tension between areas of the poem's topography of signs. Tension between above, light, measure, definitive consonantal sound, and below, dark, measureless, affective suasion of vowel sound, is a function of the system of internal references characteristic of poetry. The poem's text is a texture of differences, self-referential, as all poetry is, in what Coleridge called its primary aim—which is pleasure, language's autoerotic function. This duality that gives constant interest to the verbal fabric stretched across these poles of Heaven and Hell, sunlit dome and measureless cavern, exists as analogue of the maker's creating psyche. Though unable to explain the before and after of origin and articulation, the poem offers itself as a record of that sequence. The poem's dream music is structured by necessarily preceding, now receding experience, followed upon by language (or writing).

Our topographical paradigm representing consciousness and its origins, with the annexed mythology of creation and fall, is very much the "logocentric" pattern that Derrida deconstructs in *Of Grammatology*. He argues that a continuity between a Christian or Platonic worldview and the implied signifier/signified relationship extends into the world of Rousseau and beyond. The analyses of this study confirm the continuance of this pattern. Yet we will take the longevity of the signifier/signified relationship, making possible the very symbolizing activity of the mind in words, as evidence of a conformity between this dual structure and the dual human psyche as reflected in its art. It is not our task to deconstruct the poets' myth-implying metaphors, but rather to describe them in their detail, and to appreciate their implications for poetry as it has been, is, and still may be. Logocentrism has no pejorative connotations for a study of the art of the word. Where Derrida is severe in respect to Rousseau's account of origin, we will be sympathetic, taking his vision of language born out of a warm south as expressive of the psyche's deep longing and inclination, rather than as an account of historical possibility. Our preconception is of an artistic hunger for a wholeness and extent of being that exceeds thought's logic, but that is gestured toward in myths of origin and, in the best cases, implied in the innumerable permutations possible between the finite elements of the verbal artifact.

A virtue this study proposes for itself is at least self-awareness. The ideology or mythology or theology of the major Romantic poets and of their Modernist successors was indeed embodied in their essential metaphors. It is our purpose to apprehend these figures in their paradigmatic outline, and to treat them, as purely as possible, as phenomena of the poetic mind in operation. We will argue in effect that the ship/sea or tower/water figures, as varieties of the creation of form out of formlessness, reveal the outline of consciousness' self-ordination. The poet may have invoked nature, or the "wisdom and spirit of the universe," or God. But we will see such signification as mental signature. The poem's text will be seen as the mind's writing of the multiple names of its consciousness (through their web of differences) upon or against a fertile first water or void or chaos, which we will often refer to as the *unconscious*, and meaning, strictly, only that Before which has to be supposed because of the After which implies it. We will use *unconscious*, then, not in its particular psychoanalytic sense, but as synonym for that landscape or sleep or state of nature which consciousness in the process of the poem defines itself from and against.

Robert Langbaum argues in *The Mysteries of Identity* that the Wordsworthian self is dual, compounded of conscious awareness and an underlying unconsciousness, repository of memory and thus of continuity. According to his analysis, Locke, by equating identity with consciousness, created the problem of how the self's continuity is maintained when consciousness is extinguished, as in sleep or forgetfulness. Wordsworth's answer, he argues, was to identify memory with the landscape and to retain a palimpsest of scenes in the deep psyche, even in the absence of conscious recollection.[6] The mind, thus actively belonging to and interacting with its landscape of memory, comes in part to create the nature it perceives. If Wordsworthian place is "the spatial projection of psyche," and if the memory wherein self and nature interpenetrate is unconscious, it follows that the Wordsworthian memorial landscape is in part the projection of the poet's unconscious. The old leech gatherer in "Resolution and Independence," like something left behind by a primordial inland sea, is an archetype apprehended by "the eye of unconscious racial memory."[7] In seeing the landscape, the poet sees also our biological origins, the emotional and typological strata deposited by evolution.

Perhaps a psychological version of the poetic fiat cannot, without unacceptable reductionism, comment directly on the materials and meanings of poetry.[8] What does seem legitimate, however, is the aid of certain psychoanalytic texts in mapping more accurately for literary study the structure of consciousness in relation to its underlying sources, as implied in poetry that tends as part of its central subject to comment reflexively on the creative act. We will therefore be engaged, with the help of psychic models pro-

vided by Freud, Jung, and others, in drawing more clearly a topography of self that the English Romantics and their twentieth-
century successors tended to project within the landscapes of other
subject matters.

The development of interest in the unconscious is associated
with Romanticism—though more explicitly in Germany than in
England. Still, both Wordsworth and Coleridge use the word
unconscious in a recognizably modern sense.[9] In Germany a sequence of speculation and influence reaches from Goethe and
Schelling through Schopenhauer, Carl Gustav Carus, Eduard von
Hartmann, to Freud and Jung.[10] We are now aware that both
Schopenhauer and Wagner have in important respects anticipated
Freud. For Wagner, in many ways the epitome of musical Romanticism, a making conscious of the unconscious was a major part of
the artistic intention.[11] A tension between that unconscious di-
mension of the psyche increasingly brought into definition from
Romanticism to psychoanalysis and the poet's conscious artistry
and effort of articulation is central to the line of development from
Romantic poetry to our own.

Langbaum's version of the Romantic conscious self, "connected to the unconscious and suffused with its vitality," is thus a
union of contrasts, of opposed areas of the psyche's topography.
Yet for poets later in the nineteenth century, this vitalization from
subterranean regions encountered difficulty. Already in Arnold the
"Buried Life" of the instincts is partly beyond reach, premonitory
of Eliot's paralyzed, self-enclosed consciousness—deeply split between "unconsciousness and the consciousness that watches itself
in action."[12] By examining the duality of the more conscious and
the less conscious elements of personality as they are projected in a
typical bipolar imagery, we will be positioned to evaluate the Romantic self-conception in the poetic act as it has both continued
into modern poetry and been significantly altered. In this we will
be particularizing what is already assumed. Critics of the stature of
Geoffrey Hartman and Harold Bloom move easily from Wordsworth or Blake to Freud; a similar structure of insights seems to
prevail.[13]

Freud in *The Ego and the Id* makes explicit his "topographical terminology," portraying the obverse of the landscape's grounding of unconscious memory as described by Langbaum. Freud, positioning consciousness on the surface, in contrast to the psyche's "deepest strata," concludes that only what was once a perception can again come into awareness; "anything arising from within (apart from feelings) that seeks to become conscious must try to transform itself into external perceptions."[14] Thus, we are authorized by psychoanalysis to find, in the poet's landscapes, projections of the unconscious that could not otherwise arise. The Romantic meditation involving mind and landscape is therefore not only an interplay between subjective mind and external reality but a dynamic interchange between more and less conscious areas of the total psyche.

The unconscious, as biological process and evolutionary history, is, on its lowest levels, continuous with the nature from which individual identity has come. The unconscious mind intuitively knows this nature of which it is part, and the landscape, symbol of this nature, can serve as a vehicle into which the cumulative, otherwise unknowable strata of our dual identity can project themselves and be to some extent recognized. The clarification of the lower, "landscape" dimension of Romantic selfhood may prove our time's major contribution to the understanding of Romantic creativity. Conversely, the very modernity of analysis that makes such a clarification possible, incorporated into literary personae, may have heightened unbearably the tension between aspects of the dual self. In some of the Modernist poems we will examine, the two imagistic terms are discernible, are related to each other but are incapable of dynamic interaction—blocked by inhibition, neurosis, or the paralysis of excessive intellectuality.

We have begun, then, with a simplified scheme: the topographical model of the psyche as drawn by Freud. In *Beyond the Pleasure Principle*, a single cell-like "vesicle" (situated between an upper world of stimuli and a lower stratum into which sink the traces of sense perception not retainable within this circle of consciousness) becomes his metaphor for the ego. The origin of consciousness is compared to the origin of life itself. Drawing upon the account in *The Symposium* of Zeus's division of the original bisexual creatures into men and women (who must then seek and hunger after the missing half), Freud speculates that "living substance was at the time of its animation rent into small particles, which since that time strive for reunion by means of the sexual instincts." The condition of inanimate matter, point of origin and return, is unconsciously remembered. The death instinct, like all instincts, is conservative, a tendency "toward the reinstatement of an earlier condition." It appears to be evolutionarily derived, "historically conditioned," proof of "the organic compulsion to repetition."[15]

Various separations and reunions—religious, mythological, philosophical, literary, anthropological—associate themselves with this pattern. In the Neoplatonized Christianity as described by Abrams, "the fall of man is conceived to be primarily a falling-out-of and falling-away-from the One, into a position of remoteness and a condition of alienation from the source. . . . In all versions of the fall as a falling out of unity, redemption is regarded as a process of reintegration." Neoplatonic and Christian patterns of thought were a central influence on Romanticism. German philosophers from Kant through Schiller, Fichte, Schelling to Hegel found in the fall a favored analogy representing, as felix culpa, the progression of humankind from a state of nature submerged in instinct to the consciousness that brings moral responsibility, complexity, self-division, freedom, and, eventually, an earned higher unity on the other side of knowledge. An "opposition between the conscious self and nature was a necessary stage," part of a circuit of division that would eventually bring humankind back through conflict to a higher harmony springing "from the labor and culture of the spirit."[16] There are important resemblances to these patterns in the poetry of the major English Romantics.

Models of the origin of human consciousness such as those provided by Freud, by Carl Jung, by Jung's disciple Erich Neumann in *The Origins and History of Consciousness* and, more recently, by Julian Jaynes in *The Origin of Consciousness in the Breakdown of the Bicameral Mind*, share a need to represent an original life-matrix (analogue of Eden), whether undifferentiated stratum of animated matter for Freud or some variety of nonconscious, instinctual communal life, as for Jung, Neumann, and Jaynes. Influenced by theories of evolution, all these writers see consciousness as we know it to have come about through some primal differentiation or separation. We might include in this generalization Desmond Morris and his book *The Naked Ape*, which sees our ancestors undergoing an "expulsion from the Garden" as they moved from their ancient forest home into that stressful hunting existence on the open plains that was to impel the brain in its development toward complexity.[17] The crucial, intensely interesting moment in the evolutionary ascent is always the separation of intelligence into self-consciousness. This problematic event, as one of the profounder mysteries we face, akin to the question of the origin of life itself, inevitably invites mythological treatment, even by scientists.

Neumann sees the individual ego's self-identification as involved with, and as model of, creation mythology: a separation from the uroboros. The uroboros was originally the serpent with tail in its mouth, that without ending or beginning—a symbol used in alchemy. Neumann makes of it his representation of the unconscious as source of consciousness. It is also, symbolically, an ocean or an underworld. The division of the light of consciousness from the darkness of unconsciousness provides the psychological meaning of the creation story in Genesis. Topographically, the conscious ego is the limited island in the limitless ocean.[18] Jung, like the German Romantic philosophers, sees consciousness as having been created by man's "opposing himself to instinct"; consciousness has "split off from the unconscious—an eternally repeated event symbolized as the fall of the angels and the disobedience of the first parents." Topographically, consciousness is islands; the unconscious, the sea or a geological "deposit."[19]

For Jaynes, influenced by neurological studies involving surgery on epileptics and subsequent tests of perception and response, the brain's function in the modern person is divided, specialized into right and left hemispheres. The right hemisphere—emotional, synthetic, perceiver of symbolic meanings—has largely given over the ability to articulate speech to the left brain—now specialized as analytic and verbal. "The right hemisphere, perhaps like the gods, sees parts as having a meaning only within a context; it looks at wholes. While the left or dominant hemisphere, like the man side of the bicameral mind, looks at parts themselves." A Mesolithic culture of 9000 B.C. was, in Jaynes's speculation, ruled by the internalized voices of dead ancestors (who had become gods), and their representative, the current king. These voices were heard as auditory hallucinations, proceeded from the right brain, and directed a way of life that can only be called unconscious. The voices were able to solve problems as we do now in dreams and in instantaneous perceptions, but under the rule of this intuitive obedience to the past humans lacked the self-awareness we associate with subjective consciousness. Sometime before 1000 B.C., under the stress of changing conditions and aided by the development of written language, Mesopotamians and Greeks developed the personal identity-concept we refer to as ego and gradually began to lose the ability to hear the gods as audible speech. The most famous literary texts reflecting these changes are the *Iliad* and the *Odyssey* and the Old and the New Testaments. Yahweh speaks to the children of Israel with the ancient authority of the right brain, just as Achilles, Hector, and the other heroes are addressed by gods whom they must obey. The *Odyssey* is seen as a voyage to consciousness, just as Jesus of Nazareth's religion of the inner man appears a belief and a morality adapted to the new subjective consciousness.[20]

The pattern, in general outline, is central to our civilization's image of itself. The left brain specializes and differentiates its function from the old, intuitive, unconscious right brain, developing a concept of personal identity and the related subjective consciousness, but is haunted by a longing for the old god voices and their "archaic authorization."[21] Our ancestors separate themselves from the sheltering forest and its fruits, master fire, tools, and social complications, but miss somehow the old, easy communal life as apes. Adam and Eve acquire knowledge from the serpent (Desmond Morris suggests that our ancestors learned "to make sex sexier" as part of the pair-bonding necessary to deal with extended childhood in a hunting society) and lose their own child-freedom in Eden.[22] Prometheus's theft of fire leaves him crucified upon a cliff, to wrestle with an individual moral dilemma. Milton's Satan separates himself from divine love and the conformity of obedience, to glory in his power in a kingdom of the North. Plato and Plotinus show the soul losing immediate contact with the absolute, to descend into material incarnation. Blake's Thel is offered this option but refuses. His Urizen, however, endures the full agony of physical individuation, the definition of consciousness that is a self-enclosure, a narrowing. Goethe's Faust, after all his agonized searching and self-assertion, reclaims new land along the shore— the achievement that he has sought from the beginning and that sums up, metaphorically, his conquest of new realms of consciousness from the unconsciousness of the sea.

The English Romantic poetry of landscape may be seen as providing comparable accounts (in more consistently topographical terms) of consciousness in relation to its point of origin and return: a subtly mythologized unconsciousness of nature. Wordsworth lovingly separates personal identity from the winding waters of the Derwent that "flowed along [his] dreams" (*Prel.* 1:274). His inland journey of consciousness takes him far from such dream waters, through Cambridge to London to revolutionary Paris. It is with much ado that he is able to return, as in "Tintern Abbey," to an "inland murmur" of streams that refreshes awareness. The Titan gods in Keats's *Hyperion,* associated with the slumberous life of trees and stones, are replaced by the warmer-blooded Olympians. Young Apollo is deeply pained by his sense of loss of immediate instinctive participation in the whole cosmic drama but is consoled by a kind of racial memory imparted by Mnemosyne. The speaker in poems such as "Ode to a Nightingale" and "Ode to the West Wind" feels his limited consciousness in time called to by a wine of the underground ("a beaker full of the warm South"), or by the wind that enlivens both land and sea. On many levels, the separation that brings individuality, clear articulation, consciousness (in and of) time is penalized by loss of community with a ground of being: the One or an ocean of unconsciousness or a forest or Eden or Edenic landscape that originally sustained the soul or self in a permanent condition lacking individuality and freedom but continuous with a whole of things not visibly ending or beginning. This separation, or differentiation, of the individual from the collective, is reflected not only in religious mythology and philosophy but also in the models of consciousness provided by psychoanalysts such as Freud and Jung, and in the underlying structures of Romantic landscape poetry. All these versions of consciousness and its origins share a perception that the first condition of identity with a larger source still exerts a suasion over our thoughts, if only through dreams and other disguises. Civilized consciousness is seen in each case as partly irrational, marked by its process of evolution, and called to by symbols and compulsions from its unconscious past.

The literary critic is properly suspicious when terms such as the *One*, the *uroboros*, the *unconscious* are imported from religion, philosophy, or psychoanalysis into literary criticism. Harold Bloom reminds us that even the psychoanalyst, when writing, faces the same standards of judgment as any other writer, and should not "privilege" his own area of belief: that of the unconscious, or the realm of what Freud called the "primary process." Bloom rightly argues that faith, of whatever sort, is no substitute for precision of argument and analysis. The psychoanalytic writer "cannot invoke the trope of the Unconscious as though he were doing more (or less) than the poet or the theologian does by invoking the trope of the Imagination, or than the theologian does by invoking the trope of the Divine."[23]

Critical scrutiny of what might be called the psychoanalytic mythology of origin is represented, for example, by Derrida's treatment of psychic models proposed by Freud. In "Freud and the Scene of Writing" Derrida suggests that the late (and relatively minor) image of the psyche as "mystic writing-pad" be preferred to the more usual topographical metaphor. For Derrida, words, as a system of differences, refer primarily to other words, and the unconscious should be seen as what (for him) is implied in the writing-pad image: an accumulation of language traces. In the writing-pad essay, according to Derrida, Freud not only acknowledges the metaphoric, essentially literary status of psychoanalytic language, but enacts this process of writing that is never able to refer outside its self-enclosed system. Freud's own writing "can only try, endlessly and without success, to designate a genuine beginning, an authentic essence or real immediacy—nature, instinct, biology, sexuality—just as the psyche itself is always unable to recover its own beginning before repression."[24]

Yet without the duality of terms—consciousness and what it has separated itself from—we are unable to account for the dynamics of interchange between contrasting levels of psychic life represented in the models of the creative act given us by poets and other artists. The painter Robert Motherwell, for example, wrote that "all my works, consist of a dialectic between the conscious (straight lines, designed shapes, weighted colors, abstract language) and the unconscious (soft lines, obscured shapes, *automatism*) resolved into a synthesis which differs as a whole from either."[25]

To say, of course, that an explanation is needed is not equivalent to saying that one exists. Yet if we are to proceed in accordance with Bloom's stipulation, we can at least invoke the unconscious—the second, lower, and yet original term of the self's duality—as trope, as enabling *fiction*.[26] Therefore, as part of a particular kind of writing, an analysis of certain texts, we will propose that two terms, an upper and a lower, an eye (or I) and a landscape, be utilized in readings better able to deal with Romantic dualities than a truncated terminology wherein criticism, like post-Cartesian Western consciousness, is threatened with solipsistic self-enclosure.

Though no impartial reader of Freud is likely to come away from his works with any impression other than that of his devout belief in the unconscious, the religious aura suggested by a word such as *devout* is itself a problem for Derrida. He is concerned to reduce any illicit metaphysical construct to its constituent linguistic elements. Yet the Romantic self presented through rhetorical tropes by philosophers, poets, and psychoanalysts shows sufficient consistency and persistence to constitute a working hypothesis: a two-term psyche busily projecting its structure into the world of perception. The very writing-pad image of Freud's, which Derrida uses to undermine the unconscious as substantial psychic component, is susceptible to a very different interpretation. The "slab of dark brown resin or wax" that in Freud's day formed the base of the device (providing a retentive lower stratum below the upper layers of transparent celluloid and translucent waxed paper) corresponded for Freud to the unconscious. This wax recorded the imprint of a writing that the upper layers entertained only briefly. Perceptual consciousness and its shielding receptors of stimuli, as imaged in the waxed paper and the protective celluloid, seem relatively insubstantial when compared with this solid wax, which would truly correspond to the unconscious if it could "like our memory" reproduce from within the traces made upon it but no longer visible upon the conscious surface.

Through the very poetic weight of his imagery, Freud dramatizes his own lower term as active, substantial, mysteriously autonomous. Perception itself is energized from below, "as though the unconscious stretches out feelers, through the medium of the system *Pecpt.-Cs.* [perceptual consciousness], towards the external world." The topographical model is thus alive within the writing-pad image, the duality we have stressed presented there as *"two separate but interrelated component parts or systems."*[27] With a clear sheet of celluloid as eye, with a waxed paper temporarily retentive of sensory and meditative contents as consciousness, the Romantic poet walks again over the landscape into which the poetic mind projects the "ancestral voices" and "unhonored dead" of memorializing unconscious. Freud's wax base is, by his own metaphorical extension, the lower stratum of consciousness—perhaps an undersea floor from which stretch the tentacles of the primal psychic creature.

In spite of his reconstitution of the Freudian unconscious as a collection of language traces in "Freud and the Scene of Writing," Derrida's account of language in *Of Grammatology* seems influenced as much by unconscious dynamics of the psyche (as described by Freud) as by semiotic theory. His analysis of Rousseau's *Essay on the Origin of Languages* winds its way finally to a perception of incest prohibition as source of that gap between signifier and signified which, as "differance," the "supplementary" system of differances and deferences, links language's operation with the cultural (as opposed to natural) impulses more generally. "It [incest prohibition] is the element of culture itself, the undeclared origin of passion, of society, of languages: the first supplementarity which permits the substitution in general of a signifier for the signified, of signifiers for other signifiers, which subsequently makes for a discourse on the difference between words and things."[28] Derrida's language theory is inclined to posit an uncrossable line between the word and its object because that object, in its first manifestation, was mother, and was made unpossessable by this prohibition which created both language and civilization.

Because the essential object of passion confessed by Rousseau was an image—that of mamma, translated at times into the language of other women's gestures—and because this image/sign, linked with masturbation, necessarily deferred the reality it represented, the linguistic act is shown to be always a substitution. Rousseau's autoerotic self-enclosure, as he contemplates in all its differing forms the image whose original he must not possess, becomes the writer caught in "an infinite chain, ineluctably multiplying the supplementary mediations that produce the sense of the very thing they defer: the image of the thing itself, of immediate presence, of originary perception." Whether metaphysician or poet, the writer, like onanistic Rousseau, is engaged in "spelling out the supplements that are linked together to replace a mother or Nature."[29]

In many respects the version of language returned to us by Derrida is one in which the literate reader should rejoice. The self-referentiality of the language of poetry is in effect extended to all written discourse. The figural operations of rhetoric, at the heart of literature, are seen also as powerful determinants in philosophic texts. The textuality of writing is preserved as a precondition of thought in language, an absolute realm inhabited by writer and reader prior to specialization in a science of semiology, or anthropology, or psychoanalysis. The implications of metaphor are seen as determinative in this making (and unmaking) of the text. Yet in bringing the insights of Derrida to bear on the poetry of the English Romantics, the critic faces a major discrepancy. Derrida's model of the relation of the writer's mind to nature is masturbational: the writer never actually possesses the thing desired, but accepts words instead, whose role is to substitute for, to defer. Wordsworth proposed a different sexual metaphor for the imagination's relation to reality. He called it a marriage, and looked upon both mind and nature as active (and interactive) partners. Certainly Wordsworth of all poets seems to have known nature in the biblical sense. His metaphor of coitus between mind and object represents his belief in direct contact between words (those "emanations of reality and truth") and things. Whether or not an illusion, this faith in the connectedness between language and landscape was the basis of his poetic, the enabling condition for his poetry of place.

Langbaum evokes the Romantics' potentially solipsistic isolation in the post-Kantian world, wherein much of the value and order was known to be projection.[30] The danger that consciousness would become its own self-enclosure, its own hermetically sealed bell jar, arising with Enlightenment science and scientific philosophy, provided one of the specters that Romanticism faced—and, in its crucial poems, vanquished. Yet the skeleton would not stay in the closet. We see how later with T. S. Eliot the Dantean tower into which Uglino was locked to starve, as reinterpreted in part 5 of *The Waste Land*, becomes a symbol of F. H. Bradley's meditation on the inescapable privacy of the human soul.[31] In order to escape its towers of isolate intellect, consciousness needs to have originated from a more continuous stratum; this landscape, in the essential Romantic poems of renewal (like the landscape a few miles above Tintern Abbey), calls back to itself the self-enclosed ego, convincing it of a world outside its interior mirroring.

The organism is found to bear within it the print of its beginning. That is what calls it *Beyond the Pleasure Principle*, toward the Thanatos standing past the detour of Eros. Death is the call felt by the individual cell-circle, symbol of the lonely ego, from its inanimate and collective origin, to which it must and will by its own process return. The Romantic poet or Caspar David Friedrick's Monk, looking across a great vista of landscape or sea, is like this separated cell or ego; the landscape or sea is the originating mass, the *God-term* (to name our trope).[32] Whatever Derrida's doubts, we need a model positing a tension between terms in order to investigate the dynamic interchange between ego isolation and a landscape of origin.

Freud's landscape-like stratum of animated matter versus the single cell of ego, his writing pad divided between the wax base (matrix of memory) and the top film clear as perception—these are images, metaphorical figures expressed in words. Likewise, the Romantic poet's pleasure dome above in sunlight versus the underground spaces of a sunless sea, his self-conscious poet returning to the memorial landscape of Tintern Abbey or Derwent waters, are structured images, metaphorical figures deserving to be called models of the psyche. Like Freud's figures (when undistorted by Derrida), Wordsworth's suggest what is essential for solving the dilemma of ego solipsistically in its tower. The tower is found to stand upon a landscape, beside a stream. This base, this substratum of consciousness, is part of its identity. Consciousness is able to know the Other because the Other is, at bottom, incorporated into itself, part of the thing from which it has come.

But more precisely what, we may ask, is the content, the meaning, of this dark lower term symbolized by landscape in many forms and, quintessentially, by the sea? The poet typically reacts to a configuration of wild nature, a panorama dramatically older and other than the self, to which the individual is yet proved to have an essential relation. This spatially extended otherness, perceived through the waking senses in Somerset or through reading, opium, and inward vision, stands somehow prior to the individual's history, as a headwaters of psychological origination. Keats in the "Nightingale" ode, like Wordsworth's inland traveler, has paused in his personal journey graphed out upon the landscape of consciousness to turn and look backward toward the beginning (and ending) point prior to society and time. We can say that the sea represents a timeless uroboric source anterior to subjective ego consciousness. The hints and guesses that come as in a sea wind are experienced as the "oceanic" sensation mentioned by Freud in *Civilization and Its Discontents.*

As the rational analyst, Freud cleverly attributes immediate knowledge of this "sensation of 'eternity,'" this "feeling as of something limitless, unbounded—as it were, 'oceanic,'" to a "friend."[33] The point from which such a breeze of sensation blows stands outside the boundaries of discontented society. Like the dolphin-torn harbor beyond the Emperor's dome in Yeats's poem "Byzantium," this sea delivers the materials of time to civilization's doorstep, may resonate within the architectures of consciousness, but is not itself in and of this history, this temporal sequence. Surges of this sea's waves may freshen and empower words, but the sea itself, beyond time, is not to be rendered directly in language. We have instead landscapes in the mind, in words, on canvas, seas in poetry and music, and reminders of the sea, such as the dolphin under the piping rider: the articulating artistic consciousness. Nietzsche images Apollonian individuality as a man in a little rowboat on the "immense, raging sea" of the Dionysiac Other.[34]

The sea, then, is unknowable in rational terms. Just as the word *unconscious* only points toward, literally, that which is not conscious, so the sea image as used (along with many allied landscape images) by Romantic artists indicates that which is not the conscious self. Not, therefore, easily discussed. But the creative act, seen from a Romantic perspective, turns on a paradoxical meeting between the timeless, not conscious, not knowable origin, and a history, an articulation of symbols (including words) in art. Subjective consciousness is somehow (through oracles, divination, inspiration) infused again with what Julian Jaynes calls archaic authorization: man's "contact with his lost ocean of authority." Spatially (Jaynes says consciousness "is always a spatialization"), the Romantic vision renders significant juxtapositions of consciousness structures (peaks of vision, towers, domes, windows) with waters of *not*-consciousness: immortal seas, perilous seas, mackerel-crowded seas, seas, in Wordsworth's *Prelude* (2:407–9) echoing the life-swarming waves of original creation as portrayed by Milton in *Paradise Lost*.[35] It is precisely because this plenitude (which begets in the poet's mind images lovely as Venus born from the waves) remains outside ordinary consciousness and the articulations of language that we must pay careful attention to the typical symbols through which it announces its effects.

W. H. Auden's *The Enchafèd Flood* depicts the sea as "symbol for the primordial undifferentiated flux," representing a "state of barbaric vagueness and disorder" upon which form has to be imposed. The willingness to voyage upon this flood he singles out as one of the "distinctive new notes in the Romantic attitude." Auden is concerned to point out the singularity, in respect to earlier literature, of this willingness to enter voluntarily upon that chief symbol of the "world of conflict and disorder," which he sees as the traditional opponent of civilization. *The Enchafèd Flood* implies, therefore, a Modernist criticism of Romanticism as being insufficiently mindful of the law-abiding civilizing act on land, whereby cities were established and defended. Though classical heroes such as Odysseus and Jason are great navigators, neither "goes to sea for the sake of the voyage," and Auden is at some pains to show that from Homer through *The Seafarer* to Shakespeare, the "sea is no place to be if you can help it."[36]

Yet those great English poets who laid the foundations for modern poetry were far from simplistic or careless in their attitudes; they, no more than Shakespeare, abandoned "the world of reconciliation and order" for headlong approaches to the ocean and all that it symbolized.[37] Certainly the sea was for them no absolute opponent or enemy, but, if we except some of the passages in Shelley, the essential business of poems such as "Kubla Khan," "Tintern Abbey," "Ode: Intimations of Immortality," "Ode to the West Wind," and "Ode to a Nightingale" may be defined as a mediation between extremes such as adulthood and the child's paradise, waking and sleep, articulate individuality and mute identification with nature—between a figure on shore and the sea. It is Modernism, with its tendency toward a self-discovery by consciousness, that sets the intellect's precisions and limitations more hurtfully at odds with the Romantic landscape of origin. The Romantic duality is heightened in the earlier work of T. S. Eliot and in the *Ariel* poems of Sylvia Plath, for example, into a dichotomy that invades the central personality, threatening sterility and collapse.

By contrast, Romantic lyrics of consciousness' escape from itself and return, as represented by "Ode to a Nightingale," create patterns of psychic survival. The dichotomy, for Keats, between artistic wakefulness and inspirational slumber (as in "Sleep and Poetry"), or between the self-conscious poet and the unconscious ease of the nightingale in its forest, may after all be transcended, if only during those moments that will fructify into poetry. The greatest poetic mediations between opposites such as the poet and the

landscape, creative will and its sources of inspiration, produce a
tone of elegiac acceptance, a balancing of loss and gain that typifies
the maturing personality.

Keats is tempted, by the beauty of the bird's song, to leave his
identity in this world where "youth grows pale, and spectre-thin,
and dies"; he is drawn toward the idea of a wine embodying a
whole countryside ("the warm South"), an underground wine
("Cool'd a long age in the deep-delved earth") that would merge
him with nature, with the nightingale and "the forest dim." But
such total reidentification with this source would mean loss of articulate consciousness. Death as the ultimate aesthetic experience,
the final self-expression, wherein the poet literally pours forth his
soul in parallel with the bird's song, would leave him, he sees, a
mute, inconsequential piece of the landscape: "a sod." The journey
into the nightingale's thicket, therefore, is a temporary one, made
in imagination rather than literally in the body. The poem dramatizes a kind of ritual death and rebirth whereby the temptation of
reunion with, and extinction into, whatever underlies this field of
"alien corn" is faced, evaluated, and overcome.

The poet for a moment loses his individual identity in stanza
7, merging into Ruth of the Bible, then with some unnamed hero of
fairy tale. But the structure of consciousness is preserved in the
limiting (yet lyric) "magic casements," which open upon "the foam
/ Of perilous seas," while preserving the clear-sightedness to see
them as perilous, their "faery lands" as "forlorn." Like a visitant to
the underworld who has refused its food, the poet is able to come
back—he has been wiser than his "knight-at-arms" in "La Belle
Dame Sans Merci," who partook of the "honey wild and manna
dew." He is left at the end of the ode in his individual identity, in a
reality modified by vision of what lies beyond or beneath the specific landscape. He is left on that shore where the children sport in
the "Intimations" ode—between waking and sleep.

Nietzsche in *The Birth of Tragedy* makes explicit (if sometimes
obscurely so) what the Romantics imply: the lyrical poet is, first, a
"Dionysiac artist," one who in creation momentarily abrogates subjectivity to become wholly identified with "the original Oneness, its
pain and contradiction." The "I" loses its individuality, to dwell,
"truly and eternally, in the ground of being." The poet becomes "a

medium through which the True Subject celebrates His redemption in illusion."[38] Thus, Wordsworth on Mount Snowdon identifies for a time with that "image of a mighty mind" (*Prel.* 13:69) created by the moonlit dome of sky above those chaotic waters that roar through a rift in the clouds. Coleridge through his dream vision becomes the decreeing Khan, divider of land and dome and light above from the dark waters, the original sea of chaos, below. Yeats, great Romantic inheritor, shaped and measured the void (like Coleridge with his "walls and towers") through geometrical gyres and moon phases. He looked from the True Subject's point of view as Byzantium's Emperor, as Old Rocky Face, as the three Chinamen upon the mountain above history in "Lapis Lazuli."

But though the interaction on the strand between timeless sea and civilization's consciousness occasionally produces God-like visions, Nietzsche's paradigm is in some respects misleading or at least overstated. The lyric poet as represented by Wordsworth, Coleridge, Shelley, Keats, and their Victorian successors more typically inhabits the structure of subjective consciousness even while seeing the vision beyond. The poet incorporates the personal self, with its fears, weaknesses, limitations and sufferings, into the narrative of encounter. The poet's family situation and recent circumstances, as in "The Eolian Harp," "Tintern Abbey," and "Ode to a Nightingale," provide a dramatizing individuality of perspective from which the threateningly collective source of inspiration may be viewed, approached, invoked as continuing resource, then retreated from. We are reminded of the figure in Caspar David Friedrich's "Traveller Looking Over the Sea of Fog" who, back to us, represents the human scale of perspective while guiding our gaze out over the vast Alpine panorama of peaks and mists. Like the rational narrator in a tale by Poe who must come to terms with some monstrous manifestation of the irrational, the poet's own ego and life story offer the suffering, time-bound reader a point of identification in the drama. A central tension of Romantic poetry derives from the interaction between the rational, subjective narrator caught in time and a fertile, sustaining, threatening, nontemporal, nonrational source-principle the narrator experiences as inspiration.

Thus, though what is truly unconscious cannot be known by consciousness, we can investigate how the impingement of an ambivalent plenitude upon the ego has been embodied in archetypical configurations of imagery. Houses, towers, lonely observers on peaks, figures overlooking vast landscapes associate with the more personal part of Romantic identity. Just as the ego for Freud is itself partly unconscious, these pleasure domes, palaces of art, and houses of Usher incorporate spaces where consciousness merges with an objective underground.[39] The interaction between the sunny dome of the upper ego and the caverns and sea below, as in the convulsive spurting of a fountain, forms the dynamic of central Romantic poems. Variations on the house/landscape pattern juxtapose the poet and contemporary concerns with "immemorial" spaces, as in "Tintern Abbey," "Resolution and Independence," and the Salisbury Plain episode of *The Prelude*. This line includes, as important precedent, Gray's "Elegy Written in a Country Churchyard," wherein a narrator isolated in one stratum of time and conventions (including a rather restrictive tradition of diction) is completed and consoled by another order of history: the landscape of the anonymous dead.

The other most important model of the psyche and its sources is the figure on shore or in a boat in relation to the sea. Wordsworth walks with his French daughter on the beach at Calais and listens with her to the sound of a "mighty Being" ("It Is a Beauteous Evening"). This is the "eternal deep" of the "Intimations" ode, the "immortal sea" that brings us hither, and upon whose shores the children sport before their inland journeys. Wordsworth, Coleridge, Shelley, later Tennyson venture in small sailing vessels upon versions of this absolute, this nature-unconsciousness of the psyche's origin and return. Wordsworth shows in the "Intimations" ode how the more usual Romantic vision of origin from the oneness of nature may be assimilated to the neoplatonic pattern (or vice versa).

In a manuscript continuation of what became the Mount Snowdon experience of *The Prelude*, book 14, Wordsworth considers accounts of explorers who are drowned in accidents with small boats.[40] This material reminds us of Wordsworth's earlier cooperative labor with Coleridge on "The Ancient Mariner" during the period following the triumphant first completion of "The Ruined Cottage" (a poem dramatizing a house of consciousness as it is reabsorbed by nature). The sailing journey to revelation (or to apocalyptic dissolution), as prefigured in these *Prelude* manuscripts and "The Ancient Mariner," becomes a central theme in nineteenth-century poetry (and is visible in prose). Shelley's voyage in "Alastor" and sailing images in *Prometheus Unbound* and "Adonais," along with his own inspiration, "The Ancient Mariner," appear to have influenced Tennyson's "Lady of Shalott," "Morte d'Arthur" and "Ulysses." Poe sailed, in the fashion of the Ancient Mariner, to psychic antipodes, in "Ms. Found in a Bottle," "A Descent into the Maelstrom," and the "Narrative of A. Gordon Pym." Melville wrecked his Pequod of Ahab's projected Romantic ego onto an ice-white hypostasis of nature-unconsciousness as the whale Moby Dick. Hopkins's treatment of the wreck of the *Deutschland* and Hardy's of the sinking of the *Titanic* show the adaptability of real events to this paradigm of the psyche's self-representation. Rimbaud's "Le Bateau ivre" makes explicit the symbolism of this reimmersion of the civilized ego in waters of its primal beginning.

The sailing vessel blown along by Coleridge's storm wind or Shelley's "breath whose might I have evoked in song" ("Adonais") appears to be a version of the Aeolian harp metaphor. The ship or boat with masts and sails corresponds to the harp with its strings: both represent the poet's ego as it is acted upon. The wind (which may sweep across, come from, or be associated with, the sea) is the activating principle, inspiration from the unconscious. In Coleridge's "The Eolian Harp" (which stands at the head of this class of poems), the poet retreats, perhaps in fright, from his wind-impelled speculation on the vast plastic impersonality of this "one intellectual breeze" behind all thought. Shelley's "Ode to the West Wind" shows the poet in his boyhood running as lightly as the wind, representing a condition of identity (or at least close contact) with a sustaining origin-principle. We are reminded of the "Intimations" ode and those children who "sport upon the shore." But, as in "Hymn to Intellectual Beauty," the "unseen Power" that moves in the human psyche like "music by the night-wind sent / Through strings of some still instrument" is inconstant, frustratingly unpredictable. Ordinary consciousness succeeds inspiration, the inland journey of adulthood takes precedence over childhood, and the ancestral voices echoing in domes of pleasure turn, as in Poe, into nightmare. Various versions of individuation seen as separations from a timeless ocean—and thus as falls into the chronology of adult consciousness—occur in Wordsworth, Coleridge, Shelley, and Keats.

The conflict is dramatized most succinctly in the "Intimations" ode: between child-closeness to an "immortal" sea of origin and those conventionalized social imitations that the child is drawn toward, thus blindly "at strife" with its original blessedness. A tension between a timeless sensation of origins experienced in inspiration, and the need to live and write in time (and in society) becomes a crucial issue. There are four basic Romantic responses to the dilemma, which may partially overlap. Wordsworth is a primary exponent of all but one of these.

First, the poet may try to live, even as an adult, in a continuation of the child's perhaps mythologized proximity to the generative source. By removing with Dorothy to Grasmere, by avoiding (or attempting to avoid) ordinary responsibilities and social expectations—unconventionally keeping house with a sister—by wandering about freely and consorting with peasants to preserve inner freedom and closeness to nature, Wordsworth sought to maintain within himself an Edenic access to inspiration, to experience the landscape every day as drenched in the moisture of creation. The incomplete "Home at Grasmere," written soon after the Wordsworths' move, provides a contemporary account of living with bird-like freedom (images of birds and of flight are prominent) in a providentially favorable spot discovered in childhood.[41] The poet glimpsed Dove Cottage on a ramble from Hawkshead school and has now come back to live in "this individual Spot," this "Whole without dependence or defect" (ll. 145, 149). There are strong overtones of a mythic return. "Home at Grasmere" is concluded by what became the Prospectus to *The Excursion*. There Wordsworth suggests that mythological accounts of paradise have their origin in the human psyche, and that Edenic experience, under the proper circumstances, may prove "A simple produce of the common day" (55).

Second, the poet may come to terms with time, adulthood, and diminished contact with inspiration through an elegiac acceptance: as in the conclusion of the "Intimations" ode. Though "nothing can bring back the hour" of early pastoral splendor, the "philosophic mind" of maturity may find in the facts and sights of mortality a profounder meaning, deeper tears. This solution makes analogy with the Christian fortunate fall and indeed with the whole Christian mystery of Incarnation. Just as early in the ode the Platonic preexistence of the soul is evoked as model for direct contact with the radiance of originating plenitude (Langbaum and others have commented on the union of light and water imagery), so at the end the "sober colouring" of clouds at sunset suggests the resonance surrounding the fall into time and the body. This elegiac acceptance implies, in addition to the richer emotional tone associated with mortality, occasional sustaining contacts with the generative source: those seasons of calm weather during which the soul revisits its first shore.

The third mode of reaction to that separation from a source-principle threatened by society and time is best exemplified by Shelley (and Blake—though the situation there is more complex). The poet may envision and attempt to bring about through art a regeneration of time-bound society in the image of the timeless plenitude. Having experienced (and hymned) Intellectual Beauty, having felt the power of Mount Blanc, Shelley in *Prometheus Unbound* created the image of time wound back to its source, society and its adult inhabitants regenerated through love and child-associated creativity (see especially the "winged infant" and the sleeping child in the two mystic chariots of the moon and of the earth, act 4) so as to resemble timeless images in art. Prometheus and his entourage will apparently spend the millenium in a kind of temple of Praxiteles. Blake waged his mental fight to restore a Jerusalem of unrepressed artistic creativity.

The fourth mode of reaction is also Shelleian. The artist, having perceived that life progressively separates him from creative plenitude, may determine (more or less consciously) that society, human history, consciousness in time, are inevitably corrupt and in need of replacement. At a certain point (as for Shelley between *Prometheus Unbound* and "Adonais") the other alternatives cease to hold out hope and an impulse toward apocalypse begins to imply the destruction of the personal ego and even the collective consciousness of society. In simplest terms, this impulse is toward unconsciousness in the hope of return to an origin whose loss is unendurable. "Die, / If thou wouldst be with that which thou dost seek" ("Adonais"). The later nineteenth century is haunted by this inspired death wish, often most beautifully embodied in imagery of sailing or in imagery of architectures—structures of consciousness—destroyed or deserted.

Kubla Khan's dome, Roderick Usher's house, Lamia's love bower, and the tower of the Lady of Shalott, erected as it were out of the artist's dream, suspended (in the cases of Coleridge, Keats, and perhaps Poe) by music, seemed from the beginning tenuous, subject to collapse. Threatened by prophecy of war, by their own self-division and isolation, by the cold eye of reason or by the pressure of reality, these structures vanish, split apart, are left with mirror cracked, the weaving ruined. Wagner's Valhalla, elaborately created within a music, in the end is consumed in flames.

The major imagistic alternative to the vanishing or collapse of the man-made structure on land—a plot event rather difficult to arrange, though prefigured for the Gothic mode by the conclusion of Walpole's *The Castle of Otranto*—is the wrecking or disappearance of a ship at sea. From the bark of the Ancient Mariner to Rimbaud's drunken barge, Romantic consciousness afloat is mightily tempted toward going under. Vessels in poems by Wordsworth, Coleridge, Shelley, Tennyson, Hopkins, Hardy, and Rimbaud come to grief upon the waters. This happens, as we have noted, in the fiction of Poe and Melville. Wagner, too, ecstatically loses a ship at sea—his *Flying Dutchman*.[42] The references to Wagner in *The Waste Land* are perhaps more central than we have suspected, since with its collective architectural destructions, its voyage (more apparent in the manuscript version) and exploration to psychic extremity, it is perhaps the culmination of the nineteenth-century theme of the collapse of consciousness.

In psychological terms the issue seems to be in part the relation between the more conscious and the less conscious strata of the psyche, especially during creation. Romanticism was poised upon the brink of a modern world threatening to become precipitously more modern in a fashion capable of extinguishing divinely inspired art and life in a meaningfully sacred universe. The poet's psyche was caught in a squeeze between visionary experience of a generative source capable of bearing the earlier meanings of divinity and sacredness, and a world increasingly commercialized, secularized, and abstracted. It reacted with mythic returns to an unconsciousness in nature, with tones of elegiac acceptance and regret, with visions of Utopia and of apocalypse.

The need, of course, was a marriage such as Wordsworth calls for in the Prospectus to *The Excursion*. If the "discerning intellect of Man" can be wed to the landscape and all it represents "In love and holy passion" (as opposed to domineering over it in grandiose and defective architectures), then peace can result. Impaired imagination can be restored, the poet led back to "those sweet counsels between head and heart" (*Prel.* 11:353) that were the original birthright as creative "inmate of this active universe" (*Prel.* 2:254). Catherine in *Wuthering Heights* needs both the primal landscape associated with Heathcliff (whose name combines Romantic landscape features) and the civility of Edgar and the cultured valley of Thrushcross Grange. Unable to reconcile these violently opposed figures/forces within her own lifetime, she dies, leaving the future compromise to the second Cathy, her daughter. When cultivated plantings from the Grange are introduced at Wuthering Heights, when Hareton the surrogate Heathcliff is taught to read and to converse by Catherine's child, balance has been restored and life can continue.

In contrast, Satanic/Byronic questers such as Count Manfred, Heathcliff, A. Gordon Pym, and Ahab ram their ships upon some boreal ice of the Absolute. These Faustian magicians, driven by a bizarre combination of emotion and reason, refuse the elegiac compromise implied by the separation/interdependence of the conscious and the unconscious. Their ships, like the *Titanic*, are seagoing versions of the Tower of Babel, floating Pandemoniums.

They may be mad scientists, their monster the embodiment of this superhuman/inhuman exploration beyond the livably known, into the rarefied air of some Mount Blanc—upon whose lower slopes Dr. Frankenstein hears the tale of his monster.

Thus, the Romantics subtly psychologize the landscape and its polarities, allowing us to see that psychological possibility stretches like a playing field between the two goals of the primitive and the civilized, the natural and the human, the unconscious and the conscious, the raw and the cooked—of Wuthering Heights and Thrushcross Grange, of immortal sea and Cambridge. The livable portions are those where some proportion of mix is available. Life flourishes where the intuitive pervades artistic elaboration, where poetic consciousness articulates nature. Like the interpenetrating gyres in the system of W. B. Yeats, these opposite thrusts from dark chaotic waters and sunlit structures of order depend upon each other. As Robartes says in Yeats's "The Phases of the Moon," "there's no human life at the full or the dark." The Western mind tried, in its Romantic agony, to teach itself again what Pope knew in the eighteenth century, and what Sir John Denham had implied in the first great poem of moralized landscape. "Cooper's Hill" taught Pope's "Windsor Forest" to show the civilized and the wild as in balance through a visible mix of fertile corn and purple heath. The viable union of self-love and reason, in An Essay on Man, is a grafted plant, cultivated branches set onto a snake-vigorous sexual root. The ego in its individuating journey toward death delays that destination by balancings of superego and id. Artists in the nineteenth century dramatized even more strikingly than Freud the possibly disastrous consequences of defiantly walling away the structures of consciousness from their sources in the unconscious. In the recent Bayreuth production of Wagner's The Ring, Valhalla is strongly reminiscent of that imperial pseudo-Rome constructed for Hitler by Albert Speer.

Similarities to this archetypal presentation of the sometimes apocalyptic discontent of consciousness in modern civilization may be found in recent movies; houses haunted or possessed by demonic forces burn or explode, ships still come to grief upon the sea, airliners and spaceships (our new images of questing consciousness) in the air and in vacuum. *The Towering Inferno* presented a Valhalla of corporate boardrooms consumed in flames, and *Earthquake* showed more falling towers than *The Waste Land*. *The Poseidon Adventure* provided a *Flying Dutchman* cum *Titanic* (as seen by Thomas Hardy) overwhelmed by a wave from the giant unconsciousness—which these disaster films seem to see our civilization as ignoring or violating. The labyrinthine interiors of spaceships and stations on other planets have replaced the winding Gothic passages quarried into our subterranean psyche. Creatures, monsters, benign visitants can now come from other galaxies rather than from attics, cellars, and graveyards under the clouded full moon. Yet the vampire (as James Twitchell's book reminds us) is still very much undead, injecting his victims with irrational compulsion, draining their energies like those neuroses that prey upon our lives in the dark of dreams.[43] Our popular entertainments have so little good to say about current society as to make one uneasy about the future of civilization. Gentle, wise space creatures are misunderstood and abused by earthlings. Lord Greystoke gives up his breathtaking English estate and the love of a beautiful woman for the jungle and his apes. But true love is found by another hero with a mermaid in a life underwater.

It appears that the call of an unconscious plenitude, resisting the wear of time and the discontents of cities, is as pervasive (and as persuasive) as ever. Considering also the primitivized Wagnerian demands for apocalypse made by rock music, we may well conclude that we live in a neoromantic age, though (alas!) one that has lost the knowledge and the civilities of Romanticism. Yet the terminology and approach of contemporary literary criticism, despite some helpful countermovement, seems still marked by the Modernist misapprehension of the best Romantic achievement. In a recent volume bringing together literary assessments of Freud, the papers by Derrida and Bloom provide interesting parallels to papers by Bloom and Geoffrey Hartman in the earlier collection *Romanticism and Consciousness*.[44] Both with Freud and Wordsworth, the substantial reality of the writer's compelling subject (the unconscious, nature) is subverted or denied.

We have looked briefly at Derrida's "Freud and the Scene of Writing," wherein the writing-pad image is used to model the unconscious as a collection of language traces rather than as the vital source of energies and instincts. Bloom's "Freud and the Poetic Sublime" deals also with the issue of the unconscious, which he sees as "a purely inferred division of the psyche." Though in a strict sense this is true, Bloom does not add that the realities of the physicist's quest, those ever-multiplying (or should we say dividing) protons, pions, and quarks are equally inferential in status. We encounter directly only sense data, but this does not prevent our believing in either subatomic structure or the structure of the psyche. Bloom calls Freud's system "a science of anxiety," argues that the art of the last several centuries, an "art of belatedness," shares this essential quality, and sees "our most authentic moments" as those of "negation, contraction, and repression." We have been led back squarely to the difference between Derrida's and Bloom's versions of consciousness, as opposed to the version to be developed in this essay. The crucial issue is the account of origin. The "sublime" (or creative) moment for Bloom is a negative moment, and "tends to rise out of an encounter with someone else's prior moment of negation."[45] We are back to the argument of The Anxiety of Influence. Bloom's beginning is the striving of a writer against the father figures of earlier powerful writers. The origin of literary consciousness is thus purely literary, and purely conscious.

There is some implication that writers as successful as Milton and Wordsworth (and perhaps Freud) tend to choke off later effort. But it is more reasonable to suppose that poetry has been suffocated, not by the presence of such grand progenitors as Bloom sees later poetic "ephebes" striving against, but rather by an increasing incapacity of belief, an increasing isolation of the intellect from its sources in chaotic experience and the unconscious.[46] Comparing the views of Derrida and Bloom, Perry Meisel (in the introduction to Freud: A Collection of Critical Essays) sees them in agreement as to the structure of literary reference, which is modeled upon primal repression. It is "the retroactive installation of a referent, which language situates, through rhetoric, outside of language."[47] Such a view inevitably distorts Wordsworth, one of whose theoretical purposes was to imagine, to experience, the universe as an intelligible source of reference for poetry. The "Wisdom and Spirit of the universe," for Wordsworth, gives "to forms and images a breath / And everlasting motion" (*Prel.* 1:401–4). In the Preface to *Lyrical Ballads*, he speaks of the poet's using words that are "the emanations of reality and truth."[48]

The central thrust of Wordsworth's vision was the depiction of a kind of copulatory interchange (hence the marriage metaphor in the Prospectus to *The Excursion*) between the poetic mind and its materials—between imagination pervasive as light and those dark mist-eruptions of chance encounter, the brute imprint on the mind of the real. Idealizing, in Freud's sense *defensive* reactions, sprang from those meetings with discharged soldier, old leech gatherer, female solitaries, drowned man in Esthwaite's lake. The sequence is as most patently appears in the text: encounter, then reaction. The mind may then dread, anticipate, project future events. It may compulsively replay that which has occurred (for Wordsworth, his desertion of Annette Vallon and their daughter), to gain mastery by a reshaping in language (the story of Margaret and "The Ruined Cottage"). The oversubtle critic must not be allowed to erode the substantial reality of that primary event, that thrust from the mist that reminds the poet of the contingency of existence. Sublimity is in the mind, but, more precisely, in the mind responding as it cannot avoid to sights and sounds—blind beggar, woman with a pitcher on her head—with a grandeur that is all the nobler because mortal, compelled by reality. Take away Wordsworth's postulation of a source in nature to which his words refer, and you obviate his reason for writing, his (the term is justified) poetic faith.

This essay is founded upon the perception (opposed to the skepticism that has infiltrated criticism in our time) of a beginning point for the journey of individuation, a first shore of demarcation between that sea preceding consciousness and the inland journey into time. This first term, this sea, is admittedly and necessarily mythological, beyond direct observation. But we will see that a first, originating term, a sea continued as a renewing, stream-pervaded landscape of origin or ancestral underground, remains a necessary component of the dualistic model of the Romantic psyche projected in poems by Wordsworth, Coleridge, Shelley, Keats, and their successors. In using models of the psyche drawn from psychoanalytic texts, we are attempting to establish a dual terminology that will be just to Romantic authors and their age and yet be meaningful to our own. One of the consequences of a mythic beginning point is that it supports an intelligible reading of the myth of the fall—which Romanticism so richly adapted and continued. Without a supportive source having no visible ending or beginning, nature or immortal sea or sheltering forest or communal unconsciousness, the story of a later fall-like separation into individual identity, moral responsibility, and the frustrations of civilized society and time makes no sense at all. Without such a source principle, we are unable to account for that call of the "warm South," that suasion born by nightingale's song or sea wind that tempts individual consciousness toward a perilous reunion. Without the term associated with inspiration and the death wish, we are unable to analyze the central tensions of the crucial Romantic poems.

As we prepare to look back toward those poets in whose work the structure and themes of modern poetry arose, we should consider for a moment the profounder effects of that antiromanticism that colored the Modernist criticism of the first part of this century, and of that intellectual skepticism that is with us still. The Modernist stance we find in the early Eliot, in Auden, and later in Sylvia Plath attempts to deal with Romantic emotionalism and unrealistic aspiration through a heightening of conscious analysis and self-analysis. The result is a more extreme version of that central Romantic tension between self and the landscape, conscious and unconscious dimensions of personality. The analytic component of the dualistic landscape structure was erected into a sterile, self-imprisoned persona, as in "Prufrock," "Gerontion," and characters in *The Waste Land*. The wish to move toward, penetrate into, and know (in an almost sexual sense) the feminine unconsciousness of landscape or sea became excruciatingly poignant because of the very impossibility of fulfillment. The result was Romantic impulse interrupted by ironic self-analysis and by those harsh facts opposing the psyche's quest, producing a new and fascinating literary tone.

The Modernist attempt to deal with Romanticism through skeptical analysis, though a success in literary terms, was in terms of psychology and ultimate vision a failure. Intensifying that dichotomy between the rational and the irrational that had originally impelled the Romantics into their poetic strategies of survival—their regenerative returns to the landscape—proved a destructive course.

Admittedly, the Wordsworthian position, unsupported by any accepted theology or social organization, made rather impossible demands of its own. At the outset there was a casualty, one who fell away from the nature-faith into drug dependency—that suggestive prototype of Modernism, Samuel Taylor Coleridge. Later nineteenth-century poets found the Wordsworthian synthesis imperiled by the despair of doubt, and their poetic voyages tended to be one-way affairs. Yet it remained for Edgar Allan Poe to take the essentially modern step of embracing the analytic consciousness, the original Romantic enemy—or, at least, barrier to be transcended—as chief ally in the act of composition. The nineteenth-century dissociation of sensibility, the crack in the facade of Usher's psychic dwelling, was seized upon as literary theme. The self that wished release from that imperious rationality developed over the last several centuries was instead subjected to its probing inquisition. "The wounded surgeon plies the steel," says Eliot, having himself survived an incisive self-analysis. Sylvia Plath's poem "Cut" may stand as a kind of paradigm of the self-destructiveness implicit in Modernist analysis. Wordsworth's "We murder to dissect" becomes, in the twentieth century, self-murder.[49] The Modernist stance amounts to a partial self-loathing—one founded, we suspect, in the inability of the rational consciousness to accept for what it is the incorrigibly Romantic psyche with its roots in the slime of the unconscious. The dissolution of this judgmental structure, followed by a new birth from earlier sources, constitutes the essential resuscitation ritual of poems such as Coleridge's "The Ancient Mariner," D. H. Lawrence's "The Ship of Death," and Theodore Roethke's "The Lost Son" sequence. Roethke, a relatively recent poet, one influenced by a psychological reading of "The Ancient Mariner," makes more explicit the Romantic dynamic of the return of consciousness to underlying sources in the unconscious.

The giant figures of twentieth-century poetry in English—Yeats, Frost, Stevens, Eliot, Auden, Williams—have all in their own way got beyond the Prufrock-phase of rationality, skepticism, and limiting self-analysis. Whether through occult study, religion, or the religion of art, they have arrived at more unified perspectives in some fashion reintegrating the individual reasoning mind with those necessary sources in the irrational and the collective. It is important to understand that this sequence of development was implicit in their initial positions. Poets of our century who have genuinely triumphed have done so by a thorough assimilation and transformation of the Romantic legacy, not by its rejection, which formed the fashionable veneer of early Modernist criticism.

Ultimately, the English Romantics are not separable from our own literary identity, from where we are today. They were the first generation of writers of great genius who reacted to the modern situation, and their terms, properly translated into the idiom of our day, are our terms. It is only fair, or just, to appreciate the technical and tonal innovations of Plath, Roethke, Eliot, or Stevens in relation to Romantic precedent, to realize that the mode of Wordsworth, Coleridge, Keats, the subject of consciousness in the world, was one capable of startling alteration and variety of presentation.

If W. B. Yeats is the greatest poet of our century, it is so partly because he achieved the greatest assimilation and transformation of Romantic irrationalism. Like the Gothic cathedral as analyzed by Erwin Panofsky, Yeats's work presents the maximum possible reconciliation of the rational and the irrational, the conscious and the unconscious, craft and inspiration.[50] That is the very foundation of his system of symbols. His geometries diagram a much more intricate version of those dichotomies balanced by Romantic landscape;

cones or "gyres" representing individuality and subjective consciousness interpenetrate with those representing the unconscious, collective origin of Anima Mundi. The architecture of his system is reflected by that primal confrontation between the structured consciousness of tower or dome and the vast unconsciousness of the sea.

1 *Cosmos from Chaos:*
The Story of Individuation

Let us speculate that in the paradigm English poems of land-scape, a mythic potentiality hovers within or behind the ostensible practicalities of location and occasion. If for Pope the "groves of Eden" that "Live in description, and look green in song" are to be rivaled, as inspirational prospect, by Windsor Forest, it is so partly because this present Edenic beauty reminds us still of the mastery of chaos that produced the original garden.

> Here hills and vales, the woodland and the plain,
> Here earth and water seem to strive again;
> Not chaos-like together crushed and bruised,
> But, as the world, harmoniously confused:
> Where order in variety we see,
> And where, though all things differ, all agree.[1]

Milton presents Chaos as an unformed contention of the four elements: "Hot, Cold, Moist, and Dry, four champions fierce, / Strive here for mastery" (*Paradise Lost*, 2:898, 899).[2] Pope's land-scape in "Windsor Forest" is explicitly "Not chaos-like," in that the harshness of discord, which crushes and bruises earth into water, fire into air, and each faction of "embryon atoms" into each other in Milton's "dark / Illimitable ocean, without bound" (891–92) has been overcome, Chaos converted into Cosmos, and an intelligible order brought forth into the light. But the very richness, the variety of this intelligible landscape, does nevertheless remind us of its origin in the primordial "Illimitable ocean." There the elements earth and water contend on a level of raw matter, a striving that this present interplay of stream and hill, of sun and shade, seems elegantly to imitate.

Mircea Eliade, in *The Sacred and the Profane*, tells us that rituals such as the Persian New Year commemorated "the day that witnessed the creation of the world and man." In the celebration of these occasions, the extinction of fires, social confusion such as that of the Saturnalia, with the associated erotic license, "symbolized the retrogression of the cosmos into chaos." The wear and soiling of profane time was annulled, and man, by "participating in the annihilation and re-creation of the world," was reborn, created anew. "Symbolically, man became contemporary with the cosmogony, he was present at the creation of the world."[3] Perhaps some analogous sense of a contemporaneousness with creation enlivens Pope's response to this prospect where water and shadow balance bright hill and sun, the wild heath's purple plays off against the cultivated "verdant isles" of corn. Chaos, harsh and sterile as an absolute condition, seems nevertheless to lie below or behind this fruitfully organized landscape, and to be responsible for the richness of variety. Chaos is a starting point that, as in the Persian New Year celebration, may be returned to in a reestablishment of contact with the principle of origin.

Central Romantic meditations in verse provide parallel narratives wherein the poet's consciousness returns to an immemorial, chaos-like source symbolized by landscape with fountains, streams, lakes, and, most definitively, the sea. The theme of return in "Tintern Abbey," for example, suggests a revisiting of primal sources. Five years have intervened between the poet's present stage of awareness and an earlier participation in the vitality that this landscape represents, years rather burdened with life in cities and a concurrent "weary weight" of unintelligibility. But as the poem continues, a reidentification is discovered. From behind the untenanted trees come the "wreaths of smoke" that suggest a hermit: a hidden presence mediating between the poet and the landscape. The mountains and the sound of their springs have drawn an enclosing circle. Within that circle everything is connected, land linked to sky by the cliffs, human habitation and cultivation woven into the wider landscape by a continuous green. With the help of his sister, who has "wild eyes" and is a version of his own earlier responsiveness, the poet reidentifies with a "life of things" from which he had thought of himself as separating. Metaphorically, in "Tintern Abbey" the poet is just sufficiently removed from "that immortal sea" of the "Intimations" ode to appreciate the journey into adulthood and the "still, sad music of humanity," but close enough to be fascinated also by the "mighty waters rolling" with their note of evermore. This suggested relation to primordial sea source is responsible, in part, for the resonance of the phrase "inland murmur." As through the vision of the children "upon the shore" in the ode, the speaker in "Tintern Abbey" revisits and re-experiences a separation that is like a birth. As when identifying with those children in the "season of calm weather" that is the poem, he is close enough to the ocean to be refreshed by a sense of his origin. His meditative, elegiac perspective serves to convince himself, and us, that this fall into individual identity and maturity may be seen as qualified, fortunate.

The creation myth of Genesis, as amplified in *Paradise Lost*, held a powerful appeal for the Romantics. In his Prospectus to *The Excursion* (drafted in the same year that "Tintern Abbey" was written), Wordsworth parallels his own poetic exploration into "our Minds, into the Mind of Man" with Milton's descent into Chaos and "the darkest pit of lowest Erebus."[4] Significant echoes of *Paradise Lost* occur throughout *The Prelude*, especially in the climactic vision from Mount Snowdon in book 14. There the parallel with Milton's creation scene suggests such a contemporaneousness with the cosmogony, such a sense of the poet's being "present at the creation of the world," as Eliade finds in the Persian New Year ritual. And "Kubla Khan," written by Coleridge during the 1797–98 period of close interchange with Wordsworth that helped spark the latter's Prospectus and "Tintern Abbey," may also be read as a creation poem, with significant echoes of *Paradise Lost*.[5] Thus both the paradigm treatment of external landscape in "Tintern Abbey" and the paradigm of visionary, internal landscape in "Kubla Khan" share a mythic tendency relating them to the story of creation and the fall in *Paradise Lost*. Wordsworth portrays for us a pattern in personal experience that we may relate to the myth. Coleridge portrays for us a version of the myth that we may relate to personal experience.

Erich Neumann's *The Origins and History of Consciousness* focuses upon a continuity between the individual ego's separation from preconscious sources and creation myth, with its symbol of an original wholeness—the timeless uroboros, serpent with tail in its mouth—out of which all things come. For Neumann, "the coming of consciousness, manifesting itself as light in contrast to the darkness of the unconscious, is the real 'object' of creation mythology." Central symbols of the uroboric origin are the circle, the sea, fountains, lakes and pools, the earth, and caves and the underworld.[6] Wordsworth's "round ocean" in "Tintern Abbey" is thus a double uroboros symbol, as is the "sunless sea" of the "measureless" caverns in "Kubla Khan."

Thus, the creation (or re-creation) of the world, whether reflected in ancient ritual, creation myth, or by Romantic imagination, is in psychological terms the establishment of consciousness in the context of chaotic unconsciousness. The pleasure dome of Coleridge's "Kubla Khan" is decreed like the establishment of the firmament in Genesis, like the separation of the land and the water. Chaos is ordered by the enclosing circle of walls and towers, and by the dome that reverberates with, and allows the contemplation of, the ancestral voices from below. On a more personal level, the mythic coming of consciousness becomes the story of one man's individuation. Coleridge's intellectual architecture in "Kubla Khan" is thus thematically related to the Wordsworthian contemplation of the landscape by the poet in his own guise that culminates in *The Prelude*. The decree of the dome in "Kubla Khan" and the growth of imagination in *The Prelude* are different symbolic treatments of a central theme: the creation-like separation of consciousness from the primordial chaos of unconsciousness in identification with nature.

The "sunless sea" of "Kubla Khan" corresponds, on the level of cosmology, to the original chaos that preceded an intelligible cosmos. Before God speaks light into existence in Genesis, "darkness was upon the face of the deep." The *Oxford Annotated Bible* provides this note: "According to ancient belief, the world originated from and was suspended upon a watery chaos (the *deep;* cp. Ps. 24.1), personified as a dragon in the Babylonian creation epic." God's words, his "Let there be light," begin the divisions of light from dark, above from below, land from water, that result in a landscape.[7] In "Kubla Khan," it is the decree of a "pleasure-dome," and the extension of this fiat to the encircling walls and towers, that establishes an ordering vantage point in a context without limitation—where the river Alph ran through "caverns measureless to man / Down to a sunless sea."

Milton in *Paradise Lost* also regards the original creation as an ordering of Chaos—again, symbolically, a sea. Christ and his host view from the "shore" of heaven the "vast immeasurable Abyss, / Outrageous as a sea, dark, wasteful, wild" (7:209–10). The Word commands this sea to silence, and "Chaos heard his voice" (7:221). The next act of creation, as Milton portrays it, particularly focuses attention upon the establishment of order, form, *measure*. Christ takes up an enormous golden draftsman's compass and draws upon this "immeasurable" sea the boundaries of the universe.

> One foot he centered, and the other turned
> Round through the vast profundity obscure,
> And said, "Thus far extend, thus far thy bounds:
> This be thy just circumference, O World!"   (7:228–31)

In "Kubla Khan" the poet has also drawn a defining circle, thus creating the boundaries of a world, albeit one much smaller than Milton's.

Coleridge's poem, unlike Milton's account of creation, is enormously compressed. Only eight lines into the Khan's reiteration of God's fiat, there are "gardens bright with sinuous rills, / Where blossomed many an incense-bearing tree." But perhaps the very brevity of the process lends a note of precariousness. We are reminded by the "sinuous rills" and by the "forests ancient as the hills" that this Eden of sun, blossoms, and clear forms rests rather perilously over an underground sea. The quotation from the *Oxford Bible* is perfectly appropriate: "the world originated from and was *suspended upon* a watery chaos." Chaos remains in thrilling proximity to this landscape that has been created by word. "A *firmament*, regarded as a solid dome (Job 37.18), separated the upper from the lower waters."[8] Coleridge's dome, and the sunlit landscape it surmounts, serve this function. But, in words of Carl Jung respecting the creative personality, there is here a "permeability of the partition separating the conscious and the unconscious" (*C.W.* 8, par. 135). The Garden as described by both Genesis and *Paradise Lost* has its central fountain, which is, for Milton, the point of access through which Satan reintroduces Chaos (in the form of his serpentine seduction) into Eden. Seeking to return into the Garden, Satan finds

> Where Tigris, at the foot of Paradise,
> Into a gulf shot under ground, till part
> Rose up a fountain by the Tree of Life.
> In with the river sunk, and with it rose,
> Satan, involved in rising mist.   (9:71–75)

The fountain of "Kubla Khan" parallels this fountain of Eden, and, like it, seems to threaten the serenity of a psychic state represented in terms of landscape. There is a downward movement toward it—introduced by "But oh!"—away from the "sunny spots of greenery." It is set in a chasm, a kind of fissure or ravine in the hillside, over which is cast a paradoxical air of unholiness and paradise, of sacredness and curse.

> A savage place! as holy and enchanted
> As e'er beneath a waning moon was haunted
> By woman wailing for her demon-lover!
> And from this chasm, with ceaseless turmoil seething,
> As if this earth in fast thick pants were breathing,
> A mighty fountain momently was forced.

Probably the seductive, painful siren call from this place represents the tonality that eruptions from the unconscious, perhaps in association with opium, had for the mind of the poet. We have Jung's metaphor for "the living fountain" flowing out of the unconscious, that "deposit of all human experience right back to its remotest beginnings" (*C.W.* 8, par. 339). Coleridge's fountain produces the river Alph, which runs for a while in sunlight, then falls back again to the underground sea. Amid the tumult of such a return toward collective origins, Kubla heard "Ancestral voices"—heard, that is, the tonality of the collective unconscious.

The description of the fountain's chasm suggests dread, religious awe, and a psychic compulsion. The vowel sequence in *waning, moon, haunted, woman,* and *demon,* together with the sonorous consonants *w, m,* and *n,* produce one of the most exotic and seductive passages in English verse; the reader is pulled downward in a whirlpool of sensation, under the aura of two comparisons: the waning Gothic moon and the woman compelled to call her lover, whose coming seems to mean both ecstasy and pain. The object of this descent is a fountain, which spurts convulsively from below, as if in orgasmic release of a destructive creativity. the rebounding rocks and the panting of the ground suggest earthquake, but the implication of breathing means life itself. The relation of the conscious and the unconscious minds, as Jung portrays it, seems a similar paradox. Creativity comes from below, but such regions are dangerous. Earlier times had called that area of the psyche *hell.* William Blake seems to have begun the reinterpretation of this underworld, showing us in "The Marriage of Heaven and Hell" that both areas, above and below, both principles, the Devouring and the Prolific, are necessary to existence, that life as we know it is founded on the fruitful contention of such opposites.

Kathleen Raine in her essay "Traditional Symbolism in 'Kubla Khan'" has examined the poem in terms of Jung's "discoveries of an innate conformation of archetypes which tend to appear in similar forms in the myths of all religions." She argues that " 'Kubla Khan' both is, and is about, remembrance," linking Coleridge's unconscious rediscovery of the vision of a walled garden to the knowledge said by Plato to be "remembrance, anamnesis—not memory of events of time or of the individual life, but remembrance in time, and by the individual, of permanent intellectual realities." Comparing Coleridge's garden both with the earlier "subtle magical atmosphere of Milton's Paradise" and the later description by Yeats in the *Autobiographies* of "a walled garden on the top of a high mountain," she concludes that there are "certain typical features of the Paradise archetype . . . of which no single vision has all."[9] Yet central to the versions of Milton, Coleridge, and Yeats, in contrast to the Edenic freshness as of recent origin, is the imagery of the fall.

Satan's bitter presence as an observer of Adam and Eve in their garden qualifies our perception of its deliciousness in its first presentation, *Paradise Lost*, book 4. Yeats's garden contained a central tree with "fruit out of which, if you held the fruit to your ear, came the sound of fighting" (*Auto.*, 157). Coleridge's river Alph, falling back "in tumult to a lifeless ocean," evokes "Ancestral voices prophesying war!" The summarizing image following the river's disappearance into "caverns measureless to man" emphasizes duality, reconciliation between opposites, compromise.

> The shadow of the dome of pleasure
> Floated midway on the waves;
> Where was heard the mingled measure
> From the fountain and the caves.
> It was a miracle of rare device,
> A sunny pleasure-dome with caves of ice.
>
> ("Kubla Khan")

This emphasis on a "midway" point between above and below where a "mingled measure" may be heard from fountain in sun and caves in darkness is followed by an account of a figure of inspiration, an "Abyssinian maid," which the poet once saw. The implication is that Coleridge's access to the "hiding places of man's power" (*Prel.* 12:279), like Wordsworth's, must be limited, perhaps by the very premise of artistic creativity with its perilous balance between opposites. As Shelley put it, "The mind in creation is as a fading coal which some invisible influence, like an inconstant wind, awakens to transitory brightness: this power arises from within, like the colour of a flower which fades and changes as it is developed, and the conscious portions of our natures are unprophetic either of its approach or its departure."[10] The inevitable association of the fall with the garden of Paradise may thus be implicit in the very measuring that allows us to outline, categorize, number—in the establishment of the structure of consciousness itself as a perspective walled away from the wholeness of identity with the uroboric ocean of origin.

Blake's "The Book of Urizen" presents a bitter and one-sided account of the creation story wherein the ironically named figure Urizen ("your reason"), associated later with commandments, law, and scientific measurement, is seen in traumatic separation from the original One.[11] In the beginning,

> Earth was not, nor globes of attraction.
> The will of the Immortal expanded
> Or contracted his all flexible senses.
> Death was not, but eternal life sprung.   (ch. 2:1)

But following Urizen's separation into a subjective world of moral will and commandment, "Rage seized the strong," and "Eternity" is sundered, "Rent away with a terrible crash" (ch. 3:1, 3). We are witnessing a creation story wherein the fall is clearly simultaneous with the creation.

Urizen's exploration of newly visible nature is aided by his invention of the tools of measurement.

> He formed scales to weigh;
> He formed massy weights;
> He formed a brazen quadrant;
> He formed golden compasses
> And began to explore the Abyss,
> And he planted a garden of fruits.   (ch. 7:8)

The garden seems to depend upon these instruments of consciousness, just as Milton's cosmos does upon Christ's draftsmanship with the golden compass, and the Khan's "twice five miles of fertile ground" upon the "walls and towers" that girdle around. The condition of waking, adult existence is seen in all cases as depending upon the defining and thus limiting structures of consciousness. The question becomes what attitude the poet should take toward this limited reacquaintance with the unitary origin—all that is possible for fallen man. Blake in "The Book of Urizen" and "The Marriage of Heaven and Hell" engages in sardonic satire, comparing limited actuality to unlimited potentiality.

Wordsworth, Coleridge, and Keats deal with this dichotomy between real and ideal, between fragmentary verbal artifact and inspiration's source, through the tone of elegy.

As Schiller puts it in his essay "Naive and Sentimental Poetry," the sentimental poet is "always involved with two conflicting representations and perceptions—with actuality as a limit and with his idea as infinitude; and the mixed feelings that he excites will always testify to this dual source."[12] The application of this comment to the passages we have before us suggests that the mixtures of limitation and infinitude, cosmos and chaos, are the proper mythic elements to portray reality as we experience it. The conditions of our conscious perception and the landscape before us require, as explanatory myth, an Edenic garden reverberating with tonalities of fall—exactly what is presented in "Kubla Khan." This and other Romantic landscape poems serve as the psyche's self-representation in verse, with a characteristic division between above and below, the light and the dark, the land and the water—between, that is, the created and thus measurable clear forms of consciousness, and the measureless world below.

With inspiration, windows appear in the partition between waking and sleep, consciousness and its origin, like openings in the landscape from which springs may start. As Wordsworth puts it,

> The days gone by
> Return upon me almost from the dawn
> Of life: the hiding-places of man's power
> Open; I would approach them, but they close.
>
> *Prel.* 12:277–80

If "the mind in creation is as a fading coal," then that which has set the music and imagery in motion is beyond definition except through its effects in that music and imagery. Yet it must be taken into account as a component of the analysis; we know that the deep exists if only because Venus has risen from its waves. The Romantic landscape at its best investigates the shoreline meeting between time and the timeless—just as Wordsworth and Yeats drew inspiration and structures for their poems from walking by the sea.

Wordsworth's major myth, then, seems just this separation, development, and cyclical return of consciousness to its landscape of origin, as imaged most completely in the "Intimations" ode.

> Hence in a season of calm weather
>   Though inland far we be,
> Our Souls have sight of that immortal sea
>   Which brought us hither,
>   Can in a moment travel thither,
> And see the Children sport upon the shore,
> And hear the mighty waters rolling evermore.   (161–67)

In this moment of vision the poet has retraced the steps of his earlier travel "farther from the east" (71), initially in priesthood to nature and its more than natural light, to reverse for a "season" the decline of his original birthright: his sense of support by a divine ground, his envelopment in a capacity for seeing that combines the attributes of water and light—the light "flows" (69), there is a "fountain-light of all our day" (151). He has returned from the trek inland, into consciousness and "years that bring the philosophic mind" (186), to revisit the component of his personality/inspiration that lies ordinarily out of sight in the world of time, because prior to it.

Individualization is necessary to the poet, else he would be only a mute part of the landscape (as part of him wishes to be— Keats thinks of becoming "a sod"). Without it he would resemble his female figures who never become fully known to us but forever in imagination bear a pitcher on the head "Against the blowing wind" (*Prel.* 12:253) and walk by the sea when "The mighty Being is awake" ("It Is a Beauteous Evening") and reap solitarily, filling the vale to "overflowing" with indistinguishable song of "old, unhappy, far-off things, / And battles long ago" ("The Solitary Reaper")—or, like Lucy in her various guises, die young. Lucy is a series of figures stationed in landscapes of such loneliness and purity that she seems just born and in danger of being swallowed up again. She never, in effect, gets far enough inland into maturity and autonomy to escape a reabsorptive wave from the uroboric origin. Just as, for Neumann, the infantile ego, "feebly developed, easily tired, emerges like an island out of the ocean of the unconscious for occasional moments only, and then sinks back again," so do Wordsworth's children, still enveloped in nature, return to their source. Lucy Gray, most appropriately, is drowned.[13] Lucy of "Three Years She Grew in Sun and Shower," once nature says "This Child I to myself will take," does not live long. The figure in "There Was a Boy" who interacted so seamlessly with the landscape, blowing "mimic hootings to the silent owls, / That they might answer him," does not grow up with his "mates." Like the "simple Child" of "We Are Seven," these images of partially individualized existence have not fully experienced the separation from nature into self-consciousness; they do not, like her, know the difference between the human and the natural, between life and death. They form the frieze upon the ground of the sacred, ornamenting nature as divine unconsciousness.

The solemn yet ecstatic momentum of return that Wordsworth celebrates in "A Slumber Did My Spirit Seal" tells us that the loss of individual "motion" and "force" to the uroboric roundness of "earth's diurnal course" is, from one perspective, a consummation more than an extinction. It prevents all apology for a later condition, following "glad animal movements" and cataracts haunting "like a passion," when the poet must convince himself that other, more intellectual gifts, he "would believe," offer an "Abundant recompense" ("Tintern Abbey," 74, 77, 87–88). The original infantile condition, when the Babe on his mother's breast experiences "The gravitation and the filial bond / Of nature that connect him with the world" (*Prel.* 2:243–44), is transformed and continued into the teenaged years through an imaginative vision of nature, whereby the poet sees blessings spread around him "like a sea" (395). This continued uroboric involvement culminates in the "bliss ineffable" attendant upon the "sentiment of Being" of his seventeenth year, when intuition of symbolic origin penetrated even to "all that glides / Beneath the wave, yea, in the wave itself, / And mighty depth of waters" (*Prel.* 2:407–9)—a passage echoing

Milton's vision of fish procreating in the primal waters at the creation (*Paradise Lost* 7:400–402).

The vision, then, and the aura, of uroboric identification remained—one reason, probably, why memory is so central a means toward inspiration and metaphysical insight in Wordsworth. But he would not have become the poet we know—or any poet at all—without a contrary movement, away from nature/unconsciousness, into individuality and heroic articulation. "The ascent toward consciousness is the 'unnatural' thing in nature; it is specific of the species Man."[14] Thus the dominant action of *The Prelude*, prefigured by "Tintern Abbey," concerns a single consciousness (which is representative of us all) as it emerges from primal waters by the river Derwent, realizing first power to "sport / A naked savage, in the thunder shower" (*Prel.* 1:299–300), to climb the cliffs, row the boat, and glory in autonomy—until eventually it experiences a fall-like separation from its native source through residence at Cambridge, in London, and in France. This necessary movement toward separation and independence is compensated by the poet's returns through mature imaginative vision as in "Tintern Abbey" to preconscious sources symbolized by the landscape. The reciprocal action of these opposed yet complementary impulses is at the heart of Wordsworth's complexity. Critics of his poetry find it very difficult to do justice to both halves of his vision, to both the thrust toward consciousness and the returns to landscapes perceived, in terms of deepest symbolism, as earlier.

In book 1 of *The Prelude*, Wordsworth shows us the psyche's at first tentative, backsliding steps out of primal waters onto shore. By the Derwent he "Made one long bathing of a summer's day" (290), in and out of the water like those "amphibious" dwellers between one world and another he described in a *Prelude* manuscript.[15] As he "plunged and basked again / Alternate" (291–92), he enacted his own version of that impersonal sporting "upon the shore" of the "Intimations" ode. *The Prelude*, book 1, gives us the beginning of that inland journey depicted mythically in the ode. The early *Prelude* is the poet's most detailed and intense backward glance—during his most extended "season of calm weather"—toward the "immortal sea" of psychic origin. From the distance of maturity implied by the sophistication and epic tonalities of the verse, Wordsworth looks across the "vacancy" between his present and those days that "yet have such self-presence" (2:29–30), feeling himself "Two consciousnesses," conscious of himself "And of some other Being" (32–33). This "other Being" is strange, not merely as child, but also as symbolizing the original psyche not yet fully separated from primal unconsciousness. The poet sees his earlier self as a kind of prelapsarian child-Adam in the process of becoming what he himself now is—an individualized consciousness fallen into a loneliness and freedom that may become, if too complete, sterility. The writing of the poem represents a counteraction, as he remembers and imagines across this "vacancy," to see again toward the headwaters and revisit "islands in the unnavigable depth / Of our departed time."[16]

From the perspective of maturity, the poet is able to see that the other being's journey inland was even then not a simple, linear movement, but rather a complex struggle between alternating forces whereby progress toward autonomy and self-identification provoked responses from some dark force. On his own at night to trap woodcocks, the boy felt himself to be "a trouble to the peace / That dwelt" among the moon and stars (316–17). His new independence is both exciting freedom and a burden. The guilt that succeeds when "strong desire" overpowers his "better reason" and he steals from others' snares (318–21), though superficially the product of beginning moral consciousness, is at a deeper level the guilt implicit in the part's separating from the whole—in Adam's fall into knowledge.

It is as if the ego's movement toward separation had provoked a secret resistance. The "low breathings" and "sounds / Of undistinguishable motion" (323–24) that follow him here are premonitory of the striding mountain soon to come, behind the frightened lad in his borrowed boat. Wordsworth had defined the "life of things" (49) in "Tintern Abbey" partly in terms of motion: "A motion and a spirit, that impels / All thinking things, all objects of all thought" (100–101). Such vital motion is mysterious, and of so much greater extent than the thinking thing as to threaten its individualized existence. Just as when followed by the life-suggesting

"Low breathings," the lad in rowing upon the lake is trailed by clouds not of glory but of "unknown modes of being" (393). A mountain peak seems to loom up and stride after him. Like a knight of romance facing his first dragon or giant, he "struck and struck again" (380), if only with the oars.[17] The apparition, of course, is a sensory illusion, the product of his own psyche's interaction with the cliff and mountain beyond during the time of his rowing. So the life-motion is projected out of him, onto a peak "out there"; yet the organism of phenomena that results has a wholeness and independent identity, binding together, as symbolic form, the life of the mind and the look of the landscape. Such an endowment of "forms and images" with "a breath / And everlasting motion" is a function that the poet attributes to the "Wisdom and Spirit of the universe" (1:401–4). And it was Nature that first led him to the boat—"One summer evening (led by her)"—to encounter this experience. Thus we must feel that the poet here sees his earlier self as in the hands of a greater, wiser, and yet darker power, for the imparting of a crucial lesson. That lesson is complex.

On the one hand Nature is reminding her favored son that she, after all, is primary, that her motion, as in "A Slumber Did My Spirit Seal," "Tintern Abbey," and the ice-skating vision soon to come in *The Prelude*, "rolls through all things" ("Tintern Abbey," 102), the unitary prime mover, as the "round ocean" ("Tintern Abbey," 98) is the living source. At the same time, he, the young hero, has reached a certain stage of independence, has unloosed a small boat from its chain within a womb-like "rocky cave, its usual home" (*Prel.* 1:359). So he ventures out upon the lake, followed by the troubling, guilt-embodying "voice / Of mountain-echoes" (362–63), but moving at first triumphantly into moonlight. He is learning of autonomy and initially leaves behind, from either oar, promising signatures of the psyche's self-identification and order: "on either side / Small circles glittering idly in the moon" (364–65).

Yet the complex struggle between individualized consciousness and absorption in nature (as in the womb-cave of the cliff) cannot be so readily resolved. The peak, "As if with voluntary power instinct" (379), upreared its head, and the epic combat was joined. Ironically each oar-thrust as he "struck and struck again" contributed to the life and size of this mountain giant, which "with purpose of its own / And measured motion like a living thing" (383–84) strode after him. The measure of the motion comes from his own pulls upon the oars, suggesting that the very orderliness of individualized consciousness is contributing to the counteraction by nature. When Blake's Urizen proclaims, among other things, "one weight, one measure," soon, in reaction, "Rage seized the strong" (ch. 3:1).

The young poet, at this point, is not far enough advanced along his trek into maturity that he can, like Milton's Christ and Coleridge's Khan, draw the definitive circle upon the sea of chaos. These first inscriptions toward the poet's reiteration of God's fiat in Genesis have all melted "into one track / Of sparkling light" (*Prel.* 1:366–67). The completion of that parallel waits upon the Mount Snowdon episode at the conclusion of *The Prelude*. Though he has rowed like one "Proud of his skill" (368) and has fought heroically against the "grim shape" (381), he has been overawed. He turned "with trembling oars" (385) and "stole" back to the maternal "covert of the willow tree" (387).

He carries away, however, a renewed appreciation of nature's unconscious life, and what will become a strengthened capacity to defend his own limited vessel of ego against that vast organic whole of things, whose motion is ultimately round and therefore perfect, final. He has escaped the reassimilation that took Lucy back, to be "Rolled round in earth's diurnal course, / With rocks, and stones, and trees" ("A Slumber Did My Spirit Seal"), at one with the great womb that devours as well as creates.

Wordsworth's destiny was related to, but not the same as, that of his pure, child-like, unconscious heroines. To be articulate, he must fight free of the looming uroboric form, like a mountain symbolically risen out of water.[18] So the episode of the striding mountain is a crucial one for the in-and-out relationship to nature/unconsciousness of *The Prelude*, book 1; it leaves the growing lad for a time in "grave / And serious mood," with a sense of "unknown modes of being" (389–93), but afterward he is the stronger for it, and in the ice-skating episode feels himself "Proud and exulting like an untired horse" (432), shod with steel and in mastery of the frozen lake. The sea of chaos has become, symbolically, an inhabitable landscape, and he and his fellows are articulate: "not a voice was idle" (439).

Thus, in book 1 we see the growing boy strengthening into a heroic consciousness through the experiences of loneliness, hunting, danger (when climbing the cliffs), even a combat-like confrontation with the specter of a striding mountain. But the process is not linear (or easy), because it involves struggle between the opposed powers of human autonomy/consciousness versus nature dependency/unconsciousness. Progress toward freedom and articulation provokes resistance from the unconscious, which projects a reassimilative presence into imagined "Low breathings" and into the phenomena of perception, the "mighty world / Of eye, and ear"—particularly such forms as they "half create" ("Tintern Abbey," 105–6). Wordsworth's landscapes early in *The Prelude* thus have something of the quality of dreams. At the very outset the Derwent "flowed along my dreams" (1:274). Later the striding mountain left an impression of "huge and mighty forms" that were "a trouble to my dreams" (1:398–400), and the climactic vision while skating, the spinning of the cliffs "as if the earth had rolled / With visible motion her diurnal round" (1:459–60), seduced him to a rapt attention "Till all was tranquil as a dreamless sleep" (463). It is in keeping with the tendency of *The Prelude* as a whole, wherein traditional epic quest (and conquest) is converted into a series of psychological encounters, victories, and achievements, that the beginning episodes should embody the profoundest issues of individuation projected into imagery of landscape. One thinks of the drawing produced by the patient of Jung's: "she saw herself with the lower half of her body in the earth, stuck fast in a block of rock. The region round about was a beach strewn with boulders. In the background was the sea." The woman felt impelled to free herself from this entrapment, which symbolized "being caught in the unconscious" (*C.W.* 9, par. 525, 527). Similarly, Wordsworth felt impelled to assert his autonomy in an environment reflective of his own psychic life, animated by the interaction of objects and his senses.

Although the psychological dimensions of Wordsworth's autobiography have in part to be inferred from his landscapes, there are also terms and discursive passages that provide a context of support for such interpretations. Toward the end of book 1, after the more famous episodes, he tells us that by age ten his mind had been "stamped" by the seasons (560) and that he "held unconscious intercourse with beauty / Old as creation" (562–63). In further developing the effect of experiences that brought him "No conscious memory" (574) of similar sights and "no peculiar sense / Of quietness or peace" (575–76), he is intent to point out the continuing, intuitive feeding of his senses by the landscape, his eye moving across the water "like a bee among the flowers" (580). The line of argument serves two functions: it covers the unconscious effect on him of inadvertent, hardly noticed sights, and it reaches back to include the meanings of even those dramatic, consciously powerful episodes such as the striding mountain. Both a number of quieter experiences, and the deeper significance of those events notable at the time for sheer drama, were "doomed to sleep / Until maturer seasons called them forth / To impregnate and to elevate the mind" (594–96). Clearly, he means to designate an existence of images and experiences in some dimension of the mind below the conscious level, in a state of seed-like potentiality, so that later they could be brought up and developed.

Wordsworth asserts his psychology most modestly, of course, questioning whether anyone may know "the individual hour in which / His habits were first sown, even as a seed" (2:206–7), yet there is an admiring wonderment before the psyche's mysteries that supports the capacity for symbolic presentation. He has encountered the "dark / Inscrutable workmanship" that reconciles such "discordant elements" (1:341–43) as the conflicting thrusts toward independence and nature identification. He finds it

> strange that all
> The terrors, pains, and early miseries,
> Regrets, vexations, lassitudes interfused
> Within my mind, should e'er have borne a part,
> And that a needful part, in making up
> The calm existence that is mine when I
> Am worthy of myself! Praise to the end!   (1:344–50)

As the meditation between the guilt-projecting episode of wood-cock snaring and cliff climbing on the one side, and the striding-mountain vision on the other, this amounts to an appreciation of the dark/light, pain/pleasure balance of the poet's early mind, as he struggled to resolve the conflict between human consciousness and the larger determining power of nature/unconsciousness.

Northrop Frye's "The Drunken Boat" points out the "vehicular" momentum of the poet "united to a creative power greater than his own because it includes his own," associating this creative stance with the "image of the Aeolian harp, or lyre." Romantic poetry "identifies the human with the nonhuman world," and "tends to move inside and downward instead of outside and upward." Shelley's language about the creative process is haunted by the "Kubla Khan" "geography of caves and underground streams." This tendency to probe downward, toward regions formerly thought to be infernal, gives Romantic poetry a "deep interior" that Frye finds "morally ambivalent, retaining some of the demonic qualities that the corresponding pre-Romantic level had."[19]

The realization that the source of one's vision may be destructive, even associated with death, as in Keats's nightingale ode, is part of the new moral geography of the Romantics. They felt ordinary consciousness and the traditional heavenly direction to be mechanistic—the domain of "sky-gods" such as Blake's Urizen and Nobodaddy, "Shelley's Jupiter, Byron's Arimanes, the Lord in the Prologue to *Faust*"—and so had to probe down below, into the domain of the unconscious.[20] Wordsworth, of course, deliberately challenges this new field of exploration, in explicitly psychological terms, when in the Prospectus to *The Excursion* he promises that neither "Chaos" nor "The darkest pit of lowest Erebus" can "breed such fear and awe" as are latent in the parallel depths of "the Mind of Man"—depths that are to be the "haunt, and the main region" of his song (35–41).

Wordsworth's balance in respect to such opposed images and tendencies as childhood and maturity, nature and humanity, the sea and the shore, the direction downward and the direction upward, helped him to brave an uncharted, more directly psychological territory over a longer, more complete creative career than any of his English contemporaries save Blake. His own version of the myth of the fall, in particular, helped him reconcile the Romantic, "vehicular" experience of creation as union with a greater power and the necessarily limited access to that power available to any individualized identity interested in preserving itself from the ultimate effects of chaos/unconsciousness: madness or death.

If for Frye the "major constructs which our own culture has inherited from its Romantic ancestry are . . . of the 'drunken boat' shape," we might put forward Wordsworth as model of a more balanced relation between those Apollonian and Dionysiac components whose destructive contention seems to threaten chaos in postromantic writers. "Here the boat is usually in the position of Noah's ark, a fragile container of sensitive and imaginative values threatened by a chaotic and unconscious power below it."[21] As his reference to *The World as Will and Idea* in this same passage suggests, Frye probably has in mind the quotation from Schopenhauer in *The Birth of Tragedy:* "Even as on an immense, raging sea, assailed by huge wave crests, a man sits in a little rowboat trusting his frail craft, so, amidst the furious torments of this world, the individual sits tranquilly, supported by the *principium individuationis* and relying on it."[22] Nietzsche interprets this man in a rowboat as an expression of his Apollonian principle, cognitive, individual, clear, but locked always in a duality with the collective ecstatic Dionysiac impulse, associated with earth, animals, the primitive, and divine intoxication.

A central concern of *The Prelude* is Wordsworth's complex exploration of the Apollonian *principium individuationis* in relation to its opposite term, symbolized in the passage above by the water beneath the boat. *The Prelude,* of course, is available in several versions: as Wordsworth first completed it in the long form, in 1805; as he left this long form, with many revisions, but as essentially the same poem, to be published after his death in 1850; and, more recently, edited from the poet's manuscripts, in the two-part version of 1799. Between the two-part 1799 *Prelude* and the thirteen-book *Prelude* of 1805 was an intermediate version of five books, one including the narrative of the ascent of Mount Snowdon which, in revised form, concludes the finished poem.[23] Emerging from this complexity of versions, revisions, and interrelated manuscripts is the image of the poet wrestling, during his most creative period, with the contention of the two halves of his paradigm of individuation.

Wordsworth's poetic power was at its peak during the period when these two terms (represented by individual limited human identity in the boat, and a collective uroboric water below) waged their fiercest contention. Manuscript variants omitted from the completed *Prelude* suggest that a side of the poet strongly preferred identification, not with the man in the boat, but with the unconscious, collective life that surrounded and supported him. The following passage dates from 1799, or about the time of the completion of the two-part *Prelude:*

> what we feel
> Of active or recognizable thought,
> Prospectiveness, or intellect, or will,
> Not only is not worthy to be deemed
> Our being, to be prized as what we are,
> But is the very littleness of life.
> Such consciousness I deem but accidents,
> Relapses from that one interior life
> That lives in all things. . . .[24]

These lines associate with episodes of the two-part *Prelude* wherein the boy, led by "spirits" and "beings of the hills," receives the impress of the vaster life that made "The surface of the universal earth / With meanings of delight, of hope and fear, / Work like a sea."[25] The balance of identification, at this season, inclines toward the unconscious, the collective, the Dionysiac. The landscape itself is impregnated by a residuum of the chaotic origin and symbolizes that sea whose "mighty waters" still roll within hearing. The ego, with its plans and self-direction (its "prospectiveness, or intellect, or will"), is struggling to assert the worth of its independence in respect to "that one interior life / That lives in all things" (see above). Yet at this moment the poet is much more impressed with the unconscious, unitary life connecting his own deep psyche and the landscape than with that partially individualized human thought which, from the point of view of mountain lake, peak, and stars, seems only a "littleness."

In *The Prelude* that evolved, this crucial contest was projected into the boy "Scudding away from snare to snare," versus the "Low breathings" that followed him (1:314, 330). As he rowed upon the mountain lake, the peak that rose in the horizon, a bit like one of Schopenhauer's "huge wave crests," embodied the unconsciousness of organic evolution now projected back into the landscape by some dark, collective stratum of the poet's total psyche— a projection suggested by the contribution of sensory illusion to this form. Schopenhauer's man "in a little rowboat," associated by Nietzsche with the Apollonian principle, corresponds to the boy in his borrowed boat. His rowing, his wake of "Small circles glittering idly in the moon" (1:365), suggests an assertion of the *principium individuationis* in this domain of Dionysus.

Both the structure of Wordsworth's image complexes and the shape of his major myth—this struggle toward individuation— have at their core a duality, a contention of two terms, neither of which must be allowed to overcome or negate the other. The conscious observer must not wholly lose himself into the landscape, must not join the hermit of "Tintern Abbey" invisibly behind the trees, writing no poems. If temporarily "laid asleep" (45) to become again an Adamic "living soul" (46), he must wake into words. The child on the shore must not sport so far into the waves as to be drowned, yet the youth on his inland journey must not lose all contact with that originating sea. The "intellect, or will" must fight free of "low breathings" and contend in its boat of individuality with the collective unconscious mountain, yet if the deep sense of "that one interior life / That lives in all things" is lost, the poet will fall victim to the "meddling intellect" ("The Tables Turned") of a too-conscious age, which murders to dissect.

It has always been the role of the experience on Mount Snowdon to deal explicitly and in maturity with those components of the total psychological picture only implicit earlier. Thus, the mountain prospect provides, in the 1805 text,

The perfect image of a mighty mind,
Of one that feeds upon infinity,
That is exalted by an under-presence,
The sense of God, or whatsoe'er is dim
Or vast in its own being.   (13:69–73)

This scene is mind-like largely because of its duality—its division
into upper and lower, sight and nonsight—by the vastly extending
ocean of cloud. Having climbed through the mist into moonlight,
the poet is able to see to the circumference of an enormous hemisphere, one formed by the dome of sky with moon, as it rests upon
the horizon. The trek up has had something of the turbulence and
blindness of the earlier episodes: surrounded by "dripping mist,"
in "that wild place and at the dead of night," where the shepherd's
dog barking at a hedgehog seems "turbulent" and a "small adventure" (13:11–27). Surely this resembles in tone, though for the man
now rather than for the boy, those adventures of "low breathings"
and boat-rowing of *Prelude* 1. As if the ascent toward consciousness
were now concentrated into one climb, he "panted up," with "fore-
head bent" toward that earth, that nature which had sought to
retain him (31, 29)

He was recently involved in the mist, blinded and opposed,
but now he has perspective, and that whole irrationality of early
life, the "terrors, all the early miseries, / Regrets, vexations,
lassitudes" (*Prel.* 1805, 1:356–57) are down below, part of a "huge
sea of mist, / Which meek and silent rested" at his feet (13:43–44).
With the creation scene from *Paradise Lost* echoing in the verse,
Wordsworth presents the emergence of the distant hills into his
vision as if they were the first forms of landscape coming like consciousness through primordial waters: "A hundred hills their
dusky backs upheaved / All over this still ocean" (13:45–46).

As was suggested by the reference to Eliade's *The Sacred and
the Profane*, the poet has become, in symbolic terms, "contemporary with the cosmogony," for he has "witnessed the creation of
the world."[26] The creation is in this case a psychological one, a
renewed structuring of the psyche through return, refreshed per-

ception, and unification. The source, the beginning point of the journey into maturity, is visible far in the distance. Separation from this sea has been achieved by all the inland journeying of *The Prelude*, as the path has led, in the five-book version, through residence at Cambridge, then later, through London, the Alps, France, even through a political revolution. The child has been taken far from his first shore, into many other kinds of experience. But now mounted high on an eminence of the sort implied in the "Intimations" ode, in such a "season of calm weather," the poet is able to look backward toward his headwaters, to review and relive the process of his psychic growth. That review is a return, a return to a deeply symbolic natal landscape, as in "Tintern Abbey."

Nostalgia for this first shore, this amphibious dwelling on the border of the Derwent, this time of "glad animal movements" with no need, or knowledge, of any "remoter charm, / By thought supplied" ("Tintern Abbey," 74, 81–82), is prevented by the power of imagination. The imagistic representation of this power emphasizes the synthesis of opposed principles: below and above, mist and moonlight; turbulent blindness and sound versus brilliant clarity and sight. The "huge sea of mist" (*Prel.*, 1805, 13:43) at the poet's feet, the "still ocean" (1805, 13:46) of cloud, in stretching to the horizon, masters the real sea, symbol of origin and thus "infinity." The actual Atlantic is made to "dwindle, and give up its majesty" (1805, 13:50). This cloud-sea symbolizes, perhaps, experience of nature, blind contact with irrational actualities in childhood, as in the episode of waiting for the horses that were to bear him and his brothers home at Christmas, that sad holiday during which his father died. "Feverish, and tired, and restless" he had climbed a crag that overlooked the road down which the horses must come. With "a single sheep" and "whistling hawthorn" as companions, he had strained his "eyes intensely as the mist / Gave intermitting prospect of the wood / And plain beneath" (1805, 11:346, 358–63). Connected with his father's death that "dreary time" (364), the mist here seems symbolic of the blind involvement in unconscious process characteristic of childhood. This same mist forms the lower half of the scene on Snowdon, just as the experiences of early life remain in the unconscious.

In climbing through this mist into a perspective of clear vision, the poet has dramatized in one concentrated symbol the process of psychic development that is his subject: the story of the "growth of a poet's mind." Maturity is implied by the meekness and silence (1805, 13:44) of this mist, which he now can see across to the horizon, just as in adulthood, in moments of perspective, we can review our past lives with a sense of clarity and ease of understanding. Yet if this mist-sea of childhood's unconsciousness and irrationality has been mastered, it has in no sense been discarded. It is rather the indispensable means whereby imagination is nourished, given substance, just as the story of the early years by the Derwent and on the lakes provides material for the story of individuation. The events of his own life, expanded mist-like in memory and unconsciousness, are the very means whereby the poet comes to terms with that oceanic sensation of the psyche's origin. He deals with the sense of loss contingent upon leaving that Dionysiac shore through the consideration of his own life, through telling his story and thus revisiting that earlier landscape.

Memory alone, however, is not all the consolation. This mist-ocean is both calm and fruitful because it has been ordered by contemplation. The clear moonlight suggests the poet's meditative use of memory and the unconscious in the creation of a new vision that combines below and above, blind sensing and clear sight, the vital turbulence associated with the mist and the calm clarity associated with moonlight. Under an "ethereal vault" (1850, 14:50) more capacious than the pleasure dome of "Kubla Khan," the poet in part of his total personality identifies with the moon "in single glory" (1805, 13:53), whose mastery of the situation became, in the 1850 version, a "sovereign elevation" (14:54), suggesting a queenly or imperial rule. But another part is drawn away to identify with

> a blue chasm, a fracture in the vapour,
> A deep and gloomy breathing-place, through which
> Mounted the roar of waters, torrents, streams
> Innumerable, roaring with one voice.   (1805, 13:56–59)

We think of the "low breathings" that followed the boy in *Prelude* 1.

Here, in order that the separation from nature/unconsciousness not be absolute and sterilizing, a return has taken place.

> The days gone by
> Return upon me almost from the dawn
> Of life: the hiding-places of man's power
> Open; I would approach them, but they close.
>
> (*Prel.* 12:277–80)

The chasm beside the Khan's pleasure dome, the blue chasm beside Snowdon, and this opening toward the hidden sources of power in childhood, all associate themselves with what Jung called a "permeability of the partition separating the conscious and the unconscious" (*C.W.* 8, par. 135).

Wordsworth's attempt to define that crucial interaction—between clear moonlight in the dome above and water sound from the mist below—is of interest. His final formulation of the effect of that fountain of sound, as it pervaded and vitalized the scene, is as follows. The collective "roar of waters" was "Heard over earth and sea, and, in that hour, / For so it seemed, felt by the starry heavens" (1850, 14:59–62). The dome of consciousness reverberates feelingly with the wet resonance of the unconscious. Earlier the poet had seen the "universal spectacle" grand enough "in itself alone," yet sensed in the chasm the secret vitalizing agency of the scene:

> in that breach
> Through which the homeless voice of waters rose,
> That dark deep thoroughfare, had Nature lodged
> The soul, the imagination of the whole.   (1805, 13:60–65)

Perhaps the poet later stepped away from localizing imagination in the breach of clouds because such an attribution did not sufficiently convey the way the different elements of the scene "moulded, joined, abstracted" and endowed one another with "interchangeable supremacy" (1850, 14:83–84), as sound suffused light, to energize it, and light in turn clarified sound, so that below and above were unified in a single creation-like act. Like the fountains in the gardens of "Kubla Khan" and *Paradise Lost*, this is the point of access, and thus the spatial locus for representation of that crucial marriage between the mind and the landscape spoken of in the Prospectus to *The Excursion*. This wedding or "consummation" (58), as the poet describes it, seeks to reacquire the essential "Paradise, and groves / Elysian" (47, 48) through an exploration of the "Mind of Man" (40) as daring as Satan's trip through Chaos and the "darkest pit of lowest Erebus" (36). "Kubla Khan's" suggested union of Hell and Paradise, of bright gardens above and dark caverns below, is clearly related to Wordsworth's psychic exploration, and to his rendition of this individuating journey in landscape terms. Wordsworth's final, schematic account of this psychic origination and development in *The Prelude* uses the image of a stream and emphasizes a reciprocity between dualities of dark and light, blindness and sight, above and below.

> This faculty hath been the moving soul
> Of our long labour: we have traced the stream
> From darkness, and the very place of birth
> In its blind cavern, whence is faintly heard
> The sound of waters; followed it to light
> And open day, accompanied its course
> Among the ways of Nature, afterwards
> Lost sight of it bewildered and engulphed,
> Then given it greeting as it rose once more
> With strength, reflecting on its solemn breast
> The works of man, and face of human life.
>
> (1805, 13:171–81)

Whether this fall-like separation from essential sources occurred primarily through time and thought, as seems the case in "Tintern Abbey," or whether it was caused by residence at Cambridge, in London, and in France, it is healed by a return in maturity to the landscape symbolic of origin and by the union there of conscious understanding with unconscious experience, so that the aboriginal stream from nature's dark heart can flow in the daylight and reflect the "face of human life."

Two opposed yet complementary principles, then, like the interpenetrating gyres in W. B. Yeats's *A Vision*, contend in Wordsworth's characteristic passages. Sometimes the "one interior life" causes "intellect, or will" to seem a "littleness," overawed by something greater, like the boy in his borrowed boat below the striding mountain. Sometimes the poet to his "conscious soul" can say "I recognize thy glory," celebrating episodes when the growing boy preserves, with difficulty, his new autonomy in the face of "low breathings" and "huge and mighty forms," which pursue as if to resubsume him within their larger life. The more closely *The Prelude* is examined in its different versions and manuscripts, the more certain seems the association between this creative tension and the period of Wordsworth's greatest achievement. Yet leading critics of his poetry have difficulty in appreciating and analyzing this fruitful duality at the center of his work. The scholars and commentators of our analytic and self-conscious age find it especially hard to deal effectively with that lower symbolic term associated with nature.

Geoffrey Hartman, for example, treats "Romanticism and 'Anti-self-consciousness,'" with a recognition of tensions analogous to those we have explored, and quotes uses of the words *unconscious* and *unconsciousness* by Wordsworth, Carlyle, and Thoreau. Yet though unconsciousness is seen as the direction of escape from solipsism, Hartman does not make the term an important feature in an analysis of Wordsworth's central constructs. He provides no paradigm capable of relating the landscapes of Wordsworth and Coleridge to those of Yeats or Eliot or Lawrence or Roethke. His fear that "visionary poetry" may be a "thing of the past" is made to seem more likely by the absence of any account of continuity. "The future belonged to the analytic spirit, to irony, to prose."[27]

Hartman's book-length study of Wordsworth sees the poet as needing above all to separate his imagination from nature. The critic is most inspired and impressive when dealing with those episodes—notably that of crossing the Alps in *The Prelude*, book 6—wherein the thrust of Wordsworth's consciousness toward heroic independence is paramount. The Alps passage descriptive of imagination lifting up "Like an unfathered vapor" from "the mind's abyss" (592–95) constitutes, for Hartman, a culminating insight.

This mountain crossing and the ascent of Snowdon "are two rival highpoints of *The Prelude.*" But because the material from book 6 (on the imagination's rising nakedly after disappointment in nature) was composed last, it deserves a kind of priority by virtue of "compositional sequence." Hartman would have us read this passage from the middle of *The Prelude* as a kind of corrective of what the poet chose to say through his account of the Snowdon experience. The Alps passage, which the critic would make the final word of this great poem in praise of nature and imagination in their creative interaction, "suggests a progressive mounting of the mind toward self-consciousness."[28]

Although he has said that Snowdon provides a "culminating evidence that imagination and the light of nature are one," Hartman's analysis does not make us feel that this is so. He describes the ascent and insight as confused, contradictory. Wordsworth cannot "sustain his quest to link what makes a poet, the energy of imagination, to the energy of nature." He has failed to be "a visionary poet in the tradition of Spenser and Milton" because of the "unresolved opposition between Imagination and Nature." We are made to feel that Wordsworth mistook the quality of imagination, which in its purity is "unfathered," a "self-begotten, potentially apocalyptic force." The word *apocalyptic* implies "an inner necessity to cast out nature," and Wordsworth apparently failed to understand his own gift and thus missed the opportunity to become the "visionary poet" Hartman would have him be.[29]

Imagination does lift itself for a moment separate from nature in the Alps episode. The issue is whether this leaves the poet "in an absolute sense, lonely," and whether such loneliness represented a greater poetic destiny that Wordsworth might have chosen but did not. The poet chose to conclude his greatest poem with the Snowdon episode, which Hartman finds "a difficult one to interpret," with its attribution to nature of a power resembling the human imagination. Hartman finds here "Wordsworth's most astonishing avoidance of apocalypse." Thus, while trying to make the best of the poet's return to landscape as the originating element of his vision, one of Wordsworth's chief modern critics plainly would have preferred another outcome, a continuance in "that blindness to the external world which is the tragic, pervasive, and necessary condition of the mature poet."[30] For Hartman, Wordsworth was unfortunately not enough like Blake.

Nature as a term is finally uninteresting to Hartman, who opposes "song itself," or self-generated creative imagination, to that poetry which is "subordinate to the mimetic function, the experience faithfully traced."[31] If the presentation of landscape in Wordsworth were indeed always and only "subordinate to the mimetic function," then we would agree with Hartman and wish with him that the poet had followed his glimpse of the "invisible world" and sought a destiny "with infinitude," with "expectation, and desire, / And something evermore about to be" (1850, 6:605–8). But these abstractions and generalities sustain the verse for only a few lines, and even while we feel the excitement, we miss the vivifying imagery of other great passages. Without the account of the mistaken climb and descent and that factual disappointment, these lines would have little poetic impact.

Wordsworth is one of the fathers of modern poetry precisely because he developed the ability, in his greatest landscapes, to allow an apparent imitation of nature to be invaded and transformed by his central imaginative power. The English landscapes, especially, of his greatest period, certainly those descriptive of early life compacted together in the 1799 two-part version of *The Prelude*, are alive with expressiveness. A dark power that seems to belong both to the land and to the underlying depths of the poet's own psyche makes "the surface of the universal earth" breathe and move, even embody itself as a striding mountain. This symbolic, natal landscape is made to act or *"Work* like a sea." Its waves of expressive motion are like those beneath the man in Nietzsche's "little rowboat," symbolizing that darker, collective, Dionysiac power inevitably associated with the earth. The Apollonian power of consciousness must contend with this primordial other half, triumph over it, gain distance from it, but not discard and abandon it.

Hartman debates with himself in his 1971 "Retrospect" as to whether the "poles," at least, of Wordsworth's characteristic psychic voyaging can be identified: "They are related, clearly, to 'imagination' and 'nature,' to 'romance' and 'realism.' Yet they veer, converge, or cross."[32] The need acknowledged here for a legitimate two-term analysis is more persuasive than the suggested difficulties of such identification—difficulties that suggest an unwillingness to find any resonant term or symbol in the realm below the mist, in what Frye calls the direction "downward, into the profounder depths of consciousness."[33]

The structural impulse of English Romantic poetry, as epitomized in Wordsworth, is to assimilate the external environment for the purposes of the psyche, discovering or projecting into frost-silenced "sea, hill, and wood" ("Frost at Midnight") its emotional and intellectual concerns. This re-creation by imagination, describable as a marriage between the mind and nature, depended upon the discovery by philosophers such as Locke and Berkeley (and by poets such as Wordsworth and Coleridge) of the subjective component in perception. Imagination's very success in coloring reality may cause poetic consciousness to fear isolation in a world of its own creation. In "Dejection: An Ode," Coleridge sees the poet's vitalism, his imaginative color in nature, to be entirely projective, and external reality itself as inanimate and cold. Wordsworth realized the essential threat to his vision posed by the possibility that mind was responsible for everything. His central concepts and symbolic intuitions, his profoundest symbols, take issue with this devastating hypothesis. He understood instinctively that a metaphysical base was necessary for the validity of his most cherished constructs. He created this base, most centrally, through the accumulation of those landscape images that are charged with a sense of priority, actuality, and of vital, collective unconsciousness.

Wordsworth's greatest landscapes, then, tend to be simultaneously pictures of reality and visions of a source-principle outside the individual. Some origin represented by the earth itself or the sea proves capable of surprising self-enclosing consciousness with a conviction of human figures inhabiting a communal landscape. The old leech gatherer in "Resolution and Independence" bears relation to one of the archetypal patterns of Wordsworth's imagination, his tendency to see a real object sometimes as "an amphibious work of Nature's hand, / A borderer dwelling betwixt life and death" (*Prel.*, p. 498, 71–72). Yet we are all convinced, if we will be honest, that the poem dramatizes the old man as in the most essential sense *really there*. His point is largely that he is not created by the poet. He comes as a gift out of a mystery, an occasionally intelligible process that the poet trusts and upon which he depends, as he depended upon chance encounters for the formative events of childhood.

The volume *Romanticism and Consciousness,* from which we have already quoted remarks by Hartman on "anti-self-consciousness," forms a representative gathering of opinion as to the interplay of the poet's mind and its object, so often represented by the landscape. These central essays on a crucial topic, edited by Harold Bloom, display what appears to be a bias against appreciating Wordsworth's other, lower term in the manner his own statements authorize. Paul de Man, for example, ends with a quotation from that same Alps-crossing passage on the self-sustaining imagination so favored by Hartman, and emphasizes the possibility thus suggested "for consciousness to exist entirely by and for itself, independent of all relationship with the outside world." Romanticism's questioning of "the ontological priority of the sensory object" seems to him the essence of its legacy, one that "leaves the poetry of today under a steady threat of extinction."[34] For Bloom, "Romantic nature poetry, despite a long critical history of misrepresentation, was an anti-nature poetry, even in Wordsworth who sought a reciprocity or even a dialogue with nature, but found it only in flashes." The poet and nature represent "two powers that are totally separate from each other, and potentially destructive of the other," which try "to meet in a dialectic of love." The "reality principle" of the Romantics, unlike that of Freud, which worked through "the great disenchanter, reason, the scientific attitude," was merely "an anxiety principle masquerading as a reality principle and identical to the ego's self-love that never ventures out to others."[35] These are visions of the poet isolated within a tower of self-consciousness, like Coleridge in "Dejection," seeing all that is valuable in nature as a projection of his own thought.

Such a possibility was indeed the danger that Wordsworth addressed in his central philosophic and literary position. His tale of Margaret and her ruined cottage (*The Excursion,* 1:438–916) dealt with the morbid and self-destructive tendency of an imagination deprived of its object and shut within a house of its own deteriorating shell. Before the houses of Tennyson's "Mariana" and Poe's Roderick Usher, Wordsworth saw clearly the fallacy of mind alone in its own projection, even if that were to be, as for Tennyson, a palace of art. The most complete Modernist version of the Wordsworthian literary position and characteristic structure is to be found in W. B. Yeats, who through occultist study rather than experience of landscape came to value, like Wordsworth, the lives and language of the peasantry and to develop, as the core of his vision, two contending terms. The tower of self-enclosed, individual imagination in Yeats is bordered by a stream or the sea representing the unselfconscious life of humanity fused during time with the soil and what it symbolizes. Wordsworth's "immortal sea / Which brought us hither," collective, Dionysiac, becomes in Yeats a Spiritus Mundi, the collective reservoir of man's unconsciousness.

Hartman and de Man link Romanticism's discovery of the potential solitude of consciousness in the post-Cartesian universe with a threat to the existence of poetry itself. If the "future belonged to the analytic spirit" (Hartman), that very surrender to skepticism helps produce the "steady threat of extinction" (de Man) that poetry still faces. Consciousness' own self-discovery and development through analytic philosophy and criticism has brought about a hermetically enclosed house of intellect, like that of T. S. Eliot's "Gerontion," wherein mind sealed away from its sources faces hysteria and collapse. If our most sophisticated criticism of Wordsworth renders him, by implication if not by overt assertion, as self-regardingly cerebral, as anxiously self-analytic as the master Freud, then a distortion has occurred, one that may be seen as part of the Western development of the scientific outlook.

The critic, certainly, has the right to dislike anything suggestive of the Jungian collective unconscious, or of the irrational instinctuality of D. H. Lawrence. He may also disdain Nietzsche, and the *Vision* (as opposed to the poetry) of W. B. Yeats. Yet the paradox is that Blake, in whose image Hartman recasts the poetry of Wordsworth, had as powerful an involvement in the unconscious and its creative power as any poet in literary history. He did not project his access to this power into the imitation of landscape (though there are powerful underworld passages in "The Marriage of Heaven and Hell" and "The Book of Thel," for example), so perhaps the confusion lies especially in seeing Wordsworth's *nature* as only an attempt to replicate the visible world in words.

Imagination might well be opposed to such a *nature*, but in fact these are not the best names for the two contending principles in Wordsworth. In the Alps passage, poetic consciousness has risen into a new self-awareness. In the early-life episodes of *The Prelude,* a collective and largely unconscious sense of nature's wider life broods giant-like over the boy, like "a Master o'er a Slave" (the "Intimations" ode, 119). The Snowdon episode brings separated human consciousness back to the collective natural unconsciousness from which Wordsworth feels it has originated. Imagination is not really opposed to nature, as Hartman would have it be. Imagination is, rather, the mediating power that in maturity operates to synthesize the conscious and unconscious aspects of personality, the moonlight and the sound from the mist. Imagination may be projected into the landscape, more in the service of childhood unconsciousness and the associated unconscious component of the creative act. Or it may be encountered more nakedly by the poet, as in recalling the Alpine crossing, thus more in the service of artistic consciousness and its new self-awareness. In itself it is neither conscious nor unconscious, neither human nor natural, but rather a power mediating between the individual poet and his sometimes transpersonal sense of inspiration.

Wordsworthian imagination deals, then, with "indissoluble mixtures" such as those A. W. von Schlegel found characteristic of Romantic art and poetry: contrarieties such as nature and art, spirituality and sensuality, the terrestrial and the celestial. Animated by tensions ultimately between the conscious and the unconscious dimensions of personality, the poetry produced by such imagination "is the expression of the secret attraction to a chaos which lies concealed in the very bosom of the ordered universe, and is perpetually striving after new and marvellous births; the life-giving spirit of primeval love broods here anew on the face of the waters."[36] Wordsworth's poetic power is at its height during the years of *The Prelude*'s composition, the period that saw him attracted back in memory to the chaos of childhood and its accidents. This chaos is symbolized by the "huge sea of mist" (1805, 13:43) below Snowdon, the analogue of that Chaos (itself symbolically a sea) from which Milton first originates the order of landscape in *Paradise Lost*. If this "womb of Nature," with sea, shore, air, and fire all "in their pregnant causes mixed," might provide the "dark materials to create more worlds" (2:911–16), then Wordsworth's fertile mix of mist and water-roar was similarly an essential source of poetic raw material. This mist-sea below the clarity of the moonlit dome symbolized the reservoir of both early-life memory and that oceanic sensation of the psyche while in intuitive contact with the transpersonal unconscious.

A draft of material intended to be part of the projected five-book *Prelude* and dating from February 1804 provides evidence, even thus close to the poem's initial completion, of a continued indecision on the poet's part as to his final attitude toward individual creative autonomy versus transpersonal inspiration. This manuscript (labeled Ms.W) attempts to assemble additional analogies "betwixt / The mind of man and Nature" (27–28) and was intended as an extension of the first sixty-five lines of the Snowdon experience—that part ending with the breach in the mist in which imagination is localized (1805, 13).[37] Wordsworth's fascination here with nature's imagination-like working upon the "outward face of things" so as to produce "living pictures" (Ms.W, 11, 32) is made much easier to understand if we see his nature as acting in conjunction with what we would call the unconscious.

The distinction between individual consciousness and a transpersonal identification and empowerment seems to have been left deliberately ambiguous in the Snowdon episode. The first finished version (1805, 13) finds this "image of a mighty mind"— not explicitly the poet's, yet growing out of the experience just narrated, so indisputably his—to be one that is "exalted by an under-presence, / The sense of God, or whatsoe'er is dim / Or vast in its own being" (69–73). We have localized the "under-presence" in the mist below, the area of early life. The poet seems to be over-layering the "sense of God" with a more personal vastness of being and postulating this ambivalent Divinity/unconsciousness as the ground of the mind's existence. Later we are told that "Such minds are truly from the Diety, / For they are powers" (1805, 13:106–7). This imaged, quasisupernatural mind is not, in either the 1805 or 1850 versions, identified directly with the poet's own, but always held forth as a possible model or "type / Of a majestic intellect" (1850, 14:66–67) in its configuration and functions, a type (or *archetype*) supplied ready-made by nature.

A complete interpretation requires, perhaps, the whole body of the 1805 or 1850 text as support. The story there of a qualified fall, partially recovered from, as a result of Cambridge, London, and residence in France, gives additional substance to the personal application with which the poet rounds off his vision and meditation. "Oh! who is he that hath his whole life long / Preserved, enlarged, this freedom in himself?" he asks, referring to the whole imaginative ability to "build up greatest things / From least suggestions," to mold, synthesize, and make symbol of reality (1850, 14:130–31, 101–2). In other words, the mind-dome provided by nature represents the God-like imaginative power that might be attained by the human poet, but that this poet, because of some "falls" his "better mind" has suffered (1850, 14:147), does not explicitly have. And yet—though a "meditative, oft a suffering man," he trusts he lives "with undiminished powers" (1805, 13:126–27). So this partially fallen yet recovered poet can neither bring himself to say directly that he has, or does not have, such power. The God-like re-creation of experience is a thing to contemplate, an image providing endless interest and hope, which the individual poet need not claim—certainly not as a continuous ability. We go away as readers, however, with the knowledge that this poet has enacted the archetypal fiat at least once. These lines on the ascent of Snowdon are the record of that event.

The direction of Ms.W suggests that as late as February of 1804 Wordsworth was more attracted to a transpersonal than to a limited and personalized account of imagination. He was in effect more drawn to the irrational source, to nature and unconsciousness as determining powers, than to the individualized artistic consciousness. The encounter with the ready-made symbol on Snowdon, the moment when the poet's "sense of God" was fused with whatever was "dim / Or vast" in his own being, when his own mind corresponded to the mind of sky, was to have been followed by other "living pictures," or symbols ready-made by nature and providentially offered to the poet: like the imagination-enhancing episodes of childhood. Such incidents emphasize the transpersonal nature of inspiration, underlining the poet's role as a favored son of whatever arranges such an experience. Thus, the collective, irrational, unconscious component of the psyche's landscape comes to the fore. The first living picture offered by Ms.W is the following.

> It was a day
> Upon the edge of autumn, fierce with storm,
> The wind blew down the vale of Coniston
> Compressed as in a tunnel; from the lake
> Bodies of foam took flight, and every thing
> Was wrought into commotion high and low,
> A roaring wind, mist, and bewildered showers,
> Ten thousand thousand waves, mountains and crags,
> And darkness and the sun's tumultuous light.
> Green leaves were rent in handfuls from the trees;
> The mountains all seemed silent, din so near
> Pealed in the traveller's ear, the clouds [? ?],
> The horse and rider staggered in the blast,
> And he who looked upon the stormy lake
> Had fear for boat and vessel where none was.   (33–47)

This passage seems to emphasize the chaos we would identify with the unconscious lower term of the analysis, like the collective Dionysiac water below Nietzsche's man in a little rowboat. Although presumably imitated from reality, this scene is impregnated by a chaos like that out of which Milton shows the first landscape forms to have risen. As in his "dark / Illimitable ocean, without bound, / Without dimension" (*Paradise Lost* 2:891–93), the components of Wordsworth's picture are symbolically mixed. Light and darkness intermingle. The very dimensions of the landscape, "high and low," are endangered. The sequence "waves, mountains and crags, / And darkness" suggests a confusion of the components of an intelligible cosmos into a primordial origin, a deep "Of neither sea, nor shore, nor air, nor fire, / But all these in their pregnant causes mixed" (*Paradise Lost*, 2:912–13). Such irrationality causes fear for the boat of the individual ego. The poet, in fact, shows no such vessel on this water, but rather completes the lower term with a huge curved shape analogous to the sky-dome over Snowdon. A great rainbow stood

> With stride colossal bridging the whole vale.
> The substance thin as dreams, lovelier than day,
> Amid the deafening uproar stood unmoved,
> Sustained itself through many minutes space,
> As if it were pinned down by adamant.   (Ms.W, 52–56)

Wordsworth is not only frightened but also strongly attracted by these emblems. One's sense that the measured, limited vessel of conscious personality might fail to survive on such a surface, that Frye's fragile Noah's ark might be inundated by the turbulence, seems connected with the hope for a higher construct, a transhuman rainbow consciousness sustained by the very fertility of irrationalism that would sink the human ego. In several passages that follow, Wordsworth draws on his reading in books of exploration to depict daring voyagers in small vessels in imminent danger of being lost or drowned. Sir Humphrey Gilbert is seen most admiringly,

> Upon the deck of his small pinnace sitting
> In calmness, with a book upon his knee—
> The ship and he a moment afterward
> Engulphed and seen no more.   (91–94)

We sense in these passages an imaginative crisis, a strong tension, a mature, creative version of that early-life conflict between the boy's autonomy and the greater "life of things." At issue is the balance of relationship between the poet's creative consciousness and his unconscious sources, symbolized for Wordsworth by the landscape and especially by water. The explorer in his pinnace swept along by storm winds corresponds to Frye's portrait of the Romantic poet in "vehicular" form, "united to a creative power greater than his own."[38] Wordsworth, having experienced this Aeolian identification, seems in the manuscript passages unwilling to give it up, seems, in fact, to prefer a loss of his own Apollonian identity into that larger source to any separation from it. This is the posture of the Ancient Mariner, the poet-figure who moves beyond the bounds of ordinary personality, perhaps into madness. The pinnace represents a consciousness deliberately put at risk in relation to a chaotic sea that in this case swallows it up. "The Ancient Mariner" is a much more extended treatment of conscious personality given over to a voyage into the unknown, a voyage of discovery from which the Mariner returns both greater and lesser than human. It seems that the image of ship upon the water is one of the archetypal formulations of that consciousness/unconsciousness juxtaposition we have been exploring.

The most ancient and honorable version of this symbolism occurs in the account of Noah's flood, which is a reiteration in different terms of the creation story in Genesis. The exact dimensions of the ark as defined in cubits is another version of that introduction of measure and order into the world of primordial chaos that Milton symbolized with his golden compasses. The ark surmounts the flood because it is measured. It is enabled to ride out the upwelling of chaos because of its superior order. In reference to the story of the flood, the *Oxford Annotated Bible* emphasizes the opening of the "windows of the heavens" and the upsurging of the "fountains of the great deep," as opposed to the mere falling of rains: "Thus the earth was threatened with a return to pre-creation chaos."[39] The ark with its specified dimensions is the vessel of consciousness capable of riding out this upsurging of chaos. Noah's dove is perhaps a reminder of the dove-like "Spirit of God" which moved upon the "waters" in original creation. In his invocation to the muse at the beginning of *Paradise Lost*, Milton envisions a spirit who "from the first / Wast present, and, with mighty wing outspread, / Dove-like sat'st brooding on the vast Abyss" (1:19–21). And the rainbow is an essential part of Noah's story, perhaps analogous in its circularity to that great arc described by the golden compasses in Milton's version of creation. The Coniston passage quoted earlier has chaotic sea, the imagined vessel, and a titanic rainbow. But it has no place for the small boat of the personal ego. It represents the poet in a mood impatient of human limitation, thirsting for that transcendence implicit in an Aeolian identification with inspiration's source. It is a vision of a landscape of this world returned to the condition of precreation chaos. A superhuman act of ordination seems necessary, one represented by the rainbow.

If during the time that saw the writing of the two-part *Prelude* and Ms.W, part of the poet was attracted toward images of almost unlimited inspiration, the major direction of Wordsworth's greatest poem was not in accord with this impulse. Sometime during the year in which he finished the "Intimations" ode, Wordsworth decided upon an alternative posture. His own version of the fall as elaborated in that ode helps define a new relation to the unconscious source of inspiration, one that commits the poet to partial loss of vision through separation from the primal sea but that nevertheless permits him to maintain both those terms represented by boat of conscious personality and water of collective origin in relation to each other.[40] The major mythic pattern of Wordsworth's poetry is thus completed. The initial identification with the uroboric sea, followed by a necessary separation from that source, can now be presided over by a humanized, elegiac imagination whose visions of return toward the landscape of origin, though possible only during seasons "of calm weather," are consoling. The darkening of the radiant vision is transformed into gain, insofar as the "sober coloring" incorporates the significance of mortality. The still, sad music of humanity takes on a finer tone than any Aeolian singing, and the mean flowers bring the deeper tears. This pattern, it is true, was prefigured in "Tintern Abbey," but it seems to have cost Wordsworth a hard struggle during the writing of *The Prelude* before he could accept and emphasize it as the major direction of his work.

The paradigm of the attitude Wordsworth was tempted toward in Ms.W yet rejected recalls Shelley in his sailboat, eventually
drowned, fulfilling a prophecy made in verse.

> The breath whose might I have invoked in song
> Descends on me; my spirit's bark is driven,
> Far from the shore, far from the trembling throng
> Whose sails were never to the tempest given.
>
> ("Adonais," 487–90)

Wordsworth is not, characteristically, the poet of extreme
positions. He tends rather to retain both of his central terms in
relation to each other. Though he does resist and resent the fall into
adulthood, as seen in the "Intimations" ode, he does not cry out
against the formation of the conscious ego with the vehemence of
Blake in "The Book of Urizen," where the primal separation into
individual identity, seen through the myth of the creation, is portrayed with bitterest irony.

> Six days they shrunk up from existence,
> And on the seventh day they rested,
> And they bless'd the seventh day, in sick hope
> And forgot their eternal life.   (ch. 9:3)

Though the descent of the soul into physical incarnation, in the
"Intimations" ode, is regretted, it is not refused, as in Blake's "The
Book of Thel." Wordsworth's is not a radical vision, in the sense
that Shelley's and Rimbaud's are. He does not, like them, tend to
side with the unconscious against the conscious personality. The
passages describing small boats given over to chaotic waters in
Ms.W are, for Wordsworth, uncharacteristic, whereas the poem by
Shelley mentioned above, or Rimbaud's "Bateau ivre," truly represents the author's central impulse. Let us propose, in contrast to
the "drunken boat" constructs said by Frye to be inherited by our
culture from its Romantic ancestry, a passage from *The Prelude* as
representing Wordsworth's more balanced handling of those two
terms symbolized by measured boat above and measureless water
below. In book 4, while reviewing the condition of his psyche fol-

lowing its partial fall into time and society after residence at Cambridge, Wordsworth provides this extended metaphor:

> As one who hangs down-bending from the side
> Of a slow-moving boat, upon the breast
> Of a still water, solacing himself
> With such discoveries as his eye can make
> Beneath him in the bottom of the deep,
> Sees many beauteous sights—weeds, fishes, flowers,
> Grots, pebbles, roots of trees, and fancies more,
> Yet often is perplexed and cannot part
> The shadow from the substance, rocks and sky,
> Mountains and clouds, reflected in the depth
> Of the clear flood, from things which there abide
> In their true dwelling; now is crossed by gleam
> Of his own image, by a sun-beam now,
> And wavering motions sent he knows not whence,
> Impediments that make his task more sweet;
> Such pleasant office have we long pursued
> Incumbent o'er the surface of past time
> With like success.   (256–73)

Here is the poet in his adult role, the measured vessel of his identity drifting on the water like consciousness on the surface of its time. The present is distracting yet pleasant, gleaming with reflections of the physical environment, with his personal image, and having a mystery of its own—those "wavering motions sent he knows not whence." Yet attention is directed toward a profounder level, into the "deep," the "depth / Of the clear flood." Both "deep" and "flood" have biblical overtones and would associate this water with that original ocean. Yet this is a mastered chaos. The division between above and below, like the land's surface in "Kubla Khan" or the ocean of cloud in the Snowdon scene, is in place—perhaps all too firmly. The reflecting boundary between water and air tends to enclose the poet in a single dimension. The surface of the present, the waking separation between above and below, consciousness and its origin, allows only precious glimpses into childhood and its primordial sea. There are archetypes underwater, foundation stones of the psyche as essential as grots and pebbles. These patterns were embodied in early-life experiences, "spots of time" (*Prel.* 12:208), moments when the original chaos loomed over the poet like a striding mountain, came after him in invisible "low breathings." He glimpses these forms yet is distracted by the nature of consciousness and of time itself. Elegiac wisdom tells the poet to embrace this lot, to float upon the glittering surface with both acceptance and regret.

Wordsworth's mature, central version of the relation between those two terms represented by adulthood and childhood, observer and landscape, shore and sea, boat and water, was elegiac. Many of his most famous poems and passages of poems develop a chastened recognition that the subject of consciousness in time seems inevitably involved with the myth of fall. As a final example of this tendency, let us turn to another passage from *The Prelude*, book 4, one following closely upon the boat-drifting metaphor just examined. Concerned to diagnose in himself exactly the extent to which he has fallen away from attunement with nature and the reality it symbolizes, the poet finds himself essentially uncorrupted yet is forced to acknowledge that "there was an inner falling off." After an all-night session of dancing and revelry, he describes himself walking homeward at dawn, to be surprised by a moment that seems to focus, in terms of landscape, those contending senses of spirituality and mortality he has lately been weighing.

> Magnificent
> The morning rose, in memorable pomp,
> Glorious as e'er I had beheld—in front,
> The sea lay laughing at a distance; near,
> The solid mountains shone, bright as the clouds,
> Grain-tinctured, drenched in empyrean light;
> And in the meadows and the lower grounds
> Was all the sweetness of a common dawn—
> Dews, vapours, and the melody of birds,
> And labourers going forth to till the fields.   (323–32)

The Miltonic note is immediate, with the inversion of "Magnificent / The morning rose"; the sonorous multisyllabic "Magnificent" and "memorable" echo against one another and, together with "pomp," bring in the note of heroic ideality struck so often in *Paradise Lost.* "Grain-tinctured" recalls Milton's "sky-tinctured grain" (5:285), and the phrase "melody of birds" comes also from *Paradise Lost* (8:528). The word "Empyrean" is used by Milton to describe Heaven (3:57), and Wordsworth makes of the physical mountains an appearance associable with the walls of the heavenly city: they are, as it were, filled with light, made to seem, to quote Coleridge,

> Less gross than bodily; and of such hues
> As veil the Almighty Spirit, when yet he makes
> Spirits perceive his presence.
>
> ("This Lime-Tree Bower My Prison")

"Solid" mountains, shining cloud-like, suggest the transcendent vision, the spirit's reaching backward toward its source; this source is symbolically present in the sea, distant yet immediately visible, helping lend to the mountains their heroic ideality. But the uniquely Wordsworthian note comes through the transition of the last four lines, occurs through the transformation of the references to Milton into experience able to touch a believable moment, an earthly "spot of time"; the "meadows and the lower grounds" are of this world, participate in the "common dawn." This light is earthly, not dazzling, and we are reminded by the birds and the dew of the sweetness of a world, subject to seasons, less than ideal, where the children of Adam, laborers all, go "forth to till the fields" until their deaths. It is the juxtaposition of ideality and reality, of "immortal sea" of origin and man's fallen identity in time, that gives this passage its uniqueness. We see landscape as if it were newly defined in relation to its source, the sea of chaos. Creation is reiterated. The definite, the local, is associated with fall— Adam cast out of his Paradise is brought irresistibly to our thoughts by "labourers going forth to till the fields." Yet in this landscape that consciousness in its continual rebirth has seized and defined from the primordial unity, there is a fertilizing residuum of those original waters in the "Dews, vapours." We are reminded that after the creation, as Milton describes it, "from the Earth a dewy mist / Went up and watered all the ground" (7:333–34). This is associated in Genesis with man's tilling the soil. So Wordsworth views himself as laborer in the world of seasons, able, in fortunate moments, to see both his fall into identity and time and the mountain height of ideality and collective origins from which this fall must have occurred.

2 *Guilty Reason and the Curse of the Unconscious*

"The Ruined Cottage" is Wordsworth's most complex portrayal of imagination in a negative mode, acting to harm rather than to heal. Margaret, whose husband has abandoned her, seems hypnotized, suspended from all positive choice, by her continual projections of his return. She is, as it were, cursed by inescapable fantasies, held by them to her decaying cottage. Yet after her death the sorrowful story as refracted in the imagination of the narrator becomes the source of a consoling vision. During the fruitful months of Wordsworth's first intimacy with Coleridge, the expansion of "The Ruined Cottage" to focus upon the narrator's early experiences and imaginative resources was at the center of effort at Alfoxden House. Thus during the planning and composition of "The Ancient Mariner," Coleridge had available to him in the work of his new friend both the story of a curse-like negativity of imagination and the example of a positive transformation of that burden.[1] *Lyrical Ballads* poems such as "The Ancient Mariner," "Goody Blake and Harry Gill," "The Thorn," "We Are Seven," and "Her Eyes Are Wild" dramatize a curse or curse-like attachment of the imagination, and may be examined in relation to the line of development that led Wordsworth from *The Borderers* into "The Ruined Cottage." The essential possibility is that suffering may prove somehow fruitful, that the negative vision may be transformed (as through the narrator of "The Ruined Cottage") into a positive one, that the curse may prove either a blessing or the symbol of a benevolent judgment by some power wiser than man's.

In a poem by Wordsworth or Coleridge, a curse may prove fruitful because it expresses what the rational ego would not otherwise come to know. The curse is a kind of primitive suasion operating upon even civilized persons, reminding them (and us) that the ancient mysteries and terrors remain buried in the psyche, despite contemporary rationalisms. Wordsworth's Harry Gill, cursed by an old woman under a cold moon, spends the rest of his life as if in freezing to death. Mary in "The Three Graves" (a joint effort at a ballad by Wordsworth and Coleridge, never finished) suffers physical pain as a result of her mother's harsh words. The Ancient Mariner undergoes a torment in some respects resembling the burden of the poet. Having absorbed the moon-heightened power of his dying shipmates' eyes into his eye, he is compelled to use that hypnotic gaze in imparting to others his own initiation into regions outside the ego's usual consciousness. There is in fact a connection between the poem of curse and the poem of symbolic death and rebirth. The curse, under the proper circumstances, can lead to either a metaphoric or literal death of ego-consciousness. Some form of death is presented as the only solution to a dilemma of entrapment in the two greatest poems of the *Lyrical Ballads* period: "The Ruined Cottage" and "The Ancient Mariner."

Wordsworth's Margaret, abandoned by her husband, suffers a curse-like attachment to her decaying hut, which becomes simultaneously the location of her psychological decay and the objective correlative of her consciousness as it gradually sinks back toward its source in nature. Margaret's death of consciousness is literal, whereas the Ancient Mariner dies to his former life, his attitude that produced the shooting of the albatross. His ego-image, corresponding to Margaret's decaying hut, is a ship, worn to ghostly thinness before its sinking into the bay. When the Mariner, floating like "one that hath been seven days drowned" (552), is rescued and taken to land in the Pilot's boat, his psychic death and resurrection have been fully dramatized. The curse he is left with asserts itself as the need to take his listeners, through the spell of hypnotic language, into the mysteries of nature/unconsciousness that lie in the depths of that symbolic south below.

Wordsworth's experiences in France, his Utopian hopes for the French Revolution and his enthusiasms for contemporary ideology, especially the political philosophy of William Godwin, seem to have prepared him for his perception of the limits of rationalism. Judging from his verse play *The Borderers*, written during the time of depression and psychic suffering following his return from France, Wordsworth underwent a strong antirationalistic reaction to the events and currents of thought he had lived through. Out of his distrust of guilty reason came the poems of irrational but benevolent curses. An experience at Stonehenge during a 1793 foot journey across Salisbury Plain, described in *The Prelude* as seeing "Our dim ancestral Past in vision clear" (13:320), epitomized a polar swing in attitude. Through his own guilt and grief over the outcome of the affair with Annette, and through his dark forebodings of war between England and France, Wordsworth seems to have been brought into an empathy with mankind's ancestral heritage of violence and irrationalism. The contemporary dependence on moral calculation was replaced by a reliance on emotion and intuition, especially in association with the English landscape and the lives of ordinary people visible there in their cottages and sheepfolds.

Between his residence in France and his composition of the great poems we know him by (beginning in 1797 with "The Ruined Cottage"), Wordsworth himself seems to have died to a former attitude, and may in his own intellectual and emotional life have prefigured the pattern of the Ancient Mariner. It was Wordsworth, after all, who suggested the shooting of the albatross. Out of his fall into doubt and psychological depression came the poetry of faith and affirmation. The five-year period framed in by "Tintern Abbey"—between the first foot journey past Stonehenge and on into the valley of the Wye, and the return to this Tintern Abbey landscape in 1798—produced the mature faith rising out of darkness that is expressed in that great poem. "Tintern Abbey" is the paradigm poem of return to deeper psychic sources, of inspiration's resuscitation, of symbolic death and rebirth. Those psychic origins symbolized so often by landscape (we should see in the lovely prospect near Tintern Abbey the shadow of Stonehenge) are dark, forbidding, distasteful; they are also, like the gardener's compost, most fertile.

A ballad entitled "The Three Graves," apparently begun by Wordsworth and picked up and continued by Coleridge (though never finished by either man), suggests the paradoxical fruitfulness of imaginative states associated with guilt and a curse. The manuscript of part 2 of "The Three Graves" appears in a Wordsworth notebook dating between 1795 and 1797. It is partly in Wordsworth's hand, partly in that of Mary Hutchinson, who left Racedown in June of 1797, shortly before the arrival of Coleridge.[2] Thus this tale of a physical manifestation of psychic impression was already formulated into a ballad before the close association with Coleridge. The poem focuses on a psychic burden that is inexplicable, irrational, and inescapable. The imagination of Mary, the bride, is infected by evil words and actions of her mother. The wound has been received and must fester. The poem is an exploration of an essentially morbid state of mind, one wherein consciousness is pulled downward by an image it cannot escape. Eventually the love/hate dualities created by relationships between mother and daughter, daughter and friend, daughter and her betrothed, mother and daughter's betrothed, are symbolized by a barren churchyard. The three graves there are grown by a thorn, whose flower suggests the potential fruitfulness of such atavistic involvement with unconscious forces.

"The Three Graves," then, is much more than a literary curiosity. Deriving like "The Ruined Cottage" from that period of spiritual gloom during which Wordsworth was compelled by guilt and depression to write such darker works as *The Borderers* and "Guilt and Sorrow," it contains the seed of a theory, a style, and a structure that were later to be instrumental in the great poetry through which he won his way back into composure and affirmation. In its relation to Coleridge, this unfinished psychological ballad suggests the direction of thought, and the early impulse toward joint composition, that lay behind "The Ancient Mariner." Like "We Are Seven" and "The Thorn," "The Three Graves" focuses upon a spot of earth made unique by graves. In both "The Thorn" and "The Three Graves" this locality, marked by natural emblems, is associated with guilt. In the latter poem, the narrator questions the sexton:

> "Then tell me, Sexton, tell me why
> The toad has harbour here.
>
> "The Thorn is neither dry nor dead,
> But still it blossoms sweet;
> Then tell me why all round its roots
> The dock and nettle meet.
>
> "Why these three graves all side by side
> Beneath the flow'ry thorn,
> Stretch out so green and dark a length,
> By any foot unworn."   (*Poems of S.T.C.*, 1:7–17)

This spot seems accursed, unnatural. The flowering desolation, the fecund loneliness, is a reflection by the landscape of the perverse events that occurred in the lives of those who lie beneath the toad, the nettle, and the flowering thorn. "The Three Graves" is in fact the most illuminating handling of the curse theme from the period that saw the conception and composition of *Lyrical Ballads*. In "Goody Blake and Harry Gill" Harry is cursed with cold by the old woman; Martha Ray of "The Thorn" is cursed, in a sense, by her guilt; and certainly the Ancient Mariner is cursed by the memory of the dead sailors' eyes. But "The Three Graves" suggests that the idea of a curse is simply an extension of the theory of imagination shared by Wordsworth and Coleridge, an emblematic dramatization of a certain potentiality of that power.

In the sections found in Wordsworth's notebook, a mother confronts her daughter in an unnatural fury: she has fallen in love with the daughter's suitor. When Mary the daughter flees in shock upstairs, the mother approaches Edward, the young man, fabricates various vices she has noticed in Mary, and offers herself and her property as the more attractive match. Edward is shocked into a burst of unbelieving laughter. The rejected mother is so enraged that she falls on her knees in prayer and directs a curse toward her daughter in the room overhead. Mary hears.

> "Thou daughter now above my head,
>   Whom in my womb I bore,
> May every drop of thy heart's blood
>   Be curst for evermore.
>
> And cursed be the hour when first
>   I heard thee wail and cry,
> And in the churchyard cursed be
>   The grave where thou shalt lie." (*P.W.* 1:65–72)

The last stanzas of Wordsworth's version portray the effects of this curse as they manifested themselves at a later time.

> And she was pinched and pricked with pins,
>   And twitched with cord and wire;
> And starting from her seat would cry,
>   "It is a stool of fire."
>
> And she would bare her maiden breast,
>   And if you looked would shew
> The milk which clinging imps of hell
>   And sucking daemons drew. (*P.W.* 1:129–36)

Though Coleridge's version omits the two stanzas immediately above, he supplies, in part 3, other indications of the curse's physical manifestation. When Mary goes on to marry Edward, she feels her limbs "creep and freeze" (241) and, as the couple kneel in prayer at the altar, sees "her mother on her knees" (243). Furthermore, the introduction Coleridge supplied for parts 3 and 4 as published in *The Friend* contains a passage of great interest, which is of clearest application to the poem as a whole, including the parts conceived and written by Wordsworth.

> I was not led to choose this story from any partiality to tragic, much less to monstrous events . . . , but from finding

in it a striking proof of the possible effect on the imagination, from an idea violently and suddenly impressed on it. I
had been reading Bryan Edwards's account of the effect of
the *Oby* witchcraft on the Negroes in the West Indies, and
Hearne's deeply interesting anecdotes of similar workings
on the imagination of the Copper Indians . . . ; and I conceived the design of shewing that instances of this kind are
not peculiar to savage or barbarous tribes, and of illustrating
the mode in which the mind is affected in these cases, and
the progress and symptoms of the morbid action on the
fancy from the beginning.   (*Poems of S.T.C.*, 1:269)

Having avowed that "the outlines of the Tale are positive
facts" (268), Coleridge seems to be urging the proposition that the
mind can work injuriously upon the body and, perhaps more im-
portantly, that the mind can work injuriously upon the mind. It is
proof of the imagination's reality and power that it can have this
negative effect. The physical manifestations Coleridge has in mind
we would call psychosomatic symptoms. He is interested in manifestations and causes rather similar to the physical expressions of
hysteria that first engaged Freud's interest.[3] Thus it is clear that for
Coleridge, and presumably Wordsworth (since the idea for the ballad seems to have been his), the action of a curse was not primarily
the result of supernatural agency, even though the appeal of the
curse, as uttered, may have been to invisible powers.

The dramatic environment of the poem's narration, the barren graves with a thorn flowering out of nettles, is structurally similar to the house and landscape imagery of "The Ruined Cottage."
The story is one wherein the waking consciousness of the daughter
is preyed upon by an irrational impression deeply absorbed into
the startled imagination. The mother-daughter love rivalry suggests unconscious motivation. We would be justified in interpret-
ing these graves with the story they enclose as a complex symbol of
the power of the unconscious over the conscious mind, as an emblem reminding us that the irrational more closely underlies our
civilized lives than we are accustomed to suspecting. Looked at in
this way, the supernaturalism surrounding the graves serves a

larger symbolic purpose. The morbid locality symbolizes a subterranean power of the psyche as it rises up and repossesses those individual identities that have partially separated from their origin. Like Wordsworth's Lucy (in her various guises), Mary, mother, and friend Ellen have been reclaimed by a sometimes fruitful chaos underlying the surface of our orderly landscape.

The idea of the curse shades imperceptibly into the great bulk of the work done by Wordsworth and Coleridge during the *Lyrical Ballads* period. Martha Ray of "The Thorn" has not been cursed by any external voice, but the guilt inside her causes her to watch over her memorial objects in a compulsive vigil, in sun and in rain; her penance for the conscious choice of allowing her infant to die is to be gradually reassimilated to the condition of nature, to become year by year more closely and habitually identified with the pool, the hill of moss (a tiny grave), and the moss-hung thorn. Once, in a storm, she is mistaken by the narrator for a part of the landscape, a "jutting crag." The little girl in "We Are Seven" is in no sense cursed, yet the linkage she still feels to the brother and sister whose "graves are green" in the churchyard causes her to sit beside them, identifying with a greater continuity of life that confounds the logic of the narrator. Her emotional compulsion to maintain this linkage with those who are dead is similar in effect to that of a curse. And Margaret of "The Ruined Cottage" is Wordsworth's greatest heroine of the subjection to the irrational. While her conscious life, her family, the garden, and the cottage she had shared with her husband fall to pieces in a parallel process, her morbid, reiterated hope that his return is imminent has the effect of a curse on her psyche. She is held away from all positive action, kept in suffocating isolation until her consciousness and the house that is its objective correlative have wholly fallen back into nature and she is dead.

As for Coleridge, it may be argued that his three greatest poems—"The Ancient Mariner," "Kubla Khan," and "Christabel"—portray aspects of a curse. The mode of the Mariner's is most emphatic, and most terrible. Under an ominous moon, his shipmates stare his guilt indelibly into his imagination in the moment before their deaths.

> One after one, by the star-dogged Moon,
> Too quick for groan or sigh,
> Each turned his face with a ghastly pang,
> And cursed me with his eye.   (212–15)

This cursing by the eye is reiterated when the dead men are revived.

> All stood together on the deck,
> For a charnel-dungeon fitter:
> All fixed on me their stony eyes,
> That in the moon did glitter.   (434–37)

It is this moon-white, Gothic aspect of eye that the Mariner absorbs, and that later helps give him his hypnotizing power. The unwilling Wedding-Guest, a version of Wordsworth's young narrator who encounters an older man, the real narrator, in "The Three Graves" and "The Ruined Cottage," struggles in the beginning to get free of the tale but is overpowered by a look.

> He holds him with his glittering eye—
> The Wedding-Guest stood still,
> And listens like a three years' child:
> The Mariner hath his will.   (13–16)

This is, by the way, one of the stanzas to which Wordsworth remembers contributing. A much more significant contribution was his suggestion of the shooting of the albatross, thus introducing the guilt that originated the curse (*P.W.* 1:361).

The idea of a curse-producing guilt, of a negative aspect to imagination partly explainable by traumatic impressions made on it, partly a symbol of the mysterious and irrational forces to which man's waking thoughts are subject, was clearly one of the common premises of Wordsworth's and Coleridge's early cooperative endeavor. The term *negative imagination* should prove useful in discussing the phenomenon as it occurs in the poetry of the *Lyrical Ballads* period. The phrase implies that there is a compensatory positive imagination, and such a suggestion is amply borne out in the development of *Lyrical Ballads*, and later. In "Kubla Khan," for example, what might be called negative and positive aspects of imagination coexist in inextricable proximity. The poem has a mingled aura of Paradise and Hades, above and below, light and dark, warmth and ice. The life-giving central fountain is surrounded by the suggestion of "woman wailing for her demon-lover" and threatens with earthquake the very landscape it waters. Could the poet revive his inspiration he would be treated like a Satanic apparition, the circle, used in demonology to confine an unholy spirit, woven around him in fright by his listeners, all because his vision was too heavenly, too rich with honey-dew and the "milk of Paradise."

The curse, in most universal terms, is a way of seeing, a dark vision; it is a curse within the eye, a mode of viewing the universe that incorporates into sight those irrational fears and superstitions, those unconsciously based fantasies and terrors, that undermine the balance of waking apprehension. The dramatization of a curse in poetry, therefore, may be a way for these unconscious contents to manifest themselves to conscious awareness, and thus may offer the hope of a healthful purgation. The transformation of imagination from a negative to a positive aspect may be the central business of the poem.

Another unfinished piece by Wordsworth dating from just prior to friendship with Coleridge is entitled "Incipient Madness." With its textual relation to "The Ruined Cottage," this fragment helps us perceive the relation between guilt-ridden personal emotion and the story of Margaret, which became Wordsworth's first great synthesis between grief and consolation, between the negative and positive aspects of imagination. Several lines of the manuscript correspond to drafts of "The Ruined Cottage." "Incipient Madness," like "The Three Graves," seems to be concerned with inescapable morbidity. The poet speaks out of a state he knows approaches madness, telling us of a fixation he has suffered.

> I cross'd the dreary moor
> In the clear moonlight; when I reached the hut
> I enter'd in, but all was still and dark—
> Only within the ruin I beheld

> At a small distance, on the dusky ground,
> A broken pane which glitter'd in the moon
> And seemed akin to life. There is a mood,
> A settled temper of the heart, when grief,
> Become an instinct, fastening on all things
> That promise food, doth like a sucking babe
> Create it where it is not. From this time
> I found my sickly heart had tied itself
> Even to this speck of glass.[4]

It is now well documented that Wordsworth fathered the daughter of the French woman Annette Vallon during the period referred to in *The Prelude* as "Residence in France."[5] The plot of *The Prelude* hinges on a partial psychic fall and recovery, a descent into moral skepticism and depression that is explained in abstract terms but that lacks a particular dramatic justification, any personal involvement with events in France. The concrete focus for all Wordsworth's thoughts about social tradition versus radical innovation in the name of reason seems to have been his guilt over abandoning his child and her mother. It is certain, at least, that the figure of the abandoned mother occurs with suspicious frequency in his poems.

Dorothy, writing from Racedown in 1795, had described the poverty of the local peasants: "Their cottages are shapeless structures (I may almost say) of wood and clay."[6] Let us hypothesize, with de Selincourt, a visit by Wordsworth to some one of these cottages, one deserted and in partial ruin, during the time of depression and psychic suffering at Racedown—in 1795 or 1796 (*P.W.* 5:377). In his guilty state of mind perhaps the deserted cottage suggested to him his own desertion of Annette. The ruin seems to have associated in his thoughts with a woman, an English peasant version of the person he had wronged. The description of the fascination in "Incipient Madness" that draws the poet like a curse to the particular spot of ground seems to be an exploration of the psychology of guilt, arising from his need to encounter once again the imagery symbolic of desertion. His "grief" is the psychic obsession that forces him to play over and over again in his thoughts the theme of his wrongdoing and the effect it may have wrought. Like his characters in "The Three Graves," the poet is harmed by imagination's very power, its ability to respond to, and to create, symbols. His "grief, / Become an instinct," manifests itself in the need to convert the objective environment into imagery expressive of its burden; "fastening on all things / That promise food," this negative imagination creates its own image out of the materials at hand.

"Incipient Madness" is closely associated with the composition of "The Ruined Cottage." The earliest manuscript of the latter poem contains several passages corresponding to lines from "Incipient Madness."[7] Wordsworth may have tried without success to work his first-person description of visiting the hut by moonlight into the story of Margaret. But as "The Ruined Cottage" progressed it must have become evident that he had transferred the action of negative imagination from his own point of view into that of his heroine. The following lines were among the first composed of the poem and were quoted from by Coleridge in his letter of June 1797. They illustrate the manner in which Margaret's imagination works to her harm by continually manufacturing false hopes, thus binding her to the more and more desolate cottage.

> On this old Bench
> For hours she sate, and evermore her eye
> Was busy in the distance, shaping things
> Which made her heart beat quick.[8]

We are told that she ceases her spinning of flax to question any passerby who bears the mark of a discharged soldier or sailor. Each disappointment leaves her sadder. The decline of her cottage is associated so closely with her state that an identification is dramatized.

> Meanwhile her poor hut
> Sunk to decay, for he was gone whose hand,
> At the first nippings of October frost,
> Closed up each chink and with fresh bands of straw
> Checquered the green-grown thatch. And so she sate
> Through the long winter, reckless and alone,

> Till this reft house by frost, and thaw, and rain
> Was sapped; and when she slept the nightly damps
> Did chill her breast, and in the stormy day
> Her tattered clothes were ruffled by the wind
> Even at the side of her own fire.   (512–22)

This is the other side of the coin from Coleridge's "stately pleasure-dome"; this is the house of a defeated, deteriorating imagination, one gradually falling back into its origin, into nature or the unconscious. She is doomed, cursed, by a love deprived of its object, so that imagination preys on itself.

> —Yet still
> She loved this wretched spot, nor would for worlds
> Have parted hence; and still that length of road
> And this rude bench one torturing hope endeared,
> Fast rooted at her heart.   (522–26)

Her death is a merciful release for a consciousness caught in a trap, confined by a kind of specious object—since Robert, her husband, has not seemed wholly worthy of her love from the beginning.

"The Ruined Cottage" is a purgation of personal guilt for Wordsworth, and also an exploration of the imagination's negative effect that gives us, in the end, an image of consciousness in relation to its origins. The consolation Wordsworth has his narrator find in this story hinges on an acceptance of Margaret's return to a collective condition in death, as symbolized by the evidences that wild nature is taking back over the ruin.

> She sleeps in the calm earth, and peace is here.
> I well remember that those very plumes,
> Those weeds, and the high spear-grass on that wall,
> By mist and silent rain-drops silver'd o'er,
> As once I passed did to my heart convey
> So still an image of tranquillity.
> . . . .
> That what we feel of sorrow and despair
> . . . .
> Appeared an idle dream.[9]

This is an intuition very similar to that found in "A Slumber Did My Spirit Seal," "Three Years She Grew in Sun and Shower," "Lucy Gray," and "We Are Seven." Moreover, the reabsorptive tendency symbolized by the wild vegetation is here seen as benign, as in the opening landscape of "Tintern Abbey," where we see hedgerows as "little lines / Of sportive wood run wild" and the "pastoral farms" as "green to the very door." The surrender to nature Wordsworth chronicles in "The Ruined Cottage" is really the surrender to a psychic death, from which the poet was able to rise in imaginative regeneration, just as the Ancient Mariner has to die and be reborn in order to escape his burden.

Ultimately, then, the sad story of Margaret's repossession by a natural, collective entropy is refracted in the psyche of the narrator, who represents the poet and is seen to be the source of a religious consolation. The thorn is able to flower out of the place of the dock, the nettle, the toad. Negativity is transformed, and that transformation often seems the central business of the poem. In Blake's "The Marriage of Heaven and Hell" the narrator descends with his companion, an angel, into a subterranean void where they view a sea very suggestive of that aboriginal chaos we have interpreted as the unconscious. They see a black sun, great spiders, and an enormous serpent. When the angel flees in terror, the scene is changed into tranquility, and Blake urges, rather sardonically, that the horrifying vision was owing to the angel's metaphysic. By encountering the unconscious and sloughing off a previous attitude, a more rational, conventional, and moralistic point of view as represented by the angel, the poet has transmuted a negative vision into a positive one. Something very similar is at the heart of "The Ancient Mariner." The water snakes are illuminated by the moonlight, the albatross falls away, and the Mariner rises reborn, as it were, with regenerated vision.

The fate of imagination is thus at issue in the two early great poems whereby Wordsworth and Coleridge established the characteristic direction of their work: "The Ruined Cottage" and "The Ancient Mariner." Poems such as "The Three Graves" and "Incipient Madness" may well have been left unfinished because of their authors' inability to see how fruitfulness or consolation could be brought out of desolation and negativity, to see how, as in "The Ruined Cottage," "The Ancient Mariner," "The Thorn," "We Are Seven," "Goody Blake and Henry Gill," "Hart-Leap Well," and others, the curse might prove either a blessing or a judgment by a benevolent nature. The incompleteness of Coleridge's most fascinating fragment, "Christabel," may be bound up with his inability either to free his heroine from the curse-like influence of the lady Geraldine or to convert Geraldine into a more positive image.

The idea of a curse as a kind of filter over vision, a projection into sight of unconscious elements, is dramatized most strikingly in "Christabel." Geraldine, the "bright green snake" coiled around Christabel the dove in Bard Bracy's dream, gives to the innocent young woman such a serpentine glance that it possesses her psyche.

> A snake's small eye blinks dull and shy;
> And the lady's eyes they shrunk in her head,
> Each shrunk up to a serpent's eye,
> And with somewhat of malice, and more of dread,
> At Christabel she looked askance!   (583–87)

Just as the Ancient Mariner's vision absorbed the curse from the dead men's eyes, so do Christabel's eyes absorb and imitate this reptilian look.

> The maid, devoid of guile and sin,
> I know not how, in fearful wise,
> So deeply had she drunken in
> That look, those shrunken serpent eyes,
> That all her features were resigned
> To this sole image in her mind:
> And passively did imitate
> That look of dull and treacherous hate!   (599–606)

Christabel's curse is the admixture into her vision of a guilty knowledge, an involvement with the unconscious, sexual side of things that the serpent has represented since the loss of Paradise was recorded in Genesis. The problem of plot in "Christabel" revolves around the apparent need to free the heroine from Geraldine's influence, much as the malign vision was sloughed off by the Ancient Mariner, the distorting angel perspective escaped in "The Marriage of Heaven and Hell." But Geraldine represents something that is not entirely bad. In her mystery and beauty, her status as "lady of a far countree" (225) in the beginning, she seems a kind of psychic messenger sent to expand the world of Christabel. As serpent she suggests both the traditional seducer into the sorrowful knowledge that is mankind's common inheritance and the Jungian messenger from the unconscious.

Christabel's innocence is perhaps too great. She resembles Blake's Thel, who refuses physical incarnation, sexuality, and all the knowledge they entail. Coleridge found no means to dramatize Christabel's assimilation of the guilty involvement with unconsciousness represented by Geraldine's embrace and "look." Christabel could not go from Innocence through Experience (to use Blake's terms) into vision, like the Ancient Mariner. The negative imagination, represented by Geraldine's snake-like glance, was not able to lead into a positive transformation. Coleridge seems to have intended to have Bard Bracy, the poet, free his patron's daughter from the serpent. But as we have seen in "Kubla Khan," it is precisely the twining of such elements as "gardens bright" with "sinuous rills," of green snake and dove, the balancing of "sunny pleasure-dome" above "caves of ice," that gives to the Coleridgean poem its inimitable resonance. The best Coleridge could do, perhaps, was to leave Geraldine in the castle, unexorcised if unaccepted.

"Christabel," then, like the curious and obscure "The Three Graves," may have had incompleteness inherent in its structure. Latent within the impulse of both poems, but unrealized in their plots, is the possibility that a curse may prove somehow to be a blessing, as is the case in "The Ancient Mariner" and "The Thorn." The place symbolism of "The Three Graves" is unrealized, in that the fertility suggested by the blossoming of the thorn from the place of toads, from the meeting of "dock and nettle," never materializes in the lives of the characters. And in "Christabel" the promise of exotic beauty, of thrilling new discovery made by the appearance of the beautiful lady in the moonlit Gothic landscape outside the castle, continues to haunt the imagination but never takes shape in events. Yet the lady's apparition has expanded our sense of possibility.

> Her stately neck, and arms were bare;
> Her blue-veined feet unsandal'd were,
> And wildly glittered here and there
> The gems entangled in her hair.
> I guess, 'twas frightful there to see
> A lady so richly clad as she—
> Beautiful exceedingly.   (62–68)

It is no wonder that Christabel and her father are attracted and entranced. And the very atmosphere of owl cry and cloud-covered moon, in this setting by a castle where moss and mistletoe embrace the huge oak, lends an expectancy, a sense of mystery that demands an exotic revelation.

These may seem nothing more than the standard elements of the Gothic situation, yet if we think in terms of the potentially fruitful curse, we see Coleridge turning to his advantage tendencies that were latent all along in the Gothic mode. If the curse in its widest significance for Wordsworth and Coleridge means the presence of a certain element in vision, the representation or projection into waking sight of elements from night, below, the unconscious, then the clear manifestation of such a curse should offer the hope of fruitful recognition and resolution. But this possibility would not always be realized. Sometimes the messenger from "a far countree" must remain unassimilated, misunderstood. No other Romantic poet was as daring as Blake, who, at the end of "The Marriage of Heaven and Hell," has his angel embrace the Satanic "flame of fire" and arise as Elijah, the poet as prophet on the other side of the conflict between Innocence and Experience. For Coleridge, the embrace of Geraldine and Christabel retains something shameful, supernatural, and forbidden, like the touch of the Gothic villain-hero, or the bite of his cousin, the vampire.

In his essay "On the Relation of Analytical Psychology to Poetry," Jung argues that great art "consists in the unconscious activation of an archetypal image" (*C.W.* 15, par. 130). The poet may not consciously understand the impulse that first leads in the direction of discovery. The poet comes to understand it, at least in symbolic terms, with continued elaboration of the visions that have been, as it were, given. Management of the material on a level of consummate mastery both demands and constitutes a kind of understanding. But not all art is great, and not all material that the unconscious obtrudes into art can receive the management that implies understanding. There are levels of self-awareness in poetry and the other arts.

Yet whatever the level of awareness, Jung emphasizes the artist's utility as a translator of archaic materials into the language of the present, so making it possible "for us to find our way back to the deepest springs of life." The artist is, for society, the vehicle through which dreams out of the past of the unconscious arise into the present of our consciousness, and so serves a compensatory function, just as an individual's dreams serve to counterbalance the attitudes of waking awareness by symbolic portrayals of other, opposed attitudes that are unconscious and repressed. Art is "constantly at work educating the spirit of the age, conjuring up the forms in which the age is most lacking. The unsatisfied yearning of the artist reaches back to the primordial image in the unconscious which is best fitted to compensate the inadequacy and one-sidedness of the present" (*C.W.* 15, par. 130). This statement applies very well to the use made by Coleridge and Wordsworth of the Gothic elements and related tendencies that had developed during the eighteenth century.

The winding hallways in castles, the underground passageways, dungeons, and crypts under churches, which we find in the writings (and sometimes in the architectural designs) of Horace Walpole, William Beckford, M. G. Lewis, and Ann Radcliffe, suggest very strongly the unconscious as described by Jung. The dream through which Jung first became aware of the collective unconscious involved a descent into the cellar below a house and the discovery there of a trapdoor leading to even lower levels.[10] The figures encountered in these regions below daylight would tend to represent elements of the unconscious denied to the waking personality by personal or societal repressions.[11] The ambiguous villain-hero, Radcliffe's Montoni for example, is strongly suggestive of what Jung calls the Shadow, an archetype embodying the evil, inferior, destructive, socially unacceptable aspects of the Self: that total of the personality, including both conscious and unconscious components, whose complete extent can never be known.[12] The action of the Gothic novel therefore has largely to be hidden from daylight. The archetypes of the unconscious, like a vampire, cannot bear the touch of the sun. Mystery must take the thoughts outside the skepticism of daylight, shade them from all rationalistic glare.

The high sense of decorum and rationality in art that triumphed in the poetry of Pope and dominated criticism for much longer was well calculated to banish the irrational into shadows. It is true that Pope (and Swift) deal with the unregenerate aspect of the psyche, but Pope's insect-like creatures of darkness, Swift's Yahoos, are unsympathetic accounts of the shadow-side of the self.[13] The forbidden aspects of the psyche apparently need a portrayal that constitutes recognition and a kind of acceptance. So the Gothic novel flourished, and poets meditated in graveyards. With a few exceptions, however, the approach to the unconscious through the Gothic narrative in the eighteenth century was not a fully realized artistic mode. The archetypal symbolism of waking and sleep, daylight and darkness, public landscape and subterranean passages, was too little realized by the Gothic novelists. They were creating popular entertainments, the detective stories and science fiction thrillers of the time. But when Wordsworth and Coleridge, and later Byron, Keats, Emily Brontë, Hawthorne, and Poe, handled the mode, whether in verse or in prose, a literary mainstream of the nineteenth century had come into being.

And there were a few poems in the eighteenth century that accomplished what Jung specifies as the task of the artist: "conjuring up the forms in which the age is most lacking." Of a few of Collins's odes, perhaps, and of a few poems by Gray, certainly of his "Elegy Written in a Country Churchyard," we can say with Jung that an image from the unconscious is so used as to bring it "into relation with conscious values" (*C.W.* 15, par. 130). Gray's "Elegy" combines a refined artistic management with Gothic atmospherics (the "mopeing owl," the "Ivy-mantled Tow'r") and a central, archetypal image corrective of the age. The graves of these "unhonour'd Dead" under their "uncouth Rhimes and shapeless Sculpture" are a reproof to the imperious elevation of the literary outlook that was the poet's inheritance and is still evident in his diction and versification. But the message, the ancestral wisdom from underground, is democratic, soft-voiced. The graves say that in death all men are equal, and that there is, in the contemplation of this common origin, a consolation for the poet or any like-minded spirit who is weary with the heroisms and contentions of an ambitious, empire-building period.

> Beneath those rugged Elms, that Yew-Tree's Shade,
> Where heaves the turf in many a mould'ring Heap,
> Each in his narrow Cell for ever laid,
> The rude Forefathers of the Hamlet sleep.[14]

Jung tells us that when encountering an archetypal situation, we feel a sense of release and power. "At such moments we are no longer individuals, but the race; the voice of all mankind resounds in us." He tells us further that such archetypes are apt to be simple and rather obvious, such as the ideal of one's native land: "the archetype here is the *participation mystique* of primitive man with the soil on which he dwells, and which contains the spirits of his ancestors" (*C.W.* 15, par. 128). Gray's contemporaries apparently perceived in his ode some voice larger than life, in spite of its relative quietness. They apparently found expressed there a common origin, an identity transcending the elaborations of conscious achievement, in which they could once again participate through reading his poem. The bodies below the surface of the soil, separate in the cells of individual graves yet connected by the loam, symbolized to them, we suspect, racial forebears in the collective unconscious, a presence that the excessive rationalization of religion, society, and art was threatening to obscure. The poem was immensely popular and exerted an influence wholly disproportionate to its length. Wordsworth's images of the grave in "The Three Graves," "The Thorn," "We Are Seven," and "A Slumber Did My Spirit Seal" are indebted to Gray. Wordsworth's inclination to deal with the lives of peasants, on the one hand, and Coleridge's echoing of "ancestral voices" on the other, may be seen as related to Gray's striking reevaluation of the common folk background of the culture.

In contrast to the Gothic novelists of the eighteenth century, Wordsworth and Coleridge completed the artistic task as conceived by Jung, not only deriving images from the unconscious, not only "conjuring up the forms" in which their time was deficient, but also handling these materials on a level of mastery, bringing them "into relation with conscious values." The symbolism of the soil, of graves, was the same for them as for Gray. Through the development of their idea of imagination, they created a context of conscious understanding in which the ancestral images could take on perfected artistic form. Blake's independent and to some extent parallel developments were perhaps more original, but they came to exert influence only later, whereas Wordsworth and Coleridge directly marked the work of the younger generation of Romantics, and thus all of the nineteenth century. It was an impressive achievement for two poets, and for a body of work that, when we consider only the best, is not particularly large. Especially in the case of Coleridge, a few magical poems have captured the imagination of English-speaking people in a manner perhaps without parallel. If Jung's idea that "whoever speaks in primordial images speaks with a thousand voices" applies to any poetry at all, it ought to apply to that of Coleridge, judging by its effect (*C.W.* 15, par. 129). It is precisely our argument that the idea does apply, that the portrayal of a relationship between the conscious and unconscious areas of the psyche is the symbolism at the heart of "Kubla Khan" and "The Ancient Mariner." Wordsworth and Coleridge between them seem to have extended and developed a symbolism latent in the Gothic mode, a system of imagery balancing consciousness against memory and the unconscious, the poet against the landscape, the house against wild nature, the ship against the sea, and used imagination, in its transformation from negative to positive, as the mediating factor between the mind and its dark antecedent.

"The Ancient Mariner," like that earlier cooperative ballad "The Three Graves" begun by Wordsworth, involves a negative or cursed imagination and represents a brilliant variation on the two terms of Wordsworth's imagery in "The Ruined Cottage." The decaying cottage of Wordsworth's Margaret with its thatch growing green and vines crowding about windows and door, with stonecrop thickening against the lower panes, is analogous to the Mariner's vessel, which returns from its voyage with warped planks and sails worn thin, so that it is compared by the Hermit to "Brown skeletons of leaves that lag / My forest-brook along" (533–34). Both complex images represent a consciousness near a kind of death. Margaret actually dies, leaving the pedlar with his tale as her representative, her psychological successor. The Ancient Mariner undergoes a symbolic death when his thin, worn vessel goes under: "Like one that hath been seven days drowned / My body lay afloat" (552–53), but he is spared, saved by the Pilot's boat, brought to land to be his own narrator.

The Romantic psyche tends toward self-portrayal in verse, and the sailing vessel is one of its favored images. We have seen something of Wordsworth's use of boat imagery in *The Prelude*. The title of Frye's essay "The Drunken Boat" suggests Rimbaud's famous use of this construct, made more psychologically inescapable in intent by his letters, which advocate a return to an impersonal and collective condition through "le dérèglement de *tous les sens*."[15] Shelley's early "Alastor," clearly influenced by "The Ancient Mariner," features a wild boat trip wherein a young poet-figure, in pursuing a vision had in sleep, gives himself up in a "little shallop" (299) to the will of wind and wave. In this posture of Aeolian surrender, the lad is borne along on a tumultuous sea like "one that in a silver vision floats / Obedient to the sweep of odorous winds" (316–17).[16]

The younger Romantics and their later nineteenth-century successors understood very well the implications of the imagery in Coleridge's most famous poem. Tennyson is full of sailing boats. The idea of being borne to a death upon the waters appears in "The Lady of Shalott," "Ulysses," and "Morte d'Arthur." In "The Lotos-Eaters" the Greek warriors have been taken by ship to a land representing extreme psychological introversion, where each seems "deep asleep" while "all awake," as "music in his ears his beating heart did make" (35–36). The interplay between sea voyage, death, and imaginative vision in "In Memoriam" defies brief summary.[17] Something like the curse that comes upon the Lady of Shalott when she leaves her tower seems to bind the protagonists of these one-way voyages to a necessary dissolution of the restrictive boat-like ego.

Without wishing to suggest that Coleridge and succeeding poets deliberately labeled the two halves of a dichotomy as they wrote, let us suppose that they intuitively grasped a symbolism embedded in some collective layer of the psyche, a struggle as in the passage quoted in *The Birth of Tragedy* between the *principium individuationis* of the man in the rowboat and the collective Dionysiac water around and below him. Further, let us suppose that this struggle between individuality and the collective, the human and the natural, the conscious and the unconscious, became particularly acute following the eighteenth century because of developments in art, philosophy, science, and society that tended to emphasize the rational, the conscious, the mechanistic, the limited, and to exclude the mysterious, the intuitive, the organic, the unlimited. If Coleridge's "The Ancient Mariner" reflects these central concerns, it is only to be expected in a poem of Romantic reaction in such an age. The psyche in the grip of Aeolian inspiration is bound as by a curse to a potentially fatal voyage beyond the bounds of the contemporary rationalism.

Several features of our paradigm need to be emphasized. First, there is characteristically a representation of contrast, of balanced existence in relation to each other by structures and areas that symbolize opposite tendencies or directions. In "Kubla Khan" there is the dome above in sunlight and there is the "sunless sea," the "caverns measureless to man," below in darkness. The sound of "ancestral voices" arises with the "tumult" of this descent. In "This Lime-Tree Bower My Prison," Coleridge imagines his friends' winding down into the "still roaring dell," then ascending again into sunlight. Second, imagination moving between negative and positive aspects presides over the symbols of consciousness and unconsciousness and helps mediate the transaction represented by fountain and voices from below or imagery of descent.

Imagination is often symbolized by the sun or the moon. The image of a "waning moon" presides over the chasm and fountain in "Kubla Khan," suggesting negative imagination and its curse. The sun in a positive aspect, as "the mighty Orb's dilated glory," looks upon the conclusion of "This Lime-Tree Bower" like the eye of the universe in a mood of blessing.

All of these aspects of the pattern can be found very centrally in "The Ancient Mariner." The idea of a ship floating upon the water embodies a sense of opposites in balance and preserves also the significance of *above* and *below.* If the ship is afloat in calm water, then the above-ground consciousness is in daylight like the upper floor of Jung's dreamed house or the inhabited chambers of the Gothic novel. The vessel is of a measurable dimension, just as the size of Noah's ark was defined in cubits, the circumference of the Khan's above-ground gardens specified by "twice five miles"; under the water, on the other hand, is as "measureless to man" as the caverns underneath. Just so is the consciousness as described by Jung in relation to its unconscious base: "the ego rests on the *total field of consciousness,* and . . . on the *sum total of unconscious contents."* Consciousness in the child rises at first "like separate islands." These islands are "like single lamps or lighted objects in the far-flung darkness" (*C.W.* 9, pt. ii, par. 4; 17, par. 326; 8, par 755). The island and the lamp may be likened to the ship: defined, recognizable, in relation to the sea or a great darkness. Jung treats the possibility that the ego, when identified with a fallacious conscious attitude, can face a kind of death and so become subject to the chaos of unconsciousness, like a ship at the mercy of the sea. "A collapse of the conscious attitude is no small matter. It always feels like the end of the world, as though everything had tumbled back into original chaos. One feels delivered up, disoriented, like a rudderless ship that is abandoned to the moods of the elements." This seeming disaster, however, can be a blessing in disguise, for in reality, in becoming subject to the sea, "one has fallen back upon the collective unconscious" (*C.W.* 7, par. 254). This presumably is what happens to the Ancient Mariner, both when his vessel is subject to the chaos of storm and finally when it sinks altogether. He is committed to this voyage first by the irresistible wind, whose

Aeolian suasion is later transferred through events to the Mariner's eye, the agency through which he is able to fulfill the terms of his fruitful curse by enlarging the conceptions of his hearers.

If "The Ancient Mariner" symbolizes a psychological death and rebirth, the result of which is a curse resembling the paradoxical burden of the poet, we must consider the essential need lying behind the beginning of this voyage. The motto from Thomas Burnet that Coleridge affixed to his poem emphasizes the mysterious, spiritual nature of the universe in contrast to that perceived by "the intellect, habituated to the petty things of daily life," the intellect that "may too much contract itself." A danger latent in the paradigm of individuation as we have explored it in Wordsworth is that the inland journey away from the "immortal sea" of psychic origin may carry into adulthood and society so far as to deprive the individual of fruitful contact with that source. The great need is for returns, for reimmersions of the ego in the chaotic bath of the unconscious. That ego too much walled away in proud self-subsistence can become a sterility, a living death. In the conclusion of *The Prelude*, Wordsworth deplores the tendency

> Of habit to enslave the mind—I mean
> Oppress it by the laws of vulgar sense,
> And substitute a universe of death,
> The falsest of all worlds, in place of that
> Which is divine and true.   (1805, 13:139–43)

We are reminded by the phrase from *Paradise Lost* of the Satanic and hellish possibilities latent within the conscious ego, particularly as supported by social custom and the scientific vision. The Ancient Mariner's voyage is made necessary by something that happens to the mind in maturity, an entrapment of consciousness within itself that philosophy and science made all the more threatening.

At the time of writing "The Ancient Mariner," Coleridge had abandoned the neo-Lockean philosophy of David Hartley, for whom his first son had been named, for the ideas of Bishop Berkeley, who supplied the name for his second.[18] Looking back upon his rejection of Hartley in the *Biographia Literaria*, Coleridge places special emphasis upon the consequences for psychological free will that he had come to see as implicit in Hartley's mechanically based association of ideas. He shows that contemporaneousness of impression becomes the sole law of association possible using Hartley's premises:

> For to what law can the action of *material* atoms be subject, but that of proximity in *place?* And to what law can their *motions* be subjected, but that of *time?* Again, from this results inevitably, that the will, the reason, the judgment, and the understanding, instead of being the determining causes of association, must needs be represented as its creatures, and among its mechanical *effects.*[19]

He had come to see that the dignity and power of the mind, the creativity of mighty imagination, when viewed as the psychological by-products of the workings of the world-machine, were made mere illusions. He perceived and diagnosed the fallacy in what he called "that subordination of final to efficient causes in the human being, which flows of necessity from the assumption, that the will and, with the will, all acts of thought and attention are parts and products of this blind mechanism, instead of being distinct powers, whose function it is to control, determine, and modify the phantasmal chaos of association."[20] According to Hartley's mechanistic premises, the psyche becomes the ultimate prisoner, having not only its location and environment but also the very processes of its thought, the flow of its ideas, dictated by the dice-throwing of matter. Thus we would all be behind bars, as the Mariner is on his becalmed vessel. His being won by the throwing of dice is ironic dramatization. Subject to an abstract, mechanistic theory, the mind is the plaything of chance.

"The Ancient Mariner" sprang from a context of work by Wordsworth and Coleridge that emphasized the curse-like effect of guilt on the mind, and that, in poems of Wordsworth such as "The Ruined Cottage" and "The Thorn," dramatized these curses' expiation through penance and sometimes death. Now we will see in "The Ancient Mariner" a more metaphysically generalized account of guilt, one that relates the crime to an outlook, a conscious attitude that, as in the quotation from Jung, must collapse under the weight of a corrective penance. The Mariner himself seems representative of the outlook of a time too much taken up with rationality and science, too little sensitive to the marvels associated with nature and the unconscious. The vessel in which he voyages may well represent that conscious, restrictive ego that at a crucial point in the poem is mirrored by the skeleton ship. This reading is related both to Coleridge's personality and intellectual concerns, and to the ideas of Wordsworth with which Coleridge would have come into intimate contact just at the time of conceiving this work.

The villain of Wordsworth's blank verse tragedy *The Borderers* is an Iago-like character who has, in his youth, been "betrayed into a great crime" and who seeks self-justification by tempting others down a similar path. Wordsworth seems fascinated by the interaction between guilt and reason, analyzing his Satanic figure in a preface as a "speculator in morals," one fond of "dallying with moral calculations," a "daring and unfeeling empiric" (*P.W.* 1:345–46). Having succeeded in a plot to make another man commit what he thinks is murder, Wordsworth's monster of rationality reproves his victim's grief with the following speech.

> What! in this universe,
> Where the least things control the greatest, where
> The faintest breath that breathes can move a world;
> What! feel remorse, where, if a cat had sneezed,
> A leaf had fallen, the thing had never been
> Whose very shadow gnaws us to the vitals.   (1562–67)

We are reminded here of Coleridge's analysis of the consequences for free will implied by Hartley's mechanically based association of ideas. Clearly, Wordsworth has in mind some deterministic theory whereby the sequence of physical cause and effect is true master of our destinies, and our moral sense only an illusion, the mere figment of the ghost entrapped in a world-machine. Wordsworth has perceived and has dramatized in *The Borderers* that such theories are a murderous dissection of experience by thought. Just as the Ancient Mariner learned of moral reality by suffering guilt after his thoughtless action, so had Wordsworth apparently

learned the fallacies of a shallow rationality.[21] The following is another meditation (by the villain-hero of Wordsworth's play) on the
incommensurable relation between a seemingly random physical
event and the momentousness of results.

> Action is transitory—a step, a blow,
> The motion of a muscle—this way or that—
> 'Tis done, and in the after-vacancy
> We wonder at ourselves like men betrayed:
> Suffering is permanent, obscure and dark,
> And shares the nature of infinity.   (1539–44)

Well might the author of these lines have suggested the shooting of
the albatross. He knew by experience the carelessness of action,
the enormousness of consequence.

Alfred North Whitehead in his classic *Science and the Modern
World* sees the Romantics, and especially Wordsworth, as opposing
a kind of dichotomy in thought that the West had inherited from
the great scientific successes of the seventeenth and eighteenth
centuries. "A scientific realism, based on mechanism, is conjoined
with an unwavering belief in the world of men and the higher animals as being composed of self-determining organisms. This radical inconsistency at the basis of modern thought accounts for much
that is half-hearted and wavering in our civilization." Whitehead
finds in Wordsworth's phrase "we murder to dissect" the basis of
his criticism of science: "He alleges against science its absorption in
abstractions." Wordsworth, he says, in relation to the eighteenth-
century worldview, "felt that something had been left out, and that
what had been left out comprised everything that was most important." Whitehead is not so appreciative of Coleridge's achievement,
perhaps because Coleridge partially mirrored the intellectual evil
that he set himself to confront. But Whitehead does appreciate the
brilliance and justice of Berkeley as a critic of materialism: "Quite at
the commencement of the epoch, he made all the right criticisms,
at least in principle."[22] And Coleridge, as we have seen, in the
period of "The Ancient Mariner," had turned toward Berkeley in
order to escape Hartley and the consequence of his materialist
system.

There is, admittedly, nothing in the Mariner's character, as earlier presented in the poem, to make him seem subject to the central philosophical specter of the age. But then there is nothing much there at all, save mystery and power. His creator, though, in more autobiographical contexts, acknowledges imprisonments by thought. He shows himself, in "Frost at Midnight," in "that solitude, which suits / Abstruser musings." In "Dejection: An Ode" he describes the sterility he is suffering as a result of "abstruse research" having "almost grown the habit of my soul." "The Ancient Mariner," then, presents us with a patient diagnosing his own spiritual malady, with a physician who has himself been infected with the disease of thought peculiar to his time (and ours).

"The Ancient Mariner" is a miniature epic of the imagination's entrapment and deliverance, a poem central to its age partly because it contends with, and vanquishes, the intellectual specter of action as random in a mechanistic universe. The Mariner shoots the albatross, symbol of universal life, without thought, as if actions had no consequences. During the rest of the poem, it is borne in upon him that actions have enormous consequences. Having been hung with the albatross, he is made subject to an image of his own outlook, the skeleton ship, then cursed by the eyes of his dying shipmates. The state of mind that produced the wrong action and that many suffer from without knowledge of their malady, is dramatized more and more clearly, until the Mariner understands and is able to repent with his heart, spontaneously, more than with the intellect. The curse of guilt becomes the blessing of expanded vision.

The Mariner's crime is in one sense token, representative of the belief behind it rather than all-important in itself. He is guilty most essentially of an outlook, a limited imagination. The curse he is made in various ways to suffer is both image of, and punishment for, his consciousness that murders because it dissects. In part 3, the Mariner imagines that he sees rescue approaching. A man shut up in solipsistic nightmare, he wants nothing more than some external intervention. For a moment the sun seems benign, positive, as it almost rests on the "western wave," broad and bright; then the "strange shape" drives in between the Mariner and this burning circle of vitality.

> And straight the Sun was flecked with bars,
> (Heaven's Mother send us grace!)
> As if through a dungeon-grate he peered
> With broad and burning face.   (177–80)

This moment is bitterly ironic for the Mariner. Hoping for release, he encounters only an intensified image of his condition. This skeleton ship is like a mirror brought close up to the Mariner, the bars through which he sees the sun the dungeon-grate of his mind's self-imprisonment. The skeleton ship symbolizes consciousness in an attitude that finds nature in its essence somehow alien, and that has manifested that alienation by its rejection of the nature of the unconscious. The terrible angel-like female figure suggests the plight of the psyche in a worldview made mechanical by science. She and her ship are like the Cartesian view of the soul within the body: a ghost in a machine.[23] With a mate who is a "death," she casts dice, suggesting the randomness of the universe as portrayed by the hypothesis that all causation is mechanical.

The causes of psychic sterility are many and complex. Wordsworth links "habit" with the oppression of the mind by "the laws of vulgar sense" in the creation of a "universe of death" (*Prel.* 1805, 13:139–41). Such a hell-vision surely may be seen, however, through the bars of a skeletal consciousness trapped within itself, unable to interact with regenerative sources. The irony of the Mariner's condition is largely that he is suffering such thirst so very close to water: "Water, water everywhere, / Nor any drop to drink" (121–22). Coleridge saw "abstruse research" as the "habit" of his soul in "Dejection," and had contended with Locke and Hartley.

"The Ancient Mariner" has for us an enormously representative quality. Its portrait of sterility, its symbolic death and resurrection, bring to mind the spiritual agonies and renewals of Hopkins, Eliot, Lawrence, Roethke, and Sylvia Plath, among others. Coleridge seems the most modern of the Romantics, the strongest suggestion, within a poetry largely of the impulse toward loss of self, of Modernist self-consciousness. His "The Ancient Mariner" seems to head a class of voyage poems wherein the ship of the psyche is impelled, curse-like, toward some disaster precisely because this vessel is an impediment to the reunion that is desired.

We have seen that the sea may symbolize unconscious psychic sources. The initial removal from land suggests travel in such a direction, particularly in the form of poetic inspiration. In "The Eolian Harp" the sound of a wind upon a harp in the cottage window produces a "witchery of sound" such as elves make when they "Voyage on gentle gales from Fairy-Land." We remember that the poet is freed from the conventional structure of thought implicit in his cottage and its overgrowing abstractions, Jasmin of Innocence, Myrtle of Love, that he finds in the window with its harp an opening into a voyage of psychic discovery, that he is carried along like a floating elf by the wind and the music it makes. The cottage of conventional thought is moved away from, and then returned to, as the poet's imagination responds to the symbolic breeze of inspiration, "Plastic and vast." But suppose the conventional conscious structure was itself, in a sense, one great harp, one thing able to respond to the breeze of inspiration: not with the metaphoric voyage of music, but with voyage itself, metaphoric of psychic discovery. Such a structure would be a ship. The masts and sails, like the strings of a harp, are acted on by wind; instead of music, identified in "The Eolian Harp" with spontaneous fantasy (39–43), there is motion, travel into undiscovered regions. In a notebook entry of 1803 Coleridge said, "I will at least make the attempt to explain to myself the Origin of moral Evil from the *streamy* Nature of Association, which Thinking = Reason, curbs & rudders."[24] Taken together with the "Eolian Harp" metaphor of floating on a wind or music, *stream* and *rudder* suggest a voyage of thought wherein the ship of ego has much ado to guide or rudder itself as it is borne along by a flow—whether stream current or wind current—from quite outside its limited boundaries.

Thus, in part 1 of "The Ancient Mariner," the ship moves downward and crosses the equator, the boundary between ordinary ego awareness and what lies below it. The ship is controlled by the wind and the sea and is taken toward the south pole, into a land of fearful marvels. Just as there were "caves of ice" in "Kubla Khan," so is there ice here: "ice, mast-high, came floating by / As green as emerald" (53–54). The jewel-like color makes this land one of rare beauty as well as of fear. The sound of the ice suggests a dream state: "It cracked and growled, and roared and howled, / Like noises in a swound!" (61–62). A "swound" is a swoon, and these noises are animal-like, as if the animal origin of man's evolution were available in this lowest region. Jung's dreamed descent into the cave below the cellar of his psychic house made him feel that the "primitive psyche of man borders on the life of the animal soul, just as the caves of prehistoric times were usually inhabited by animals before men laid claim to them."[25]

In emblematic recognition of this rapprochement between the ship of consciousness and the bottom level of the deeps to the south below it, the albatross comes, a kind of messenger, a native of this far region bringing assurance that even to this place, "where no living thing was to be seen" (gloss., 57–58), the continuity of the organic universe extends. The Mariner rejects this living symbol, refusing both it and its habitat. The result is a return to the borderline region of the equator, which functions rather like the landscape's surface in "Kubla Khan"; it marks the boundary between the rational world and the vast spaces underneath.

All in a hot and copper sky,
The bloody Sun, at noon,
Right up above the mast did stand,
No bigger than the Moon.   (111–14)

His Berkeleian universe is as the Mariner perceives it, and his eye wears a hellish filter. The ship of consciousness is marooned, stuck on this equator.

After the Mariner's shipmates, with their last glances, shine back his cursed, horned-moon vision into his eyes, there follows in part 4 a seven-day living death in which the time of original creation is as it were inverted. He must suffer sterility until his own guilty consciousness can die. When the moon goes up the sky easily, naturally, imagination is freed of distortion. Under its power he can see down into the ship's shadow, where water snakes play and are enhanced by the moon so that he spontaneously loves them. The albatross falls off, is reabsorbed into the sea.

In his condition of alienation, the Mariner had suffered from drought and a lack of wind. But here in part 5 the Aeolian play is almost too abundant.

> The thick black cloud was cleft, and still
> The Moon was at its side:
> Like waters shot from some high crag,
> The lightning fell with never a jag,
> A river steep and wide.   (322–26)

What may well be a wish of the Mariner's appears to come true: the dead sailors are brought back to life. Did he, Christ-like, bring it about through the power of his thought? It is at this point that the Wedding-Guest cries out in fear. The Mariner has apparently seemed too powerful for the comfort of his listener.

When the crossing of the equatorial boundary back to ordinary consciousness is attempted (383–84), the Mariner falls into a swoon. He is brought back to land by forces outside the control of his will (389–439). When he sees his own native country, it is transformed by moonlight, and from the bay rise crimson shapes, angelic forms with the color, and from the direction, of the traditional Hell. These seraph-men occasion his rescue by waving to the land. The Mariner's ship of consciousness, so transcendentalized by his experience as to seem spectral, finally goes under, reiterating in other imagistic terms the death of part 4. The Mariner is taken to land in the Pilot's humble rowboat, symbolizing his rebirth. What persona he may wear among his fellows is now a grave problem. He speaks, and the Pilot's boy goes crazy, and even the Hermit is hard-pressed to keep his equilibrium. The Mariner yearns toward society and conventional piety (601–9) but is set apart by his power and vision. Like the speaker of "Kubla Khan," he has accepted into his reborn personality so large an admixture of angelic/hellish inspiration that ordinary people fear him. He is an outcast, a force of nature, passing "like night, from land to land" (586). A mouthpiece for the collective history of man, he is both greater and less than human, a prophet speaking to our unwilling ears as if the earth had opened.

The Mariner, then, has completed a psychological voyage away from his time. Having had the bars of a skeletal consciousness lifted from before his eyes, he sees a world made new, wherein all life is connected in a web of moral significance and all acts are sacramental rather than random. He initiates his hearers into a chaotic, fertilizing inheritance, like that described by Wordsworth as our "dim ancestral Past" (*Prel.* 13:320). If the world had been deadened by rational thought, then the Romantic poet practices resuscitation rituals whereby intuition rediscovers the "life of things" through particular landscapes, recovers a correspondence between areas of himself and hidden declivities toward water that result in a better understanding of his own life and of its relation to the cosmos. "The Ancient Mariner" may be the most complete and suggestive of the poems that do this, and exists in a kind of counterpoint relation to the work of Wordsworth.

Both Coleridge and Wordsworth were concerned in their different ways with the guilt of reason. Evidence of this theme in Wordsworth comes in part from *The Borderers* and the preface for it that he supplied. The totality of his experiences in France — his love affair together with his observations on the course of the revolution and the psychological reaction that he suffered—left him with a profound distrust of the new rationalism as applied to human affairs. In book 11 of *The Prelude* Wordsworth describes his initial enthusiasm for the upheaval in France, making clear that he cherished Utopian hopes for the betterment of man. He had an optimistic view of the essential human nature, together with a faith in the good that reason could accomplish in the renovation of society.

> Bliss was it in that dawn to be alive,
> But to be young was very Heaven! O times,
> In which the meagre, stale, forbidding ways
> Of custom, law, and statute, took at once
> The attraction of a country in romance!
> When Reason seemed the most to assert her rights

> When most intent on making of herself
> A prime enchantress—to assist the work,
> Which then was going forward in her name!   (108–16)

Yet later, when the revolution had degenerated into terror and finally war had broken out between England and France, reason became the focus of a kind of intellectual disease in the poet. In the absence of encouraging events, he succumbed to "speculative schemes— / That promised to abstract the hopes of Man / Out of his feelings" (224–26); succumbed, that is, to the particular brand of rationalistic optimism formulated by William Godwin. Looking back on this period, Wordsworth gave voice to some of the most biting irony of which he was capable—part of it directed at himself.

> How glorious! in self-knowledge and self-rule,
> To look through all the frailties of the world,
> And, with a resolute mastery shaking off
> Infirmities of nature, time, and place,
> Build social upon personal Liberty,
> Which, to the blind restraints of general laws
> Superior, magisterially adopts
> One guide, the light of circumstances, flashed
> Upon an independent intellect.   (236–44)

His rationalism led him, not to triumph, but to a kind of despair. Burdened with guilt over Annette, faced with the prospect that the event he had hoped would better the world was leading only to a war in which the English peasants he loved would bear the heaviest burden, Wordsworth seems to have discovered the hollowness of his calculations. He had become a Descartes of the ethical sphere, "Dragging all precepts, judgements, maxims, creeds, / Like culprits to the bar" (11:294–95). The demand for formal proof in this area led only to an endless relativism, so that, in the end, he "Yielded up moral questions in despair" (305). "This was the crisis of that strong disease" (306), he concludes, the low point of his psychic fall. A verbal parallel with *The Borderers* points up a connection between the self-deceptive rationalizings of its villainous Oswald and the kind of Utopian calculations practiced in the name of liberty by partisans of the revolution. Thinking that Marmaduke has killed Herbert, Oswald congratulates him, saying:

> You have obeyed the only law that sense
> Submits to recognize; the immediate law,
> From the clear light of circumstances, flashed
> Upon an independent Intellect.   (1493–96)

Thus Oswald can justify murder. The partisans of the revolution had likewise shaken off "the blind restraints of general laws." Wordsworth in his maturity apparently felt the revolutionary reasonings and speculations of his youth self-deceptive and potential extenuation for great crimes. By comparison with nature and tradition, with the sanity of self-possessed emotion, reason had proved guilty.

The aftermath of Wordsworth's complex involvement with the guilt of reason produced the darkest period of his career. On his return from France in December of 1792, he spent the year of his adult life most obscure to his biographers, living for the most part in London.[26] He seems to have continued to need close contact with political discussion and the latest news relating to France. It must have been during this period that he practiced an Oswald-like moral calculation. He too had gone into the world and been "betrayed into a great crime," at least in his own eyes. The later, purgative poetry written at Racedown and Alfoxden grew out of this period of spiritual gloom and moral relativism. And an experience on Salisbury Plain in July of 1793 seems both to have focused his vision of human suffering and to have opened his thoughts toward some deeper source than Godwinian rationalism. Partly through accident, he undertook a foot journey that led him past Stonehenge.[27] The sense of a new possibility in poetry that sprang up in connection with this dreary place and time is recounted in *The Prelude.*

He has hypothesized that poets, like prophets, may each have their "peculiar dower," their insight that allows them to perceive "something unseen before," and has dared to hope that a special "influx," a "privilege," has been given to him, so that some

work "Proceeding from the depth of untaught things" may come
from his pen with "A power like one of Nature's." Here again we
have the image of a source prior to the critical intellect—from the
"depth of untaught things"—welling up from below. The passage
continues:

> To such mood,
> Once above all, a traveller at that time
> Upon the plain of Sarum—was I raised:
> There on the pastoral downs without a track
> To guide me, or along the bare white roads
> Lengthening in solitude their dreary line,
> While through those vestiges of ancient times
> I ranged, and by the solitude o'ercome,
> I had a reverie and saw the past,
> Saw multitudes of men, and here and there
> A single Briton in his wolf-skin vest,
> With shield and stone-axe, stride across the wold.
>
> (1805, 12:312–23)

As Mary Moorman indicates, Wordsworth's reading contributed to
this vision, yet there is no mistaking the archetypal direction his
imagination has taken.[28] And it is chiefly the landscape itself that
seems to evoke this encounter with images from the collective racial memory. In 1793, his immediate response was to begin a poem
then called "Salisbury Plain," a work never published in its original
form.

The early manuscripts of "Salisbury Plain" contain a more
Gothic and terrible work than the poem published in 1842 as "Guilt
and Sorrow."[29] A man traveling alone, on foot, is caught by a storm
near Stonehenge; the atmosphere is portentous, with gathering
clouds and darkness, imagery of raven and buzzard. As the gloom
threatens rain, he sees what seems "an antique castle spreading
wide" (78) and runs toward it hoping for shelter. It proves to be
Stonehenge, and a supernatural voice comes from the ruin itself,
warning him away with terrifying descriptions of the powers that
inhabit it: "To hell's most cursed sprites the baleful place / Belongs,
upreared by their magic power" (84–85). Wordsworth seems to

have intended these inhabitants to be ghosts of the past, presences memorializing our ancestral savagery and violence. The voice describes a hellish light that illumines the ruin,

> "While warrior spectres of gigantic bones,
> Forth-issuing from a thousand rifted tombs,
> Wheel on their fiery steeds amid the infernal glooms."
>
> (97–99)

This ancestral vision was dark, painful. Wordsworth was pulled toward it by depression, personal guilt, and foreboding. He tells us in the note appended to "Guilt and Sorrow" of his state of mind in 1793, "having passed a month in the Isle of Wight, in view of the fleet which was then preparing for sea off Portsmouth at the commencement of the war" (*P.W.* 1:94). The rupture between England and France, that blow to his psyche that made his likings and loves run "in new channels, leaving old ones dry" (*Prel.* 11:185), was at the forefront of thought, with all its implications for the affair with Annette. He knew from his experience of the French spirit that the war was likely to be long and disastrous, and that the English poor especially would bear the heaviest burden (*P.W.* 1:95). Pulled downward by his negative imaginings, he connected the current sorrows with our immemorial inheritance as represented by Stonehenge and the Druid rites of which he had read. In attempting to dramatize this racial burden, this inheritance of guilt, he gave to the structure of stones a voice, had them speak of the past and its terrors.

The dreary walk in 1793 through the plain of Stonehenge had led on into the valley of the Wye. Given the association of that earlier journey with depression and the guilt of reason, we can well understand the special significance Wordsworth must have felt when he revisited the landscape around Tintern Abbey accompanied by Dorothy in July of 1798. Brother and sister had moved into Alfoxden in July of the previous year. Following that first great period of interchange with Coleridge during which "The Ruined Cottage" had been expanded, Wordsworth's poems for *Lyrical Ballads* largely written, and "The Ancient Mariner" planned and executed, they were obliged to give up the lease. Wordsworth and

Dorothy planned to go with Coleridge to Germany in the fall. On a spontaneous three-day trip in high summer they followed the River Wye past Tintern Abbey, perhaps as a kind of farewell to the landscapes associated with so much suffering and creativity.[30] The result was Wordsworth's most complete meditative lyric of psychic regeneration. "Tintern Abbey" may be read as a personal version of that more magical scenario of death and resurrection seen in "The Ancient Mariner."

The background music is in a minor key. The poem is permeated with a darkness that must be transformed. The ability to "see into the life of things" (49) is won with difficulty, aided by experiences such as that represented in the organic landscape of the beginning. The seamless vitalism of green plays against suggestions of deadness, of a failure of perception and meaning. This spectrum of trees and cliffs is *not* "As is a landscape to a blind man's eye" (24). Certain "hours of weariness" lie in the past with a "darkness," with "many shapes / Of joyless daylight" (27, 51–52). Godwinian thought, the life in London, guilt over Annette, have been transformed into a positive vision. The very fact of physicality can be overcome during those moments when "we are laid asleep / In body, and become a living soul" (45–46). Adam created in the garden "became a living soul," and Wordsworth has envisioned a return through the sleep that lies below reason to an Adamic unity with nature. This wiser sleep occurs in the context of the eighteenth-century scientific worldview, the domain of the "meddling intellect" ("The Tables Turned").

When Wordsworth speaks of the *"motion* of our human blood" (44), he is simultaneously raising the specter that we and the world are machines, and laying it to rest. The words *burden, heavy,* and *weight,* when connected to *unintelligible world* (40), suggest the universe as described by Newtonian mechanics, where motion and mass are crucial terms. Wordsworth raises the specter of weight as only burden, motion as only a "fretful stir," part of "the fever of the world" (52–53). It is as if life in cities were identified with abstraction, deadened imagination and perception, the intellectual and social construct of a past that has to be sloughed off. Like the specter bark, this entrapment of the psyche by a hardened, conscious attitude must be exposed as fallacious. From the sleep of intuition the poet resurrects his world, and in it, the descriptions of science are transformed, Newton is transcendentalized.

When Wordsworth describes, then, in "Tintern Abbey" "all the mighty world / Of eye, and ear, —both what they half create, / And what perceive" (105–7), he is indicating the universe as brought freshly back into life by an inspired empiricism, and doing so in a terminology taken over from the scientific philosophy that his vision both reproves and completes. He is conscious of Locke as well as of Newton, indebted to Locke's distinction between primary and secondary qualities for his recognition that our senses create part of the world they perceive.[31] Something "whose dwelling is the light of setting suns" and present equally in "round ocean," "living air," and the "mind of man" is described in terms reminiscent of science, but science transformed by imagination (97–99). The poet feels

A motion and a spirit, that impels
All thinking things, all objects of all thought,
And rolls through all things.   (100–102)

Here the ocean is round, seen in completeness and harmony, not as the sea of chaos. We have brought also into our thoughts the whole solar system as held in circular, rotational balance by the gravity Newton described—and which he himself interpreted as a universal, vitalistic attraction.[32] In the light of suns, a great motion rolls, circular, harmonious, the signature of life rather than of mechanism and death, the turning upon itself of what Erich Neumann calls the uroboros, that original circle and ocean from which individual consciousness splits off.[33]

It was the unique privilege of Wordsworth and Coleridge to stand at a kind of crossroads of thought at the end of the eighteenth century and to make, in symbolic and dramatic terms, the necessary, salutary criticisms of the age of which they were a part. Wordsworth's psyche, as he dramatized it in autobiographical verse, reenacted the evolution of consciousness from the time of that "single Briton clothed in wolf-skin vest" (*Prel.* 13:322) whom he "met" on Salisbury Plain, up to his own. In recalling his own childhood and in talking with figures such as the little girl in "We Are Seven," he returned the psyche to its primitive condition. He allowed his consciousness to encounter the unconscious as part of its interaction with nature, which is precisely what Jung sees as happening when the savage projects the contents of his imagination into the landscape.[34] As *The Prelude* developed, Wordsworth brought that primal psyche, having won independence from its origin but still very much rooted in nature and the unconscious, into contact with education at Cambridge, then into contact with the bustling life of London. Finally, in relation to the French Revolution, that pivotal moment in the swing of history toward our modern world, he showed his psyche as suffering a fall, and a fall of the sort peculiar to the West in its modernity: overmuch involvement with abstract reasoning.[35] He then dramatized his recovery from that fall, suggesting that a life in tune with nature and the unconscious remains a possibility, if we can but muster the wisdom to learn from children and the landscape.

Wordsworth and Coleridge were the most influential poets of their age partly because they encountered and came to terms with its central intellectual challenge. The Mariner becalmed under a hellish sun, trapped by the vision in his eyes, is perhaps our first hero of alienation, a modern figure. Oswald of *The Borderers* is like a character from Dostoevski, free of the moral illusions of the past, who approaches crime like a scientist in his laboratory. The poet in "Tintern Abbey," like figures in *The Waste Land*, is searching for meaning in a society where the root-like connections of the psyche to its environment are endangered. That Wordsworth so unambiguously finds the answer to his quest is perhaps the only element in the poem that does not consort with the modern situation.

3 Symbols of Dichotomy and the Failure of Resuscitation

Symbols of a psychological dichotomy, of a disunity of being, may be traced through the premodernist writers of the later nineteenth century and into the twentieth. Some of Tennyson's loveliest poems—"Mariana," "The Lady of Shalott," "The Palace of Art," "The Lotos-Eaters"—feature overly sensitive, perhaps pathological psyches that can function only in the subjective atmosphere of a setting (whether house, tower, palace, or luxuriant dream landscape) so set apart from the ordinary world that there is no viable interaction between the realm of imagination and the realm of actuality. Mariana suffers a negative fixity of thought in a lonely hut, like Wordsworth's Margaret of "The Ruined Cottage." The Lady of Shalott tries to leave her tower for a more vital existence but dies in the attempt. The poet's Soul in "The Palace of Art" manages to escape the solipsistic contemplation of his mind-palace's rich imagery, but at the cost of all he holds most dear. Matthew Arnold's "The Scholar-Gipsy" portrays a figure that has reacquired the vitality of nature and the intuitive life at the price of a total withdrawal from current society.[1] His "Stanzas from the Grande Chartreuse" depicts himself and his spiritual kindred as children raised in a forest beneath "some old-world abbey wall" (170), cut off both from the Victorian triumphs of science, empire, and commerce and from the traditional faith symbolized by the abbey. He and his fellows can only sympathize from a distance with the loveliness and order of religious observance—with the yellow candle flames that symbolize a hope for immortality not shared by the poet. Like the figures in Eliot's *The Waste Land*,

Arnold can hope in the end only for a despairing quiet: "—Pass, banners, pass, and bugles, cease; / And leave our desert to its peace!" (209–10). This failure of relation between psyche and environment suggests not only the poet's increasing isolation from a real world as defined by society, science, and philosophy, but also a separation within the self. A more conscious dimension of personality associated with the lonely figure is seen to have lost contact with some deeper, more instinctive level of existence symbolized by landscape or by water.

The house upon the landscape or the ship upon the sea may serve as alternative versions of an archetypal presentation of consciousness in relation to its primordial origins in the unconscious. When a barrier between measured structure of house or ship and limitless foundation in the earth or sea is enforced by artificial means—by science's reasoned program of abstraction, by Cartesian doubt, even by society's development of a manufacturing and technological civilization—then the total psyche represented by house and landscape, ship and sea, may choose to sacrifice the rational half in preference to losing contact with an origin that it perceives as divine and as the source of its inspiration. The image of a one-way Aeolian voyage may be the result. Consciousness in a trap, frozen into a purely rational mode, may choose self-extinction as a way out. This is the sense behind the poetic of Arthur Rimbaud. He would not, in another age, have needed to derange all the senses, to throw overboard the rudder of his barge. And the historical precedent for Gerard Manley Hopkins's "heart, / O unteachably after evil" ("The Wreck of the Deutschland," 18) is the guilty reason of Wordsworth and Coleridge, which murders to dissect. The Oxford Movement that influenced Hopkins was itself part of that larger reaction against rationalism and the increasing secularization of society including, as its initial and leading indicator, the Romantic poets. In "God's Grandeur" Hopkins voices the contention between a sacred nature and a profane society.

Generations have trod, have trod, have trod;
    And all is seared with trade; bleared, smeared with toil;

And wears man's smudge and shares man's smell:
   the soil
Is bare now, nor can foot feel, being shod.

The natural foot in the confining boot is one humble symbol of a civilization-enforced separation between man and his origins. In the sonnet's sestet, nature is found "deep down things," and the "Holy Ghost," reminding us of the spirit that presided over the waters in original creation, springs dove-winged from the darkness with dawn, suggesting that the scared principle of creativity is latent still in nature/unconsciousness if we can but reach the primordial soil and that "deep down" darkness that precedes new light.[2]

Helpful clarification of the symbols of a disunity within existence may be found in Shelley, who also featured imagery of sailing. The small boat given over to the will of wind and sea is a version and symptom of a dichotomy within the creative self, one offering a final (and fatal) solution to the problem. The loss of the vessel of consciousness is, for individual personality, a metaphoric suicide. In order to understand the driving need that sends the poet off onto his one-way voyage, whether metaphoric or actual (Shelley, of course, was drowned in a sailing accident), we need to see more clearly the opponent of unity between conscious poet—symbolized by the masculine principle, light, the eye, seeing, the house, the tower, or the ship, the upward direction—and unconscious inspiration—symbolized by the feminine principle, darkness, hearing, scent, or touch, the landscape (especially underground), the sea (especially with wind and storm), and the downward direction. We find several images of small boats given over to the sea in Shelley's *Prometheus Unbound*. This work offers us also an archetypal embodiment of the sterile, masculine, misguided, and misguiding consciousness in Jupiter, the tyrant-god who is overthrown through the process symbolized by the returning of vessel to ocean.

Prometheus, symbol of man's collective psyche and primordial unity with nature, has been pinned upon a cliff in torment. He is separated from Asia, who is his feminine other half, his anima, the Eve to his Adam. The world is sadly fallen, original unity ripped apart, and all because Prometheus has brought the higher consciousness symbolized by fire to mankind. Prometheus as a character is indebted to Satan, but unlike Milton in *Paradise Lost*, Shelley permits himself to brand the ruling god, the opponent of the heroic rebel giant, as evil. Jupiter has fixed Prometheus to the cliff, just as Milton's God has cast his Satan into Hell. Shelley has taken the step implied by Blake in his comments in "The Marriage of Heaven and Hell": he has acknowledged the rebel Titan as hero and branded the ruling god as an oppressor.

Shelley's Jupiter is closely associated with the ordering machinery of civilization. After he has been overthrown, Shelley celebrates the processional passing-away of

> Thrones, altars, judgment-seats and prisons; wherein
> And beside which, by wretched men were borne
> Sceptres, tiaras, swords and chains, and tomes
> Of reasoned wrong glozed on by ignorance,
> . . . .
> And those foul shapes, abhorred by god and man—
> Which under many a name and many a form
> Strange, savage, ghastly, dark and execrable
> Were Jupiter, the tyrant of the world.   (3.4.164–83)

The collective mind of man has somehow purified itself of the Jupiter-principle and no longer needs the codified limits to individual liberty that society has developed. The heavy-handed male ruler with his sceptres, swords, and chains is representative of civilization's moral and legal consciousness. Demogorgon is Jupiter's counterpart and comes from an underground, mist-shrouded world to overthrow him.[3]

In an essay written late in his life on *Prometheus Unbound*, W. B. Yeats looks back upon Shelley, the poet whom, even more than Blake, he singles out as having "shaped my life." One element of *Prometheus Unbound* still troubles his thought. In his much earlier essay "The Philosophy of Shelley's Poetry" Yeats had accorded Shelley's verse play a certain place "among the sacred books of the world." Now toward the close of his career, Yeats asks, "Why, then, does Demogorgon, whose task is beneficent . . . bear so terrible a shape, and not to the eyes of Jupiter, external necessity, alone, but to those of Asia . . . ? Why is Shelley terrified of the Last Day like a Victorian child? It was not terrible to Blake." Yeats quotes a passage that is Blake's version of the undoing of the fall, wherein "the cherub with the flaming sword" is made "to leave his guard at the Tree of Life" so that the world of experience can be regenerated in Edenic terms, "the whole creation" appearing "infinite and holy." This is an apt parallel to the action of *Prometheus Unbound* and its theme of imaginative regeneration in the style of "The Ancient Mariner." Man is converted from "a many-sided mirror / Which could distort to many a shape of error / This fair true world of things" into "a Sea reflecting Love" (4:382–84). Yeats's questioning, therefore, is appropriate. Why should the instrument of beneficent regeneration be seen as so dark and terrific? Yeats concludes that Shelley's conception of Demogorgon is the central weakness of his play, and a weakness representative of a flaw in his vision: "Demogorgon made his plot incoherent, its interpretation impossible; it was thrust there by that something which again and again forced him to balance the object of desire conceived as miraculous and superhuman, with nightmare" (*E.&I.*, 424, 65, 420).

"The Marriage of Heaven and Hell" speaks of Titan figures associable with Prometheus. But Blake's work does not advocate the freeing of the Titan from his necessary adversary/other-half:

> The Giants who formed this world into its sensual existence and now seem to live in it in chains are in truth the causes of its life & the sources of all activity, but the chains are the cunning of weak and tame minds, which have power to resist energy; according to the proverb, the weak in courage is strong in cunning.
>
> Thus one portion of being is the Prolific, the other the Devouring; to the devourer it seems as if the producer was in his chains, but it is not so; he only takes portions of existence and fancies that the whole.
>
> But the Prolific would cease to be Prolific unless the Devourer as a sea received the excess of his delights.[4]

In spite of his sympathy for the chained Giants, Blake recognizes that both halves of the opposition are necessary. Seeing the Prolific and the Devouring as "two classes of men," Blake says that "whoever tries to reconcile them seeks to destroy existence." In *Prometheus Unbound* Shelley is seeking to destroy existence as we know it. He cannot tolerate the rule of moral consciousness, repressive legality, and all the imperfect ordering of society by the masculine Jupiter-principle that he sees in man's evolutionary past. Because the thrones and "tomes / Of reasoned wrong" are so entirely hated and rejected, Shelley has to advocate a revolution wherein the figure from underworld darkness whose very name is borrowed from Milton's enumeration of the powers of chaos (*Paradise Lost*, 2:965) overthrows the psyche's representative of consciousness, order, and tradition. Jupiter's defeat is yet another version of the swallowing up of the vessel of consciousness in a chaotic sea.

The implication of such imagery seems unhappy, even desperate, suggesting a disunity of being in which the components of the psyche are on the point of being torn apart. In the early "Alastor" the poet's figure becomes emaciated, his hand hanging "like dead bone within its withered skin" (251). As physical being wastes away, the spirit burns with feverish intensity in his eyes. He abandons himself to a fragile craft, is blown across a sea, to a new land and the beginning of a spring, and follows the stream, reliving the stages of his life until he gradually weakens and eventually dies on a precipice beside a waterfall. There the stream scatters itself "to the passing winds" (570). The surrender of ship to stream and sea wind is a different version of that subjection to a collective inspiration indicated in Coleridge's "The Eolian Harp." The final giving over of organic harp to that "one intellectual breeze" is death, the dissolution and return dramatized in "Alastor."

Shelley seems, then, to have used the idea of Aeolian surrender to image for himself more ideal relationships between the ship of consciousness and its sustaining water and enlivening wind. "Lines Written Among the Euganean Hills" begins with the extended image of a sea voyage in search of some restorative "green isle." In the beginning of "Julian and Maddalo" the narrator and his friend, the gloomy count, view Venice at sunset from a "funereal bark" (88), and for a moment "Its temples and its palaces did seem / Like fabrics of enchantment piled to Heaven" (91–92). "Ode to the West Wind" is Shelley's most impassioned Aeolian wish, and, though there is no boat image, the leaf, the cloud, and the wave form alternative versions of wind-impelled things with which the poet seeks to identify. The witch of Atlas moors her magical boat upon a fountain of light, or travels in it through her landscape, "like a cloud / Upon a stream of wind" ("The Witch of Atlas," 369, 370).

Prometheus Unbound uses boat imagery in crucial passages to represent the succumbing of the psyche to an occult, inspirational force. A wind or stream of music moves "All spirits on that secret way, / As inland boats are driven to Ocean" (2.2. 45–46). Asia describes such an experience in the following terms:

> My soul is an enchanted boat
> Which, like a sleeping swan, doth float
> Upon the silver waves of thy sweet singing,
> . . . .
> Till like one in slumber bound
> Borne to the Ocean, I float down, around,
> Into a Sea profound, of ever-spreading sound.
>
> (2.5.72–84)

The sea journey she describes is a version of the reunion of individual consciousness with its collective origin. As the passage continues, Asia passes beyond the bounds of ordinary experience and personality: "Where never mortal pinnace glided, / The boat of my desire is guided" (93–94). Like the poet-figure in "Alastor," she retraces the course of her life and moves beyond it.

> We have passed Age's icy caves,
> And Manhood's dark and tossing waves
> And Youth's smooth ocean, smiling to betray;
> Beyond the glassy gulphs we flee
> Of shadow-peopled Infancy,
> Through Death and Birth to a diviner day.   (98–103)

The life-denying potentiality of Shelley's vision is evident most especially in "Adonais." The negative ideality of such images as "Life, like a dome of many-coloured glass" (462) exists in a compensatory relationship to the moldering "leprous corpse" (172) of Keats, which is kept onstage much longer than seems decent. The rotting of the dead poet's body, however, has a symbolic purpose: it comes to typify the infection and "contagion" (356) that is spread through all the physical world by the "eclipsing Curse / Of birth" (480–81). The advice of the poem is succinct: "Die, / If thou wouldst be with that which thou dost seek!" (464–65). All beautiful earthly things seem only fragmentary facets reflecting the great beauty beyond. The poem ends with a complex, apocalyptic image of a small boat as Aeolian harp destroyed in the process of making its music.

> The breath whose might I have invoked in song
> Descends on me; my spirit's bark is driven,
> Far from the shore, far from the trembling throng
> Whose sails were never to the tempest given;
> The massy earth and sphered skies are riven!   (487–91)

This craft never returns to land, but instead of sinking, is blown by extreme inspiration completely off the surface of the earth. The sky splits and the poet's vessel voyages into the Absolute.

An interesting lineage of postromantic poems portrays small boats or ships that do not ever make it back to land. The association between a kind of one-way voyage and some death of consciousness seems central. The heroine of Tennyson's "The Lady of Shalott" drifts down a river into Camelot in a boat bearing her name, which arrives intact, though she lies dead within it. The hero of the same poet's "Ulysses" cannot bear his life on land and intends "To sail beyond the sunset, and the baths / Of all the western stars, until I die" (60–61). In "Morte d'Arthur" (incorporated later into the *Idylls of the King* as "The Passing of Arthur") the wounded Arthur sails away from land on the funereal barge, "till the hull / Look'd one black dot against the verge of dawn" (338–39). Arthur Rimbaud, though heir to the Romantic legacy in a different language, employed the same symbol. "Le Bateau ivre" follows the revolutionary progress of a river barge as it speaks in the first person of its indifference to crews and cargos, its liberation from haulropes and rudder. This surrogate consciousness is swept out to sea for delirious immersion in waters that the poet associates with stars, the milk of childhood, drunkenness, and the divine—the wave's rhythms are stronger than alcohol, dawn as exalted as a flock of doves.

Imagery of boat given over to the sea may be associated with some radical choice or sense of desperation in the poet's life. Gerard Manley Hopkins's original resolution to give up poetry as part of his commitment to Catholicism and the Jesuit Order was in its own way as extreme as Rimbaud's renunciation of literature for the life of a trader in Ethiopia. If Rimbaud's most characteristic work describes a river barge washed out to sea, the pivotal poem in Hopkins's career was "The Wreck of the Deutschland." This loss of a vessel in which five Franciscan nuns were drowned, though urged upon the poet-priest by his rector, must have implied a symbolic appropriateness, for the subject brought him out of a seven-year silence and in treating it he established the technical innovations that mark him as a poet.[5] In recalling the circumstances of his conversion, the "walls, altar and hour and night," he transforms this situation into the testing of a ship by waves and wind. God is a stormy sea, and the poet remembers

> The swoon of a heart that the sweep and the hurl
>   of thee trod
>   Hard down with a horror of height:
> And the midriff astrain with leaning of, laced with
>   fire of stress.   (st. 2)

Under extreme tension, "The frown of his face / Before me, the hurtle of hell / Behind" (st. 3), Hopkins, in an act of desperation, chose conversion; he "fled," "dovewinged," "from the flame to the flame" (st. 3).

A stubborn, sinful consciousness had to be pushed to a breaking point, a kind of death, before it could experience a reacquaintance with its origin in the divine. Hopkins portrays through traditional religious terminology the same pattern as Wordsworth in the "Intimations" ode, wherein our souls sometimes "have sight of that immortal sea / Which brought us hither" (163–64). For Hopkins, however, the transaction of consciousness with its origin is a desperate enterprise. The sense of guilt felt by the poet in his heart, "O unteachably after evil" (st. 18), his participation in "Man's malice" (st. 9) must be overcome "with wrecking and storm" (st. 9). As the whole poem exemplifies, Hopkins finds his inspiration in the story of a disaster; it is the image of the tall nun, arisen like "a lioness" (st. 17) in the confusion and horror of shipwreck, that touches his heart, brings "tears! is it? tears; such a melting, a madrigal start!" (st. 18). As the nun cries out upon Christ from amid the fury of the waves, she offers an alternative version of Wordsworth's basic symbol of the regenerated imagination in immediate contact with the source of its inspiration: the child upon the seashore. Hopkins's guilty heart is melted into tears that are the beginning of poetic song. The consciousness of the poet has enacted a pattern of death and resurrection like that to be found in "The Ancient Mariner." The old restrictive attitude has to be wrecked before imagination's rebirth, before reacquisition of the sources of fertility. Though couched in Christian terminology, the pattern of Hopkins's poem of death and new life is unmistakably Romantic.

In spite of the apocalyptic reunion with the divine envisioned in "The Wreck of the Deutschland," the most impressive works toward the end of Hopkins's all-too-brief career are sonnets exploring the terrible separation he seems still to have felt, even after his radical choice for Catholicism and the priesthood, between himself and the psychic fertility needed for creation. He ends sonnet 51 with a juxtaposition between his own sterility and the fecund, symbolic landscape of the more natural sinners from whose ways the logic of his position has forced him to turn away.

> See, banks and brakes
> Now, leavèd how thick! lacèd they are again
> With fretty chervil, look, and fresh wind shakes
> Them; birds build—but not I build; no, but strain,

Time's eunuch, and not breed one work that wakes.
Mine, O thou lord of life, send my roots rain.

Though Hopkins has idealized the masculine, ordering God, in contrast to Blake and Shelley with their Urizen and Jupiter, the effect for the poet is unfortunately the same. He feels painfully divided between morality and fertility, between his conscious devotion and the unconscious landscape of foliage, birds, and the inspiration associated with their song.

Thomas Hardy, who was born actually a few years earlier than Hopkins, lived on and wrote on into the twentieth century. His brooding vision is notorious for its perception of ironic incongruity. A sense of disunity of being is so widely prevalent that we can attend only to the more obvious and celebrated instances. Hardy desired the sense of inspired participation in the grand organic unity that Wordsworth had glimpsed in "Tintern Abbey." His intellect, however, as instructed both by science and by unhappy experience at the hands of society, was pessimistic. In the conclusion of "Hap," for instance, Hardy savors the bitter thought that his disappointments and losses are the result neither of a beneficent natural order nor of the malevolent power he would prefer to indifference. He is instead the victim of blind chance, of the dice-throwing randomness of physical reality as described by science.

—Crass Casualty obstructs the sun and rain,
And dicing Time for gladness casts a moan. . . .
These purblind Doomsters had as readily strown
Blisses about my pilgrimage as pain.[6]

The version of consciousness offered by science and current society seemed, as for Shelley, purely rational and repellent. As a result Hardy's vision discerns a pathetically truncated quality in existence. In "Nature's Questioning" the landscape resembles a schoolroom of chastened students, the "early zest" of field, flock, and tree worn away through the "long teaching days." Nature, like the unconscious, provides motive, questioning, but cannot complete itself without the intervention of a sympathetic consciousness, of a theory capable of appreciating and understanding the organic source and basis of life. Such, in Hardy's day, was not forthcoming. Hardy therefore has the landscape speak in this vein:

> "Has some Vast Imbecility,
>   Mighty to build and blend,
>   But impotent to tend,
> Framed us in jest, and left us now to hazardry?"   (st. 4)

Darwin had extended the principle of random combination according to the laws of chance from physics into biological evolution. Natural selection was seen as the principle that guided nature. This dice-throwing, or "hazardry," struck Hardy as a very disappointing explanation of the "mighty world / Of eye, and ear" ("Tintern Abbey," 105–6). He was therefore denied "those sweet counsels between head and heart" (*Prel.* 11:352) to which Wordsworth returned after his fall into rationality. Hardy's thought, confronting nature, was guilty of the crime or sickness that Wordsworth had diagnosed: "We murder to dissect" ("The Tables Turned"). He was not able, like Blake, and, in their different ways, Wordsworth and Coleridge, to analyze and reject the overanalytic, too-conscious component of thought, to escape the skeleton ship with its dicing figures and the outlook it represented. He could only reflect the dichotomy in his verse. This he did, over and over, in different forms. The dualism of a sad, ironic juxtaposition is the source of his characteristic tone.

The tendency toward dialogues between different voices that we see so widely in his work is related to this sense of dichotomy. In "Doom and She" the two voices of the "mighty pair" of symbolic figures representing the powers behind existence are sadly out of relation with one another, unable to communicate and establish better harmony. One voice is feminine: that of the originating and unconscious nature that brings life into being but that lacks sight and thus the ability to harmonize and plan. The other voice is masculine and seems to represent the determining natural laws as described by science. This voice has the sight that nature needs to complete her task, but it is useless to her because it lacks an appreciation of joy and pain. Like scientific laws, it is indifferent to human value. On a psychological level, it represents a consciousness like that of Jupiter or Urizen, insensitive to the motives, impulses, and leading tendencies of the unconsciousness that it should complete by understanding.

It is remarkable that Hardy could endure through a long and productive career, given the pessimistic nature of his thought. He shows himself cut off like Arnold from religion in "The Impercipient." In "The Darkling Thrush" he both evokes Romantic inspiration in the symbol of the singing bird and indicates the inaccessibility of this "blessed Hope" to his own imagination. If the Romantic poem such as Wordsworth's "Tintern Abbey" or Coleridge's "This Lime-Tree Bower My Prison" may be seen as resuscitation rituals, invocations designed to bring the mind back to life, then "The Darkling Thrush," "The Impercipient," and many other poems by Hardy may be seen as resuscitation rituals that fail. They are, like Hopkins's sonnet 51, unanswered prayers for rain, cries for the reanimation of imagination's process that are partial explanations of the failure of that process.

The invocation of inspiration that ends in sterility, the prayer for regeneration that goes unanswered, as in Hopkins's "Thou art indeed just, Lord, if I contend," the perception that the "blessed hope" symbolized to some by the bird's singing does not apply to the poet in Hardy's "The Darkling Thrush," are literary precedents for "The Love Song of J. Alfred Prufrock," "Gerontion," and *The Waste Land*. Matthew Arnold's recognition of the futility of Romantic hopes for a later generation too much schooled in skeptical reasonings in "Stanzas from the Grande Chartreuse" is also part of the background for this ironic Modernist development of the Romantic landscape structure and its characteristic statement of renewal.

"For rigorous teachers seized my youth, / And purged its faith, and trimmed its fire" ("Stanzas from the Grande Chartreuse," 67–68), says Arnold, describing the beginning of a separation between intellect and emotion, conscious and unconscious dimensions of personality, which we may name by Eliot's term "dissociation of sensibility."[7] Arnold's "Dover Beach" may be the great nineteenth-century landscape meditation (other than "Dejection") that utilizes the form of return toward renewal but finds the healing vision of solace through nature/unconsciousness ironically thwarted. The sea, with its associations of fertility, is evoked at the outset in "Dover Beach" but becomes unavailable as a spiritual presence through a recognition on the poet's part of the decline in religious faith. Likewise, in "Prufrock," "Rhapsody on a Windy Night," "Gerontion," "Sweeney Erect," and *The Waste Land* Eliot evokes the haunting, generative sea but keeps it, as fertilizing presence, beyond the reach of his characters. The form of Romantic landscape meditation as ritual of resuscitation is partially realized, but unfulfilled, producing a unique tone, as Romantic expectations collide with a too-harsh reality.

The essential features of this pattern are prefigured in "Dejection." At the outset the poet's hopes for rebirth are powerfully evoked. The new moon with the old moon in her arms from "Sir Patrick Spence" predicts fresh winds, and already the "Aeolian lute" in the poet's window is making some sound, if not music. And the thin clouds, the "lake" of evening sky, the moon, are beautifully described and make us expect the lyric response, which fails to come. There is, later, strong emotion, but it is the pain of disappointment, the chaos of unassimilated experience, symbolized by the wind (st. 7). The poet fails to relate himself to the world, to reintegrate his faculties, to reestablish harmony with the unconscious. The poem ends with a prayer that his friend may have better luck (*Poems of S.T.C.*, 1). The form of the landscape-meditation with its resuscitory pattern is used for an exploration of emotional possibility, and the conclusion is in some respects ironic, a perception of limitation, of modified hopes.

The poems of Eliot provide central Romantic symbols of the hope of resuscitation, such as the sea, recesses of the landscape, the harp, and the singing bird.[8] But in his earlier poetry the resuscitation is never certainly accomplished. Instead, one might argue that the failed resuscitation is the major genre of his earlier work. The famous (or infamous) formulation of a "dissociation of sensibility" that was supposed to have "set in" in the seventeenth century provides a critical version of a dichotomy that is reflected often in Eliot's own verse.[9]

> Between the conception
> And the creation
> Between the emotion
> And the response
> Falls the Shadow ("The Hollow Men")

A peculiar complexity attaches to such symbols of disunity as we have so far analyzed. Poets, in diagnosing and opposing a tendency of the age such as the Jupiter-principle in *Prometheus Unbound*, are dealing with a flaw in the civilized psyche that they share, a split within themselves. The dominant tonality of Romantic poetry is positive, triumphant because in the crucial passages that best define its direction and tone the essential opponent is encountered and defeated. But the opponent *has been there*, and may remain, is, finally, something within the poet, an inheritance from the age. It is the self-divisive, skeptical knowledge that is the price of an intellectual life in a modern world.

The pattern we have discerned in Blake, Wordsworth, Coleridge, and Shelley, and, rather too sketchily perhaps in Tennyson, Arnold, Hopkins, and Hardy, may help clarify the relationship between Romantic and Modernist poetry. The Romantics we have discussed, and their Victorian successors, all find themselves, in differing degrees and from different sources, subtly flawed in the creative imagination, separated to some extent or other from what seems the natural birthright of inspiration. Their access to an unconscious source of creativity symbolized by recesses of the landscape, underground caverns, the sea, or some combination of these elements is imperiled by the process of maturation, conscious learning, and ego development. To this extent their myth of separation from an original source is only one version of the personality's necessary self-definition and self-defense against the unconscious. But there is also an aspect of the threat they face specific to their times: the worldview developed by science and scientific philosophy, beginning in the seventeenth century. This dissection of thought, this substitution of a mechanical model for the universe as intuitively perceived, was accepted by the more powerful Romantics as a challenge to the dignity and power of the imagination, and as an implied threat to the possibility of a full and free life in a world perceived as alive. Wordsworth probably felt himself justified, in his days of wandering the landscape of Westmoreland and Cumberland, because his vivid experiences in mist, rain, or by moonlight, whether the sources of poems or not, were nevertheless refutations of the world as a "universe of death" (*Prel.* 14:160).

The peculiar lyric pressure of the Romantic landscape poems derives, then, from a separation overcome, a threat to imagination transcended. These are poems of return, against the odds, to an intuitive and unconscious origin. That is perhaps why Wordsworth's "Tintern Abbey" seems the indispensable Romantic landscape: the revisiting of a place associated with an earlier, more spontaneous stage of life exactly parallels this symbolic return. When the poet confronts a landscape perceived as alive, it represents an artisitic and spiritual response to the specter of the post-Cartesian age: that mind ineffectually inhabits, like an alien ghost, the mechanical universe whose workings proceed according to deterministic laws. The poet's lyric emotion serves as a kind of proof that what is responded to must be other than it has been described by scientific reason. A sample landscape-event, an exemplum of amplified feeling in relation to an actual place in the universe, is substituted for the theoretical model. When the poet's intuitions have been led out into the countryside, the triumph in practice over the looming abstraction may equally well be viewed as the passing of rational consciousness (associated with the theory of mechanism) through its narrow boundary into a refreshing reunion with unconscious energies and spaces.

The poet's emotional process, as it is rendered into words, serves as a rite or conjuration by which to revive imagination. In facing sterility, the poet is fertilized, through death finds life, in darkness a kind of light. The form of the paradox is familiar from religion and anthropology. The year-god, Attis or Adonis, of Jessie Weston's *From Ritual to Romance*, who is thrown into the water and fished out, or buried and exhumed, and who turns up later in Grail romance as the Fisher King, provides an analogous pattern.[10] But though T. S. Eliot brought these related figures into the forefront of literary consciousness in the twentieth century, it was the Romantics who first realized, in poetry, the experience of resuscitation. It was this quality of coming back from a kind of death that gave to their poems the lyric afflatus. And the failure of this lyrical hope for rebirth brings the peculiar tone of poignancy or irony to later inheritors of the Romantic legacy such as Tennyson, Arnold, Hopkins, Hardy, and Eliot.

In his work up to and including *The Waste Land* Eliot presents a residuum of Romantic consciousness embodied technically in reminiscence and echo of Romantic aspiration: an upward flutter of image and rhythm. Both the consciousness and its incipient lyrical flight are counterpointed by sound and association of the prosaic, the unheroic, the mundane. There are, before *The Waste Land*, descents of sound and implication amounting almost to mock-heroic, especially in "Prufrock," where the heroic Romantic imagination is held against the poor present descendant of that tradition. In "Gerontion" and the first four sections of *The Waste Land* we see more clearly that a disembodied ghost of Romantic poetry of place is hoveringly present, but that there are no vital unitary identities capable of penetrating through the social and rational surface to know the landscape.

Resuscitation ritual and the poem of significant place are allied. We see this more clearly in Eliot because there are both echoes of revivifying rituals and hints of the potential significance of places. Especially in "Gerontion" and the first four parts of *The Waste Land*, names of many places together with references to spring, flowering judas, dogwood, lilacs, the potential sprouting of tubers surround hints of the Eucharist. But there is no attachment to these places and no metaphysical significance to be got out of them, just as the hints of regeneration ring hollow. Eliot's world of this time holds only a sense of disembodied eyes passing over a landscape never possessed. "What are the roots that clutch?" (*The Waste Land*, 19) phrases the central question, but the generalized "Son of Man" (20) cannot answer, because he knows only a surface, the wreckage of civilized consciousness symbolized by a "heap of broken images" (22).

"Gerontion" presents a house of echoes, a haunted house that is the Western mind in its present condition; it contains no whole persons capable of enacting the enlivening ritual of Christ's body and blood become the bread and the wine. Instead, names suggestive of Europe and decay—Mr. Silvero, Madam De Tornquist, Fräulein von Kulp—perform pathetic mimes of the communion, of placing candles on an altar. This "decayed house" of a cumulative history with its "cunning passages, contrived corridors," this consciousness trapped within itself, is tantalized by rumor of salvation. It has heard of the "word within a word," but the Logos has degenerated into a Babel, is "unable to speak a word." There is a whisper and murmur of the merely social, an accumulation of sensibilities (to use Eliot's word) that can speak to each other and to themselves without significance in a "thousand small deliberations" that only "Protract the profit of their chilled delirium." This last phrase is itself an imitation of their sententious verbiage.

"Gerontion" is the house as symbol of consciousness as we may see it from Gothic fiction through "Kubla Khan," "The Ruined Cottage," and the chambers of Keats and Tennyson. Eliot's version is remarkable for the absence of any underground passages, any "caverns measureless to man" ("Kubla Khan"). This mind is trapped in the conscious dimension, and its final vision is of extinction, of the fragmentary identities of its names—"De Bailhache, Fresca, Mrs. Cammel"—reduced to elementary particles, "whirled / Beyond the circuit of the shuddering Bear / In fractured atoms." Such envisioned dissolution brings the one glimpse of fruitful reunion with the unconscious source to be had in the poem: "Gull against the wind, in the windy straits / Of Belle Isle, or running on the Horn, / White feathers in the snow, the Gulf claims." The straits between Labrador and Newfoundland, the route about the tip of South America, suggest passages through restricting boundaries into wider spaces of ocean. But there is no glimpse further than that of the white bird of a last soaring of consciousness lyrically distributed as feathers upon the snow. As in Tennyson, Hopkins, and Rimbaud, there is a dual impulse toward Icarian ascent and collapse. The prose analogue of "Gerontion" is Poe's "The Fall of the House of Usher," wherein the desiccated consciousness of Roderick Usher as symbolized by his house, trapped within its own atmosphere and cut off from regenerative sources, finally splits apart and sinks into the tarn.

The Waste Land dramatizes the questing, lyrical, half-paralyzed descendant of Romantic consciousness. An extended landscape superimposes European places, rooms, ruins. As in "Gerontion" there are many voices, many named identities, the majority of whom seem cynically reconciled to a death in life. "April is the cruellest month" (1) because it arouses the painful thought of regeneration, hidden usually under "forgetful snow" (6). Eliot's use of the questing Knight, the drowned or buried fertility god and his descendant the Fisher King, makes explicit the idea of resuscitation, of a bringing of the dead back to life. *From Ritual to Romance* traces the influence on medieval Grail romances of pre-Christian fertility cults in which a figure named perhaps Tammuz or Adonis, representing the life, fertility, and potency of nature, was mourned as dying in autumn and celebrated as arisen in the spring. In rituals based on this belief, Adonis figures were buried and exhumed. In Grail legends featuring Gawain, Percival, and other knights, the mysterious, wounded, or greatly aged "lord of the castle," the Fisher King, is identified by Jessie Weston as descendant of Tammuz or Adonis. In what she regards as the earliest and least contaminated version of the Holy Grail story, the Fisher King is in reality dead, and "the task of the Quester that of restoring him to life." There were many variants, however, and often he was depicted as maimed or aged. As a descendant of Adonis, wounded in the groin by a boar, one version of that "Being upon whose life and reproductive activities the very existence of Nature and its corresponding energies was held to depend," the Fisher King as used by Eliot must be suspected of impotence. The task of the Quester is to restore him to life, either literally or metaphorically. The Fisher King's lands are as sterile as he is, for he is the unresurrected "Spirit of Vegetation" as well as the source of human sexual and spiritual fertility.[11] Eliot had found in the anthropological scholarship of Jessie Weston and Sir James Frazer a way of uniting landscape imagery with his concern at the dichotomy between the spiritual and the physical. *The Waste Land* is a more elaborate expression of horror that physically potent Sweeney tends to be totally distinct from the spiritual consciousness that alone gives significance to human life.[12]

The Waste Land landscape seems influenced by anthropology. The more obviously symbolic passages resemble the sites of ancient cities in deserts. The reader is presented with a "heap of broken images" and a central question: "What are the roots that clutch, what branches grow / Out of this stony rubbish?" (19–22). As in Romantic landscape poetry, there is a symbolism of above ground and below. The personages who move on the surface in the present moment of the poem are confronted in various ways with a legacy of things underground. The question of roots becomes the further issue of a corpse planted in a garden (71), evoking Adonis and the resuscitory pattern of *From Ritual to Romance*. To reestablish connection with such ancient mysteries as Weston describes would be to reestablish connection with the fertilizing unconscious, symbolized by the underground and the sea. "Death by Water" reminds us that sometimes the year-god was thrown into the sea as alternative to burial.

Eliot goes beyond the Romantics partly by making explicit the sexual dimension of inspired contact with unconscious sources, or at least the implications of the failure of that contact. In *The Waste Land* sexual failure is the ultimate symbol of a lack of relation between the psychic and the physical. Romantic sensibility in the hyacinth garden fails to actualize itself in an emotional, and perhaps physical, response. The resuscitation possibility is implicit: "I was neither / Living nor dead" (39–40). But this voice is trapped in subjectivity, like Prufrock in his fantasy of the mermaids in the waves. On the other hand, there are those for whom sex is mechanically successful, like the women in the pub, Sweeney and Mrs. Porter, the "typist home at teatime" (3:222), and the woman in the Thames canoe. Yet the poet is horrified that sex can take place on a mechanical level. Sweeney is brought to Mrs. Porter by the "sound of horns and motors" (3:197), which echoes strangely with the "noise of horns and hunting" that brought "Actaeon to Diana" (Eliot's note).

The one copulation described in the poem is preceded and followed by images of things mechanical. The lyric "violet hour" of

evening calls for a more emotional response, but "the human en-
gine waits / Like a taxi throbbing waiting" (3:216, 217). Androgy-
nous Tiresias for a moment solves the poet's distaste for the purely
male identity as he sees this encounter of typist and clerk. Their
perfunctory union is given its symbolic resonance by Eliot's alteration of the quatrain by Goldsmith:

> When lovely woman stoops to folly and
> Paces about her room again, alone,
> She smoothes her hair with automatic hand
> And puts a record on the gramophone.   (3:253–56)

Like the hand of the child in "Rhapsody on a Windy Night," the
typist's is "automatic," but here the implications of that word are
greatly heightened by contrast with the momentousness of guilt in
Goldsmith's song, wherein the fallen woman must die to wash it
away, and by the parallel between her hand and the hand or arm of
the "gramophone." Her arm moves to her head; its arm moves to a
record. Human consciousness, her "brain," which "allows one
half-formed thought to pass" (251), has become perfunctory, automatic, mechanical. The specter, encountered by Wordsworth and
Coleridge, of existence as without spiritual or moral dimension in
a deterministic universe had been dramatized in more explicit
terms.

The Waste Land before cut by Pound included an imitation of
Augustan couplets, a Popean, mock-heroic description of the lady
poet Fresca in a toilet scene rather more naturalistic than that of
Belinda in "The Rape of the Lock."[13] It is as if Eliot had to reenact
the Romantic revolt within his own literary personality [14] In addition to these couplets, the manuscript included an extended Romantic image of sailing. The original "Death by Water" concerns an
American fishing vessel sailing outbound past "The Dry Salvages
to the eastern bank." The voyage is ill-omened, the crew refractory.
Eliot seems influenced here by Melville and other prose writers of
sea adventure. But when the cod begin to come, complaints are
forgotten until a gale springs up and drives the vessel ever north-
ward. Like the Ancient Mariner's ship in the grip of the wind,
theirs is helpless to do anything but pass "the farthest northern

islands" into "the horror of the illimitable scream / Of a whole world about us." The narrator recounts his vision of three ghostly women in the rigging one night, then the final disaster wherein the ship is driven upon "a long white line" that proves to be the Arctic ice.[15] We are forced to think of "The Ancient Mariner" with its voyage to where "ice, mast-high, came floating by" (53).

Both "The Ancient Mariner" and *The Waste Land* are highly compressed poems full of allusions written by philosophic poet-critics of enormous intelligence and learning; both poems confront the philosophic specter of a deadened life in a mechanical, deterministic world. Both are in effect miniature epics that invoke the idea of resuscitation, of a bringing of imagination back to life after its ritual death. Both employ the image of a ship given over to storm, wind, and ocean and ultimately sinking or being wrecked to symbolize rational consciousness transcended as the necessary precondition to visionary experience. Both are concerned with the imagination's access to its revivifying sources in the unconscious as symbolized by the sea in juxtaposition to the vessel of the conscious personality.

In *The Use of Poetry and the Use of Criticism,* Eliot begins the lecture on Wordsworth and Coleridge with a quotation from "Dejection: An Ode." Coleridge's words of self-indictment for having imperiled imagination through the habit of "abstruse research," says Eliot, "strike my ear as one of the saddest of confessions that I have ever read." There seems a personal empathy, a perception of analogy in situation. Eliot comments on Coleridge's experience of inspiration as follows: "For a few years he had been visited by the Muse . . . and thenceforth was a haunted man; for anyone who has ever been visited by the Muse is thenceforth haunted." These words date from 1932, ten years after *The Waste Land*. The last sentence of this group of lectures, delivered at Harvard, reads: "The sad ghost of Coleridge beckons to me from the shadows." The last use of poetry that Eliot had recognized was that it "may make us from time to time a little more aware of the deeper, unnamed feelings which form the substratum of our being, to which we rarely penetrate."[16] Eliot's sense of identity with Coleridge derives partly from a similar relationship to inspiration, one implying the "substratum" that is the unconscious. Both poets had experienced, in the writing of their miniature epics of the imagination's death and rebirth, an onset of autonomous creativity that fused enormous learning from many sources into a unitary pattern symbolizing the very process involved in creation. Both had found such access to be temporary. Both, implies Eliot, were haunted afterward by the experience. For Eliot, the pattern of incomplete visionary response, as established in Coleridge's "Dejection," may be definitive for his earlier career.

In *The Waste Land*, the image of a corpse newly buried, awaiting an exhumation that is never accomplished, parallels the situation of the Fisher King, whose sterility is investigated but not relieved. A further analogy is provided by the various vessels upon waters that carry personalities toward crises or dissolutions of consciousness seeming to offer hope of regeneration in the style of "The Ancient Mariner" but fail of such conclusion. Section 3 ends with a river sequence in which Wagner's profaned Rhine-daughters sing from the Thames, Queen Elizabeth and the Earl of Leicester are rowed downstream in a barge reminiscent of Cleopatra's as described by Shakespeare, and a contemporary Thames maiden tells the story of her seduction in words that echo Dante. The earlier grandeur of Elizabeth and Leicester, itself perhaps incomplete, since a marriage was proposed but not performed, becomes the pathetic tale of a woman seduced in a canoe. In emotional content yet a further version of the typist home at teatime, the canoe episode offers a new dramatization wherein a failure of relation occurs between the psyche and a body of water symbolizing the unconscious. In words like those of Pia de' Tolomei of Sienna, murdered at Maremma, the Thames-maiden tells how "Richmond and Kew / Undid me" (3:293–94). She seems almost dismembered: "My feet are at Moorgate" (296). As she floats downstream, her consciousness disintegrates: " 'On Margate sands. / I can connect / Nothing with nothing' " (300–302).

The paradox is that both "Dejection: An Ode" and *The Waste Land* are inspired poems, but typical in a special way of the modern situation, in which the poet achieves breathtaking technical virtuosity at the price of having within himself a critical and learned self-consciousness whose demands are so severe as almost to extinguish inspiration as it had formerly existed. We are reminded of the "House of Usher" with its fissure down the facade, inhabited by a man capable of extemporizing both poetry and music simultaneously on a guitar, though unable to bear contact with the outside world. We think of Poe's almost morbidly ethereal poetic impulse, conjoined with his mathematical literary theory as expressed in "The Philosophy of Composition." The pure rationality that coexisted, calculatingly, with his lyrical impulse was given dramatic form in Dupin and the narratives of deduction in solution of crimes. Eliot, we are told, was able to quote whole passages from the tales of Sherlock Holmes.[17]

In a lecture entitled "From Poe to Valéry" Eliot sets out to appreciate the importance of Poe, especially as his poetic example and theory had influenced Baudelaire, Mallarme, and Valéry. These "three literary generations, representing almost exactly a century of French poetry," represent also "the development and descent of one particular theory of the nature of poetry . . . ; it is a theory, which takes its origin in the theory, still more in the practice, of Edgar Poe." Eliot sees this development as coming to an end in the work of Valéry: "The penetration of the poetic by the introspective critical activity is carried to the limit by Valéry, the limit at which the latter begins to destroy the former."[18] Our analysis of the work of Eliot suggests that this perception is rooted in personal experience. Eliot, like Baudelaire, Mallarme, and Valéry, was to some extent, as poet and critic, a descendant of Poe, just as his Prufrock, and Valéry's Monsieur Teste, as characters, were somehow descendants of Roderick Usher. How, we may ask, are these characters linked to the literary theories of their authors? Perhaps the essential resemblance resides in the duality whereby one dimension of the total personality, associated with the pure intellect, self-consciously observes and analyzes the portion of the self associated with emotion, instinct, the irrational.

Eliot distinguishes between poetry that directs attention "primarily to the sound" and poetry that directs attention "primarily to the sense" of the words. Sound and sense may never be completely disjoined, of course, in successful poetry, and it is part of

Poe's deficiency as a poet, Eliot suggests, that the "dictionary meaning" of words in his poems is so nearly disregarded. Yet, paradoxically, this carelessness of exact denotation is associated with the powerful aesthetic calculation of the account of the writing of "The Raven" in "The Philosophy of Composition." Poe's relative disregard for meaning seems to have been associated with his concern with language in abstraction, or at least to have been so interpreted by his French admirers. If, in "the development of the consciousness of language," there is a movement from an initial stage of poetry wherein "the attention of the listener is directed upon the subject matter," through a middle stage wherein both subject and style are present to awareness, and onto a final stage wherein "the subject may recede to the background" and interest be directed to the style, then Poe was an important precedent in the achievement of this third and final phase of poetic possibility. Poe's indifference to meaning in regard to subject matter was a sign and symptom of his interest in language itself, as a thing apart. "This process of increasing self-consciousness—or, we may say, of increasing consciousness of language—has as its theoretical goal what we may call *la poesie pure*." Though poetry wholly pure of subject matter, of meaning, would cease to be poetry, yet a movement toward the pole of purity reminds us of an important aesthetic fact: subject matter "is important as *means:* the *end* is the poem." Baudelaire saw this implication in Poe: " 'A poem does not say something—it *is* something'—that doctrine has been held in more recent times." And one of the more recent holders of this doctrine was Eliot himself.

Eliot sees in Valéry the culmination of two related "notions" that have their origin in Poe: that a "poem should have nothing in view but itself," and the associated premise that "the composition of a poem should be as conscious and deliberate as possible, that the poet should observe himself in the act of composition."[19] The pure poem, it would seem, concerned with itself, its own inner relationships and processes, is a product of pure consciousness, one abstracted from real subject matter and the fecundity of sources in the unconscious. This is the self-conscious isolation of the ghost in the machine. This purity of the first notion is achieved partly through the attitude with which the self-observation of the second is carried out. A detachment between the critical intellect and its emotional sources and materials is implied, a separation between two aspects of the artist's personality that is potentially dangerous. Valéry in his essay "The Position of Baudelaire" provides a definition that applies more readily to Eliot's Modernist neoclassicism than to traditional classicism: "A classic is a writer who carries a critic within him and who associates him intimately with his work." The sense of self-division, of opposed tendencies held in tension within a single literary personality, is made more apparent by the application to Baudelaire: "That is why Baudelaire, although originally a romantic, and even a romantic by taste, sometimes appears as a *classic*."[20]

Eliot's own version of this detached, self-conscious, and formally rigorous stance of the artist in respect to his own emotions occurs in his essay "Tradition and the Individual Talent." Seeking to portray artistic activity as impersonal, Eliot compares the mind of the poet to a catalyst, a filament of a material that influences the combination of elements but that is not itself present in the new compound: "The mind of the poet is the shred of platinum. It may partly or exclusively operate upon the experience of the man himself; but, the more perfect the artist, the more completely separate in him will be the man who suffers and the mind which creates; the more perfectly will the mind digest and transmute the passions which are its material."[21] More sophisticated, more compelling in expression, less extreme, this is nevertheless a version of that dichotomy in the creative act implied by Poe when he declared that the writing of "The Raven" proceeded "step by step, to its completion with the precision and rigid consequence of a mathematical problem."[22] Both versions of the poetic process imply the presence of a critical consciousness that looks upon its materials as if from a distance, coolly, the tone of the description controlled by an analogy drawn, in the one case, from chemistry, in the other, from mathematics. In contrast to the positions of Blake and Wordsworth, which were opposed to scientific rationalism, this amounts to an adoption of the methods of the enemy, to an internalization of the "abstruse research" that had threatened imagination for the

Romantics. As for the Ancient Mariner, trapped behind the bars of "the skeleton of a ship" (gloss., 177–78), the price of the author's artistic abstraction, for both Roderick Usher and the narrator of *The Waste Land*, is utter isolation. Coleridge, as in "Dejection: An Ode," is again the grand precedent. This is an artistic theory that deliberately exploits the split induced in the Western psyche by Cartesian skepticism, a split that in the end produces a debilitating division between the conscious and the unconscious areas of the psyche.

There is thus an intriguing relation between the literary theory of the artist and the artist's character-types. We can see this with especial clarity in Eliot and Poe. Poe in his literary theory divided himself between artistic calculation and the emotional "effects" to be produced, between this "induction" and his innate grasp of the emotion-producing properties of language. Usher is likewise divided. The two modes of his voice are "alternatively vivacious and sullen." He is also divided between assured and intense artistic creativity and a nervous irritability amounting to hysteria. Closed within his own world of intense self-consciousness, Usher is an abstract expressionist painter—"If ever mortal painted an idea, that mortal was Roderick Usher"—and a guitarist-poet of superhuman dimension. His musical compositions and poems are the "result of that intense mental collectedness and concentration" that the narrator associates with opium frenzy.[23] Poe has imagined a kind of omnipotence: the inspiration that produced "Kubla Khan" made subject to the aesthetic will, to be mobilized by reasoning.

It is one of the paradoxes of Poe's theory of verse that a highly conscious, calculated technique is employed in the service of effects that strike the reader below the conscious level. That is one of the implications behind Eliot's remarks on the development of "the consciousness of language," leading to the position of Poe wherein the attention of the reader is directed more exclusively toward style, with the importance of word-meaning receding into the background. Poe employed great intellectuality, great self-consciousness, to secure effects that were almost entirely emotional, unconscious, in their impact on the reader. This aspect of the

poems and stories reflects the calculated exploitation of unconscious sources by the aesthetic will rather than a more healthful
(and more human) integration of the elements of personality.
Wordsworth's acceptance of his limited access to the sources of inspiration is associated with an elegiac tonality; the principle of fall
seems close to the center of the human condition. His characters
are of the human scale, and the ideal of health animates both his
criticism and poetry. Poe, in contrast, would have the rational faculty mine the unconscious landscape with inhuman efficiency. His
characters are often monsters, the emotions involved perverse or
morbid. Roderick Usher is in some respects a portrait of the self-
divided, self-exploited artist. His house is a pleasure dome gone
sour, the symbol of an artistic consciousness so flawed (and intensified) that, after the incredible flare-ups of creativity, it collapses
into its unconscious sources in the tarn. Poe's myth of unlimited
inspiration leads, paradoxically, to the failure of inspiration. We
recall Eliot's remarks on the "penetration of the poetic by the introspective critical activity" that he sees as having been "carried to the
limit by Valéry, the limit at which the latter begins to destroy
the former." Such a process is dramatized already in "The Fall of
the House of Usher."

For the clearest fictional formulation of an analogue to the
critical theory, we must turn to a cousin of Usher's, Monsieur
C. Auguste Dupin. Dupin's new friend, the narrator of "The Murders in the Rue Morgue," comes gradually to recognize in him "a
peculiar analytic ability." The following is a description of Dupin
during his moments of startling deductive flight:

> His manner in these moments was frigid and abstract; his
> eyes were vacant in expression; while his voice, usually a
> rich tenor, rose into a treble which would have sounded
> petulantly but for the deliberateness and entire distinctness
> of the enunciation. Observing him in those moods, I often
> dwelt meditatively upon the old philosophy of the Bi-Part
> Soul, and amused myself with the fancy of a double Du-
> pin—the creative and the resolvent.[24]

Poe's invention of the detective story, of the narrative of extreme
"ratiocination," grows out of, or is related to, the poetic theory that

abstracts the aesthetic will from its emotional and unconscious materials. Dupin in "The Murders in the Rue Morgue," through sheer contemplation and deduction, unravels the mystery of violent killings perpetrated, not by a human assailant, but by an "Ourang-Outang."

We have here a symbol of Poe's art: the dispassionate, conscious observer looking from a distance upon the primitive and irrational, the source of emotion (of whatever sort) and thus the origin of the writer's material, but a source to be regarded skeptically, almost with distaste. Dupin, in his moments of analysis, is as much a monster as the ape: he is all mind, as it is all irrational body. His analysis is as complete as is his disengagement and is made possible by it. A new character has stepped onto the literary stage. Sherlock Holmes, with his complete mastery of deduction, his life of isolation with Watson, his morphine, is surely representative of this superhuman and inhuman new relation of the intellect to existence. The remark in "From Poe to Valéry" that Holmes had found his violin "in the ruins of the house of Usher" is an implicit acknowledgment of the relation of Dupin and Holmes to the aesthetic theory that Eliot traces from Poe to Valéry.[25]

The reader needs hardly to be reminded of the self-division or single dimensionality of Eliot's earlier characters. The narrator of "Sweeney Among the Nightingales" regards his "apeneck" protagonist with approximately the detachment displayed by Dupin in respect to the "Ourang-Outang." Sweeney resembles the ape, and he is contemplated and analyzed from a similar perspective. Whether the split is between the observing poetic consciousness and the alien physical world it contemplates, as in the Sweeney poems, "Rhapsody on a Windy Night," "Preludes," and portions of *The Waste Land*, or between thought and action, imagination and the unavailable object of desire, as in "Prufrock," "Portrait of a Lady," and other portions of *The Waste Land*, the effect is to portray a character type as self-divided as Roderick Usher, one isolated in a ghostly house of self-consciousness: the symbolism of "Gerontion." Eliot concludes "From Poe to Valéry" with a suggestion that the line of development he has traced, the "extreme self-consciousness," the "extreme scepticism," the refusal of belief epitomized in Valéry, "has gone as far as it can go."[26] This lecture, delivered in 1948, represents an act of self-analysis on Eliot's part, a consideration of his earlier career and its premises and an admission, or declaration, that these premises will no longer serve for the creation of fresh art.

We must suspect, therefore, that the elegance, concision, and incisiveness of Modernist poetry derive in part from sources whose ultimate implications for the health of imagination are ambivalent: from the same intellectual direction that produced the triumphs of seventeenth-century science and philosophy—from the discovery of Cartesian doubt and critical self-consciousness, from the ability to abstract crucial elements from reality in order to hypothesize, experiment, and thus to simplify, to generalize, and to compress. Galileo abstracted the problem of gravitational acceleration from all ordinary cases of movement on earth's surface, wherein the resistance of friction comes into play. "Galileo moved as far as possible from day to day 'reality' by setting up experiments which provided a model for an abstract universe. Aristotelians regarded mathematics as an escape from the problems set by the real world of constant change; Galileo, on the other hand, invented a mathematical world in which speed, time and distance were the only considerations."[27]

In detaching motion from its usual context, Galileo prepared the way for Newton's formulation of his first law of motion, which presents what the kinetic energy of masses would do on earth, except for frictional resistance, and what they appear to do in space: keep on indefinitely.[28] Aristotle's teleological considerations were well on their way out of physics, and God on his way out of the physical universe.[29] Galileo also initiated the distinction between primary and secondary qualities, which was continued by Descartes and by Locke.[30] Descartes' reconception of the universe took the principle of abstraction to more radical lengths. "The Cartesian universe was mechanical in the sense that it existed as a machine and *nothing else*. Descartes stripped away from his view of the universe all that was extraneous to its mechanical functioning. It became the equivalent of a blueprint which was transformed into matter (extension). It was thus more mechanical than a machine, which at least possessed certain qualities such as color."[31]

This line of thought is the origin of that skeletal consciousness dramatized by Coleridge as the specter ship in "The Ancient Mariner." As E. A. Burtt points out in *The Metaphysical Foundations of Modern Science,* the reconception of reality in terms only of "bodies moving in space and time," even as initiated by Galileo, left no intelligible place in the cosmos either for man or for God. "We forget that we are no longer part of the real world of modern metaphysics."[32] Coleridge in "The Ancient Mariner" faced and banished this abstraction and mechanization of the world of experience and the isolation and alienation of man that it implied. The Mariner's plight, alone with his dead shipmates, presents the self-isolated skeptical consciousness through the image of a ship, but we are also aware of the mysterious source that continues to underlie it in the form of the great deep, which is both nature and the unconscious. But later in "Dejection" we find the poet isolated by a thought that sees the life of nature as a projection from his mind. The character types presented by both Poe and Eliot are related to the poet's situation in "Dejection," in part through literary influence and in part because both the narrator of "Dejection," Roderick Usher, and Eliot's protagonists share a common intellectual background.

Pure poetry as discussed in "From Poe to Valéry" is a literary version of abstraction, an idea analogous to Galileo's invention of a "mathematical world in which speed, time and distance were the only considerations."[33] If, as Eliot describes it, the poem "should have nothing in view but itself," then it becomes a self-enclosed system separated from reality, a harmony of relationships wherein the images and sounds have reference only to each other, for the purpose of assuming a final order, but refer to nothing outside. Thus we see the significance of Poe's lack of interest in the dictionary meanings of words: such meanings point beyond the poem, whereas the elements of the pure poem have reference only to one another. The technique of artistic abstraction, therefore, seems in the broadest sense related to scientific theory that isolates from the actualities of the environment certain ideal systems of masses in motion in order that physics may have the elegance, symmetry, and essentiality of mathematical formulation. Usher's art has something of the brilliance and concision of scientific achievement, but in making the composition of the poem, in Eliot's words, "as conscious and as deliberate as possible," he embraces a self-division that is ultimately destructive of personality.

Poe, of course, was melodramatic, and much Modernist poetry is the reverse: understated, ironic, limited in intention. Yet the fissure that traverses the wall of Usher's house, the self-division we perceive in him and in his "cousin" M. Dupin, has analogies in the characters of many Modernist poems. For Prufrock and his fellows, the self-directed satiric edge, the ironic and reductive analysis, reveal both Romantic impulses and the hopelessly opposed circumstances that thwart their enactment. It is as if the poetic consciousness were seen as inhabiting a world so different from itself that all action save thought was preempted. Eliot's earlier poems, Pound's "Portrait d'une Femme" and "Hugh Selwyn Mauberley," Ransom's "The Equilibrists" and "Captain Carpenter," Tate's "The Last Days of Alice" and his "Ode for the Confederate Dead," Stevens's "Peter Quince at the Clavier"—in short, a number of the most often reprinted and often discussed poems of the earlier twentieth century—have concerned themselves with the ironic futility of characters divided from themselves, from self-realization, by a thought that is its own unrealistic ambience, its own suffocating atmosphere, separate from nature, like that of "The Fall of the House of Usher." Modernism, even at its height, seems in a sense to be prophesying its own demise. Captain Carpenter is hacked into pieces on his futile Romantic quest, the woman of Eliot's "Portrait of a Lady" abandoned to her own "atmosphere of Juliet's tomb." The narrator's consciousness fades out, in Pound's "Mauberley," into "scattered Moluccas / Not knowing, day to day, / The first day's end, in the next noon."[34] The clarity of vision allowing these characters to be presented so dazzlingly and unsparingly has also tended to deprive their authors of a confidence in the imagination and the poetic act that would have enabled their creations to be more than futile or mock-heroic.

A central issue for Modernist poetry has been, therefore, and must continue to be in the post-Modernist era the relation between the imagination and the skeptical and self-critical inheritance of the poet. The line of development that Eliot identifies as leading from Poe to Valéry stretches, in the larger sense, from Galileo, Descartes,

Newton, and Locke through Wordsworth and Coleridge—from the great self-critical awakening in the Western consciousness that allowed it to develop the science of chemistry from alchemy and to replace the physics of Aristotle by theories susceptible of experimental verification. This is also the line of development that has made it increasingly difficult for Westerners to apprehend the marvelous, to sense the presence of the sacred, and to suspend disbelief in respect to the great myths that in the past had inspired new creation and had related humanity and its destiny to a cosmos intelligible, at least, to the emotions. Although the Romantics profited from this scientific sharpening of vision, this heightening of critical self-consciousness, they also realized—especially Wordsworth—that the tool was double-edged, the dissection of thought by skepticism and abstraction a threat to imagination. The great Romantics all seem to have devised defenses through which the most destructive effects of scientific method and vision were kept from the life of imagination. Most notably, they discovered the ability to transcend the rational mode of consciousness and to reach depths in the landscape where lay preserved, in what Jung would call the collective unconscious, the powers and images that had inspired their poetic forebears.

Modernism seems to have repeated much of this Romantic scenario, with the difference being, especially in the line of development seen by Eliot as stretching from Poe to Valéry and, by implication, to himself, that the dissecting scalpel of self-conscious analysis has been even more brilliant and even more murderous in its effects. "The wounded surgeon plies the steel," says Eliot, and nowhere is the effect of self-dissection more evident than in the work leading up to and including *The Waste Land*.[35] How may the Modernist knife be so managed as not to disable the guiding hand? It is not too strong a formulation of the problem to suggest that this rigorous dissection, practiced upon the self, may amount to self-murder—or suicide. The case of Sylvia Plath is instructive. In *Winter Trees* and *Ariel* an enormously keen intelligence cuts itself apart until, in the end, extinction is the only possibility. It is no accident that the imagery of physical cutting is so prominent in her work.

The possibilities opened in this century for both the literary and the visual arts by the willingness to break up the representational surface in the service of more compelling aesthetic forms have been enormous. Whether Cezanne's pioneering suggestion of the volumes of boulders and pines, or Picasso's cubist rendition of a more primary mask behind the surfaces of faces, or Wassily Kandinsky's dispensing "with subject matter entirely" in order to "use color to express his own states of mind," the principle of abstraction has been crucial for Modernist art.[36] The use made of French symbolism by Eliot, Yeats, and Wallace Stevens hinges on the omission of many elements from any imitation of nature, together with presentation of certain charged particulars that sum up, make quintessential and symmetrical, both their own values and those that, though omitted, stand behind. Eliot's use of quotation in *The Waste Land* is instructive. A few lines or line, even a phrase or a verbal echo, may evoke whole works by Shakespeare, Spenser, Dante, Goldsmith, Baudelaire, or Nerval, bringing these metaphysical and tonal associations into ironic contact with the outline of a contemporary action or situation. The music "upon the waters" from *The Tempest* harmonizes with the ghost of pre-Christian fertility gods fished from the sea, and rings ironically against images of the contemporary Thames (3:257). In a poem by Stevens or Sylvia Plath, the subject, in the sense of biographical occasion or stimulus for composition, may be almost wholly disguised behind, or omitted from, the presentation of something more poetically essential: the sequence of verbal associations, with implied emotional tonality, that rises like a clear exhalation from the body of event or fact.

Poetry in English of the first half, at least, of the twentieth century has reflected an impressive consensus, certainly in respect to the technical means of expression. Yet there are implications destructive to the life of imagination, and, by extension, to the life of the poet, within the very premises upon which the Modernist triumph was constructed. The presence within the modern poet of an alien rationality, of the masculine pure reason of an Apollonius at the feast of poor Lamia, of an exclusive Urizen in the aboriginal psychic cosmos, of a tyrannical Jupiter in Prometheus's very self, of the scientific "Nazi" daddy within Sylvia Plath's memory (her father was an eminent German entomologist) has provided both a dazzling clarity of analysis and expression and has threatened to initiate a potentially fatal disunity within the total personality, setting reason at odds with imagination, skepticism against the impulse toward faith, surgical self-analysis against the impulse toward synthesis. In most inclusive terms, the division has been between the more conscious and the less conscious aspects of the psyche. Purely conscious Dupin has looked upon irrational ape with cold calculation. The ape, misunderstood, has responded with outrage and violence.

4 Romantic Duality and Unity of Being

That shoreline meeting between opposed principles typical of Romantic landscape is also central to the poetry and vision of W. B. Yeats. Yeats's poetry, criticism, and visionary prose constitute our century's most complete and impressive assimilation and transformation of the Romantic legacy. His images of tower next to stream, of Byzantine dome beside the chaotic harbor, provide versions of the juxtaposition of individual consciousness and its collective origin that we have traced from Coleridge and Wordsworth. His interpenetrating gyres, his moon discs divided between dark and light, may be read as geometrical hypostases of the Apollonian-Dionysian tension latent within Romantic depictions of nature.

A central thrust of his vision is toward reunification of those opposites of thought and emotion, truth and imagination, consciousness and unconsciousness, reason and intuition seen in hurtful separation in poets from Shelley to Hardy. Yeats's ideal of Unity of Being is associated with some of the more compelling moments in his poetry, as when in "Among School Children" he sees the "chestnut-tree, great-rooted blossomer" as one unitary presence of leaf, blossom, and bole, the dancer indistinguishable from the dance. Yeats realized the danger posed by disunity between imagination and reason, heart and head, and gives us compelling images of dichotomized existence: in "The Second Coming," the falcon out of touch with the falconer; in the *Autobiographies*, a portrait of Woodrow Wilson alive only in the eyes, the rest dead and mechanical; in *A Vision*, interchangeable bodies sculptured in togas upon which could be screwed a personalized head, at a time in

Roman history analogous to our own.[1] But rising beyond his perception of disunity and its threat is a grasp of the great Romantic moments of synthesis—between above and below, light and dark, the individual and the collective—as when Coleridge associated his "dome of pleasure" with "ancestral voices" and Wordsworth meditated upon Snowdon.

Yeats's success in completing and extending those confrontations implicit in Romantic landscape constructs is associated with the most elaborate defense since Wordsworth against the debilitating effects of Western skepticism and analysis. His work, in fact, assumes its fullest intelligibility in the context of scientific abstraction and a related tendency that he saw toward disunity in both personality and society. In this light, his occultist study appears a central defense of imagination's prerogative rather than obscurantism or idiosyncrasy. His contact with both Romantic inheritance and the opposing rationalism, moreover, was thorough and in many cases personal. Poorly educated by university standards, inept at math and even spelling, Yeats was nevertheless the recipient of marvelous early life experience in the west of Ireland, the home of his mother's people, where he heard tales of the supernatural directly from the peasantry. Meetings with William Morris and other Romantic heirs also helped counterbalance the threat from science Yeats felt as a young man.

Yeats records in the *Autobiographies* a detestation of Huxley and Tyndall, who deprived him of "the simple-minded religion of my childhood," and who were a chief source of "those scientific generalizations that cowed my boyhood." He tells us further that "I had learned from Blake to hate all abstraction," and allows us to see the connection between abstraction and the disunity of the modern world, which seemed to him "but a bundle of fragments." The vision of fragmentation is developed in contrast to a past unity that he sees as ending in approximately the historical epoch that witnessed the birth of modern science: "Had not Europe shared one mind and heart, until both mind and heart began to break into fragments a little before Shakespeare's birth?" He quotes from "The Second Coming," juxtaposing to that great image of how "things fall apart" his speculation that, in his own day "abstraction had reached, or all but reached its climax"; yet "individual men might still escape."[2] Thus Yeats had sensed from childhood, then analyzed in maturity the threat posed to imagination (and to life at large) by scientific generalization and an attendant abstraction and fragmentation in thought and in society, and had organized his psychic resources from early on to meet this threat, partly by opposing to it an ideal of unity that he saw in the earlier history of his culture.

He had reacted to his deprivation of religion at the hands of Huxley and Tyndall by assembling for himself "a new religion, almost an infallible church of poetic tradition, of a fardel of stories, and of personages, and of emotions, inseparable from their first expression." His dream in young manhood was to work toward a new unity of culture, using the folklore of the Irish peasantry as Shelley had used Greek myth: "Might I not . . . create some new *Prometheus Unbound;* Patrick or Columbkil, Oisin or Fion, in Prometheus' stead; and, instead of Caucasus, Cro-Patric or Ben Bulben? Have not all races had their first unity from a mythology, that marries them to rock and hill?" The great bulk of Yeats's work may be seen as the fulfillment, in other terms, of this intention, though he proved to need the "international" sources he had hoped to avoid (*Auto.,* 71, 119).

Yeats's response to the modern world's "Grey Truth" that had succeeded upon the "antique joy" of dreaming in the "woods of Arcady" was on the one hand to seek a knowledge quite outside the rationalist perspective, and on the other to develop for himself an ideal of unity that transcended the self-division induced in personality by abstraction.[3] The narrative of the four crucial years 1887–1891 in *The Trembling of the Veil* turns very largely upon acquaintance with persons (or images) that provided him clues either to occultist wisdom or to the ideal of Unity of Being, which he had first absorbed from his father. He records, first, associating himself with Madam Blavatsky, in whose circle one evening he had an experience (of an apparitional painting) described by her as "clairvoyance," as opposed to "mediumship." Next he encountered Macgregor Mathers, author of *The Kabbala Unveiled;* "it was through him mainly that I began certain studies and experiences, that were to convince me that images well up before the mind's eye from a deeper source than conscious or subconscious memory." A few years later he was associating with the visionary poet George Russell (Æ) and his house of theosophists. He envisioned "a mystical Order" after his visit to a castle on an island in Lough Kay. Then at Sligo he practiced thought-transference and the summoning of mental image by symbol with his maternal uncle George Pollexfen, apparently with some success.[4] We hear of him addressing "his fellow adepti in the Order of the Red Rose and the Cross of Gold" in 1901.[5] Repeated experience of what he terms "supernatural events" raised for him a question that reveals a profound distrust of rational skepticism. How may one "trust historian and psychologist that have for some three hundred years ignored in writing of the history of the world, or of the human mind, so momentous a part of human experience?" (*Auto.*, 159).

In these years during which Yeats was forming the bases of his mature thought and art, therefore, we see him constructing strong defenses against skepticism, abstraction, and the attendant self-division of personality. He seems to have arrived at the conclusion that the "first unity" of "all races" in the mythology "that marries them to rock and hill" has a deeper underlying cause in something very like the Jungian collective unconscious. He recounts both in *The Trembling of the Veil* and the essay "Magic" the experience of a literal-minded young man who, in a trance, envisioned Eden as "a walled garden on the top of a high mountain, and in the middle of it a tree with great birds in the branches, and fruit out of which, if you held a fruit to your ear, came the sound of fighting." Dante's *Purgatorio*, which neither he nor the young man had read, seemed a possible source, as did "a mediaeval diagram, which pictured Eden as a walled garden upon a high mountain," which he found "years afterwards." But in either case, the correspondence between spontaneous imagery and the unknown literary parallel helped convince Yeats "that there is a memory of Nature that reveals events and symbols of distant centuries."[6] He knew himself "face to face with the Anima Mundi described by Platonic philosophers, and more especially in modern times by Henry More, which has a memory independent of embodied individual memories, though they constantly enrich it with their images and their thoughts" (*Auto.*, 158).

In his long essay *Per Amica Silentia Lunae* (which in many respects prefigured *A Vision*) Yeats discusses further this Anima Mundi, this "Great Memory passing on from generation to generation," and identifies it with the symbol of the sea, which we have found so prominent in Romantic poetry. Convinced, as in "Magic," that "the borders of our mind are ever shifting, and that many minds can flow into one another, as it were, and create or reveal a single mind, a single energy," he suspects rather humbly the comparative shallowness of a modern individual's consciousness in relation to the immemorial depths of the past with its great explorers (*E. & I.*, 28). "Our daily thought was certainly but the line of foam at the shallow edge of a vast luminous sea; Henry More's *Anima Mundi*, Wordsworth's 'immortal sea which brought us hither,' and near whose edge the children sport, and in that sea there were some who swam or sailed, explorers who perhaps knew all its shores" (*Myth.*, 346). This passage not only links Yeats with the line of development we have traced but provides a context for the interpretation of one of his most central poetic symbols: the "murderous innocence of the sea" of "A Prayer for My Daughter," the "mackerel-crowded seas" of "Sailing to Byzantium," the "frogspawn of a blind man's ditch" of "A Dialogue of Self and Soul," the underground water of "Coole Park and Ballylee, 1931," the "gong-tormented sea" of "Byzantium," the "many-headed foam at Salamis" of "The Statues," and the "great water" that "sighed for love" in "News for the Delphic Oracle."

As has been suggested, Yeats's earlier search for a new religion for himself and his associates through their common artistic and philosophic inheritance and his seeking for a reunification of Irish life through a revival of Irish mythology gave way in the end to a belief in a common racial inheritance underlying the individual consciousness, and having its roots in nature and humankind's history from the beginnings. "Was not a nation, as distinguished from a crowd of chance comers, bound together by this interchange among streams or shadows; that Unity of Image, which I sought in national literature, being but an originating symbol?" (*Auto.*, 158, 159). Yet given this sea about whose edges an individual's thought was only bubbles in the foam, how could he explain the abstraction and disunity of particular personalities and of the time in which he lived? Yeats was eventually to evolve in *A Vision* a cyclical portrayal of history whereby certain ages, like certain persons, were more divided from themselves, more dichotomized, than others; individuals like himself and those whom he admired, who had largely escaped the curse of modernity, could be explained as born "out of phase," as unitary individuals cast by the "gyres" into a time of abstraction.[7]

Perhaps the most important such figure portrayed in the narrative of Yeats's early intellectual quest in *The Trembling of the Veil* is William Morris. Yeats wished to use Unity of Being "as Dante used it when he compared beauty in the *Convito* to a perfectly proportioned human body." Though he does not specifically apply the term to Morris, his description of "the broad vigorous body" that suggests "a mind that has no need of the intellect to remain sane," together with the "little tricks of speech and body that reminded me of my old grandfather in Sligo" and the associated "spontaneity and joy," helps convince us of Morris's centrality to his ideal (*Auto.*, 117, 87, 86).

Morris, after all, was one of the chief Pre-Raphaelites, student of Rossetti, poet, painter, designer of fabrics and furniture, and founder of a successful company intended to reintroduce handicrafts and older patterns of taste in opposition to machine manufacture and the Victorian grandiosities in home furnishings and art. One may still purchase fabrics designed by William Morris at Liberty of London. In a portrait of Morris by Watts, Yeats saw "grave wide-open eyes, like the eyes of some dreaming beast," saw "the resolute European image that yet half remembers Buddha's motionless meditation, and has no trait in common with the wavering, lean image of hungry speculation. . . . His intellect, unexhausted by speculation or casuistry, was wholly at the service of hand and eye" (*Auto.*, 87). We suspect Morris as prototype of Lady Gregory's dead son in the elegy "In Memory of Major Robert Gregory," especially since the major is portrayed as painter and as "he that practised or that understood / All work in metal or in wood, / In moulded plaster or in carven stone." Morris was probably the closest Yeats ever came to knowing someone like the wonderful figure that *A Vision* posits in Byzantium "a little before Justinian opened St. Sophia and closed the Academy of Plato." "I think I could find in some little wine-shop some philosophical worker in mosaic who could answer all my questions, the supernatural descending nearer to him than to Plotinus even, for the pride of his delicate skill would make what was an instrument of power to princes and clerics, a murderous madness in the mob, show as a lovely flexible presence like that of a perfect human body."[8]

Can we characterize more precisely this Unity of Being, which Morris especially seemed to have symbolized for Yeats? "The statues of Mausolus and Artemisia at the British Museum, private, half-animal, half-divine figures" seem to have represented for the youthful Yeats this quality, with their "unpremeditated joyous energy." Morris's eyes, "like the eyes of some dreaming beast," had also this quality of joining seamlessly the animal, natural, unconscious being with the human consciousness (*Auto.*, 92, 87). But it is not a painful self-consciousness. In his essay "The Happiest of the Poets" Yeats praises Morris for a vision "that sets mind and body at ease," regarding him as one blessed to see the original unity of things before the modern fragmentation: "His mind was illuminated from within and lifted into prophecy in the full right sense of the word, and he saw the natural things he was alone gifted to see in their perfect form" (*E. &. I.*, 61, 62). Yeats was aware of the limitations of Morris's poetry, attributing it to the exhaustion of language by "abstraction," but nevertheless expresses this preference: "If some angel offered me the choice, I would choose to live his life, poetry and all, rather than my own or any other man's" (*Auto.*, 87). This idealization seems to involve the thought that Morris was not only a "dreamer of the Middle Ages," a European with an aspect of the Buddha, a modern man with an ancient, animal ease and spontaneity, but that he had actually somehow avoided or transcended that fall which we have associated in Wordsworth with a separation from nature and thus from unconscious inspiration.[9]

Though the poetry of Morris "often wearies us as the unbroken green of July wearies us," Yeats seems to see this as the fault of our own fallen state, "for there is something in us, some bitterness because of the Fall, it may be, that takes a little from the sweetness of Eve's apple after the first mouthful"; Morris, in contrast, seems Adamic, unfallen: "But he who did all things gladly and easily, who never knew the curse of labour, found it always as sweet as it was in Eve's mouth." Morris, thought Yeats, possessed the unfallen vision. "All kinds of associations have gathered about the pleasant things of the world and half taken the pleasure out of them for the greater number of men, but he saw them as when they came from the Divine Hand" (*E. & I.*, 61). This praise becomes intelligible as we realize that Yeats felt he had found in Morris the realization of a crucial possibility: that some few representatives of a past "Unity of Culture" may be born into this fragmented, self-divided modern age. Morris, as Yeats sees him, embodies a prelapsarian wholeness (*Auto.*, 162).

Remarks by Yeats on the creative process make clear the elements that seemed unified in Morris, as contrasted with the tendency of modern times. Mentioning a letter of Goethe's opposing "evocation" to a "literary sterility" that is "too intelligent," Yeats describes his discovery that access to the unconscious may be gained through the free play of association, once the critical consciousness is suspended.

> If you suspend the critical faculty, I have discovered, either
> as the result of training, or, if you have the gift, by passing
> into a slight trance, images pass rapidly before you. If you
> can suspend also desire, and let them form at their own will,
> your absorption becomes more complete and they are more
> clear in colour, more precise in articulation, and you and
> they begin to move in the midst of what seems a powerful
> light. But the images pass before you linked by certain asso-
> ciations, and indeed in the first instance you have called
> them up by their association with traditional forms and
> sounds. You have discovered how, if you can but suspend
> will and intellect, to bring up from the "subconscious"
> anything you already possess a fragment of.   (*Myth.*, 344)

This occurs in *Per Amica Silentia Lunae*, in close association with references to Anima Mundi and the sea image he links to Wordsworth's "Intimations" ode. In "The Symbolism of Poetry"

Yeats argues that the regularity of rhythm in a poem serves "to prolong the moment of contemplation, the moment when we are both asleep and awake, which is the one moment of creation . . . in which the mind liberated from the pressure of the will is unfolded in symbols" (*E. & I.*, 159). Poetic rhythm, then, is a minor hypnotism, giving access to the unconscious. Artistic genius is defined by Yeats in terms of access of the individual to what he has called Anima Mundi and compared to Wordsworth's "immortal sea." "I know now that revelation is from the self, but from that age-long memoried self, that shapes the elaborate shell of the mollusc and the child in the womb, that teaches the birds to make their nest; and that genius is a crisis that joins that buried self for certain moments to our trivial daily mind" (*Auto.*, 164). This passage links, in fact, what Wordsworth called nature in "Tintern Abbey" with what we have called, following Jung, the collective unconscious, and which Jung himself called the "Pleroma" and regarded as something akin to Yeats's "general cistern of form."[10]

Yeats also approximates Wordsworth in saying that the union to the "buried" source obtains "for certain moments." We remember Wordsworth's "the hiding-places of man's power / Open; I would approach them, but they close" (*Prel.* 12:279–80). We have argued that Wordsworth's concept of man's fall is rooted in this conception of limited access to inspiration. Yeats, in presenting William Morris as an ideal, seemed to exempt him from any such limitation on artistic creativity even while ruefully attributing to himself and all others "some bitterness because of the Fall." We can see in the following passage in which Yeats explained to himself the artistic defect of George Russell a more realistic assessment of the conscious and unconscious components of the creative act than that totally unhindered one implied in his portrayal of Morris. Was Russell's unevenness and sudden decline "precisely because in Swedenborg alone the conscious and sub-conscious became one . . . ?" Leaving aside, then, the case of prelapsarian William Morris, and that of Swedenborg, which is like a "marriage of the angels, which he has described," Yeats seems to be saying that the condition of the modern artist involves some degree of separation between the daily self and the "buried" self (*Auto.*, 148). This is the barrier an artist must somehow overcome, for the sake of those moments of unification that will determine genius. The critical faculty must learn, for crucial periods, to suspend itself, just as intellect has learned to appreciate the value of what may come to it in a Wordsworthian "wise passiveness."[11]

Such self-consistency as Morris and Swedenborg represent, therefore, such unity between intellect and emotion, between conscious and unconscious aspects of personality, is by no means the usual condition in the modern world. Along with his visions of unity, whether Morris, Swedenborg, the dancing girl of "The Double Vision of Michael Robartes," or the "chestnut-tree, great-rooted blossomer," of "Among School Children," Yeats presents very powerful images of an opposing disunity: "Things fall apart; the centre cannot hold" in "The Second Coming"; "There lurches past, his great eyes without thought" in the conclusion of "Nineteen Hundred and Nineteen"; "That insolent fiend Robert Artisson," representing all the insensitive masculine pure power that threatens, in the modern world, to trample underfoot such offerings of beauty as those peacock feathers laid down by "the love-lorn Lady Kyteler."

Founding his position from the beginning, therefore, on his perception of the limitations of science and its rational perspectives, Yeats responded to the threat posed for imagination by the modern world with a vision of contrasting possibilities: on the one hand there is a "tragic minority" of individuals like himself and his idealized William Morris who reunify, or attempt to reunify, heart and head, soul and body, conscious and unconscious dimensions of personality; and on the other hand there are individuals, and perhaps even inhuman presences such as the "shape with lion body and the head of a man" of "The Second Coming," who do not embody the balance between intellect and emotion, the cultured and the wild, the conscious and the unconscious, which we have associated with civilization in the past, that balance which defines for us the fully human (*Auto.*, 175). All this suggests that a significant continuity extends from Yeats's vision of unity or disunity within the individual personality to his vision of history, and that, whether for a person or an age, a crucial issue is the relation between individual intellect and Anima Mundi, or, in Jung's terminology, the conscious ego and the collective unconscious. We run the risk of oversimplification, for in Yeats's final mythology *A Vision*, the contending principles within both a person and the age are translated from the original Subjectivity and Objectivity into Antithetical and Primary, then elaborated into four faculties, Will and Mask, Creative Mind and Body of Fate, which in the closing sections take on, as analogues, Husk, Passionate Body, Spirit, and Celestial Body.[12]

Behind the complexity of terminology and diagrams, however, there are very basic juxtapositions analogous to those we have seen symbolized in Romantic poetry by poetic observer, mountain prospect, pleasure dome or ship, on the one hand, versus the landscape with its underground spaces and the sea on the other. Yeats's pleasure dome is that of Saint Sophia's in "Byzantium," and the originating water to which it is related is as turbulent as Coleridge's fountain in "Kubla Khan." Conscious art and unconscious nature form a symbolic strand—one of the best presentations of that interface between conscious and unconscious, human and divine—as the "Marbles of the dancing floor" seem flooded about by "That dolphin-torn, that gong-tormented sea." In "A Dialogue of Self and Soul" the tower of art and intellect overlooks the stream of sensual life, "the frog-spawn of a blind man's ditch." In "Coole Park and Ballylee, 1931," the poet says, "Under my window-ledge the waters race," placing the essential juxtaposition of consciousness-structure and unconscious water into the opening line. In "A Prayer for My Daughter," "The Statues," "News for the Delphic Oracle," and a number of other poems, the confrontation as between tower, dome, golden bird, statue or mosaic, and the sea crowded with mackerel or torn by dolphins goes on, with human life and civilization both threatened and refreshed by the "murderous innocence of the sea."

On the shore between what is rationally measured and limited and therefore fails to satisfy us, and what is irrationally whole but beyond comprehension, human perception does the most that it can do: looks toward the land of consciousness, architecture, and civilization, then toward that frightening divinity that is permanent, fruitful, unconscious and that creates new forms, wreckage, and division while remaining itself changeless and one. The poet creates symbols for this encounter, which is on one level always that of the individual consciousness with the uroboric sea of its origin, and on the other that of civilization and its fallen history with the preceding Eden.

One of the basic symbols elaborated in *A Vision* is the gyre, or cone-shaped spiral. The uroboros is symbolized by the circle, the snake with its tail in its mouth. Yeats makes clear in relation to the gyres of Plato's *Timaeus* and an account of gyres in Saint Thomas Aquinas that his symbol does in geometrical terms precisely what the juxtaposition of dome and sea does in "Byzantium": establishes an annunciation principle, if you will, whereby the timeless is seen to descend into time, the one become many, the Edenic origin produce fallen history. If "the same" of the *Timaeus* is a circle, and if Aquinas's angels in their "circular movement" imitate this perfect "same," and if the human intellect, in geometrical terms, is a "straight line," then the combination of changeless divine circle and time-conscious line would be the spiral, or gyre, the figure "made by the ascent and descent of angels between God and man." For living men, the "serpent has not its tail in its mouth," and so, perhaps, we lack wholeness by birth.[13] Yet some men, like some ages, have more of a unity with their "buried self" than others.

An excellent illustration of this contention between being and becoming in terms of differing effects for human character occurs in Yeats's contrast of two portraits in the Dublin National Gallery. We can see here a basis for his original terms *Subjectivity* and *Objectivity*. He has been describing the attainment to "Unity of Being" around 1450 in European culture whereby great numbers of men exemplified that balanced personality as of "a perfectly proportioned human body" that was later to be approached by only "a tragic minority." Juxtaposing "a portrait of some Venetian gentleman by Strozzi and Mr. Sargent's painting of President Wilson," Yeats is able to typify in visual terms the leading tendencies of two opposed cultural moments.

Whatever thought broods in the dark eyes of that Venetian gentleman, has drawn its life from his whole body; it feeds upon it as the flame feeds upon the candle—and should that thought be changed, his pose would change, his very cloak would rustle for his whole body thinks. President Wilson lives only in the eyes, which are steady and intent; the flesh about the mouth is dead, and the hands are dead, and the clothes suggest no movement of his body, nor any movement but that of the valet, who has brushed and folded in mechanical routine. There, all was an energy flowing outward from the nature itself; here, all is the anxious study and slight deflection of external force; there man's mind and body were predominately subjective; here all is objective, using those words not as philosophy uses them, but as we use them in conversation.   (*Auto.*, 174–75)

We might compare Yeats's image of thought feeding upon the body like the flame upon the candle to the adaptation by Coleridge in the *Biographia Literaria* of a poem by Sir John Davies descriptive of the soul. These lines, he says, "may with slight alteration be applied, and even more appropriately, to the poetic IMAGINATION."

> Doubtless this could not be, but that she turns
> Bodies to spirit by sublimation strange,
> As fire converts to fire the things it burns,
> As we our food into our nature change.[14]

For Yeats, it is precisely this conversion of bodily to spiritual energy by a flame-like "sublimation" that produces the unity and expressive power of a whole body that seems to think. Strozzi has accomplished on canvas the creation of a living symbol that Coleridge attributes in poetry to the activity of imagination. The human body is animated by—made expressive of—human thought. Such fusion of the physical and the spiritual, the unconscious and the conscious, is the ideal toward which Yeats aspired, both in his life and in his art.

Wilson, by contrast, exemplifies abstraction: the separation of life energy from its source in nature for a concentration in the head, the eyes. Describing the cyclical movement of history after "Unity of Being" has passed, Yeats says that "great men must live in a portion of themselves, become professional and abstract" (*Auto.*, 175). Here is that dichotomy between the rationality of science and the fullness of experience, between Dupin and the ape.

Subjectivity, or the Antithetical principle, as Yeats symbolizes it by one of two interpenetrating gyres, means "our inner world of desire and imagination," and is "emotional and aesthetic," as opposed to the Objective or Primary gyre, which is "reasonable and moral." The Objective principle stresses "that which is external to the mind" and tends to deal in "outward things and events" and "actual facts, not coloured by the opinions or feelings."[15] The two gyres of Subjectivity and Objectivity, Antithetical and Primary quality, are presented as two cones nosed point for point inside one another, and are drawn on the page as overlaid triangles, the apex of each touching the base of the other. One is shaded dark, the other left light. On the simplest level, we see represented geometrically the contention between moon-symbolized Subjectivity and that "inanimate cold world" ("Dejection: An Ode") of hard facts in the absence of inspiration. Yeats, however, no more than Wordsworth, wanted to celebrate a lonely, self-enclosed sensitivity shut up in a solipsistic tower like the Lady of Shalott.

Thus he was by no means content to remain in his early literary position, founded, as he says in "Art and Ideas," upon the principles "of Arthur Hallam in his essay upon Tennyson." Hallam had advocated "the school of Keats and Shelley," who "wrote out of the impression made by the world upon their delicate senses." Yeats became dissatisfied with such pure subjectivity: "Impressions that needed so elaborate a record did not seem like the handiwork of those careless old writers one imagines squabbling over a mistress, or riding on a journey, or drinking round a tavern fire, brisk and active men." His experience of the common folk of Ireland formed a counterpoise to the rarefied isolation of the Lady in her tower and the mind alone with perception: "I sought some symbolic language reaching far into the past and associated with familiar names and conspicuous hills that I might not be alone amid the obscure impressions of the senses" (*E. & I.*, 347–49). Perception was to be given again its public dimension, based upon the traditional associations that make up the language of place and upon objective symbols founded in the memory of the race.

A Vision depicts the sometimes fruitful, sometimes destructive contention and interaction of Subjectivity and Objectivity. It was crucial to Yeats's direction that he conceive the world of the Objective in terms other than as the mechanistically determined physical reality that formed the machine about the Cartesian ghost, a reality so opposite to the mind that the possibility of interaction was made suspect. Yeats's solution to this problem was, like Coleridge's, in essence Berkeleian. In his late essay "Bishop Berkeley" he resoundingly rejects "the new realist philosophy which thinks that the secondary and primary qualities alike are independent of consciousness," feeling compelled by ancestral memory to "reject whatever—to borrow a metaphor of Coleridge's—drives mind into the quicksilver." Berkeley is for Yeats "idealist and realist alike," in that he returned men's attention from the abstractions of science to the unarguable finality of perception (*E. & I.*, 405–7). Thus with the help of Berkeley, magical experiment, and the traditions and tales of the Irish peasantry, the objective world is to be seen as a language of landscape, a body of traditional symbols (or archetypes) whose origin is in Anima Mundi. Envisioning in "The Second Coming" that frightening "lion body" with "the head of a man," its "gaze blank and pitiless as the sun" (prefiguring what may be the Annunciation of a new Objective, Primary, solar civilization), the poet encounters a "vast image out of *Spiritus Mundi*." Objectivity, like Subjectivity, comes ultimately from that collective source he calls elsewhere "the murderous innocence of the sea."

The brute objective force we see entering the world anew in "The Second Coming" is opposed to the sensitive imagination of the artist, but it is not the indifferent mechanism of the Cartesian world-machine. It is a passionate irrational power more like Blake's Tyger than the mills of Locke and Newton that Blake satirized. We are subject to power beyond our individual control, but it is a kind of power to which we have *some* relationship, since it is living, animal and organic, even if terrifyingly impersonal. Each of us has the same source in the depths of the unconscious. Like Jung, Yeats sees our drama and tragedy as the result of a confrontation, age after age, with different outcomes, between the human consciousness and its collective and Dionysiac source symbolized by the sea. And although we cannot identify Subjectivity any more than Romantic imagination with consciousness alone, we can see nevertheless that Yeats's Subjectivity represents the human type, phase, outlook, or historical era most able to assimilate the irrational source and bring it into expressive consciousness.

Yeats has added to the Romantic vision of this primal confrontation an appreciation of the irrational and destructive capabilities of a source that he realizes is the origin of the sexual impulse as well as of artistic inspiration. Yeats shares with Jung a sense that the individual mind's attempt to deal with the immemorial flood of unconscious imperatives is both heroic and tragic. Yeats's old warrior Cuchulain, after many battles, fights the waves and is drowned.[16] And Yeats, of course, deals more inclusively with history and civilization than do the Romantics. His is not merely the introspective poetic observer on the shore in the Byzantium poems, but an entire culture. Yet the principle of contention and potential balance between principles symbolized by pleasure dome and sunless sea, moonlit dome and dolphin-torn harbor, is the same.

In Yeats's cyclical scheme as represented by the interpenetrating gyres, therefore, it is less the names given to the contending principles than the equality of proportion between them that determines the character of a given historical moment. *Primary* and *Antithetical*, as designating terms, are manipulated with a dizzying complexity in *A Vision*. Yet it is clear that in the times Yeats favors— Europe in 1450, Byzantium around A.D. 560—the gyres interpenetrate more equally, so that the contending opposites, whatever their names, are in balance.

Roman civilization at the time of the coming of Christ, A.D. 1050, and our own time as it advances toward the year 2000 have in common, by contrast, the widest possible imbalance and separation between the two contending spirals. "Turning and turning in the widening gyre," as Yeats puts it in poetic imagery, "The falcon cannot hear the falconer." The disunity of culture and individual being in "The Second Coming" is reflected in the irrational and impersonal force of the lion-bodied figure with pitiless solar gaze that has come to the poet as a portent out of Spiritus Mundi. President Wilson of the portrait and other great men who become "professional and abstract," as well as this terrible unthinking lionman, are both characteristic of times when Subjectivity and Objectivity have been split far apart, one cone expanded, the other only a point. Since head can no longer know heart, since "President Wilson lives only in the eyes," the fully human synthesis that assimilates the unconscious and translates it into expressiveness is undermined (*Auto.*, 175). Thought loses passion in abstraction, and therefore lacks force and conviction. Dupin regards the ape from a distance, coolly, with distaste. "The best lack all conviction, while the worst / Are full of passionate intensity." We are in the condition of Roman civilization at the time of the birth of Christ.

> The Roman Empire stood appalled:
> It dropped the reigns of peace and war
> When that fierce virgin and her Star
> Out of the fabulous darkness called.[17]

Yeats distrusts passionate irrationalism without the completing imagination and intellect, whether in the future or in the past. His ideal is a synthesis, not a warring separation, of the contending principles. The images of human-animal fusion without human awareness in "The Second Coming" and of mind-body division in the portrait of Wilson best express his aversion to the separated extremes of conscious and unconscious dimensions of personality.

A passage in *A Vision* descriptive of Rome of the first and second centuries presents an era analogous to our own, and an image of mind-body dichotomy parallel to that in the portrait of President Wilson. Again, Yeats works in terms of art, contrasting those "riders upon the Parthenon" who were part of "a movement that seemed, so were the hearts of man and beast set upon it, that of a dance," with the static portrayal of individual character evolved by Roman sculpture out of its Greek beginnings. In contrast to the Parthenon's dance-like movement linking beasts and men (and thereby suggesting Unity of Being), Yeats describes a situation in Rome wherein "the delineation of character as shown in face and head, as with us of recent years, is all in all, and sculptors, seeking the custom of occupied officials, stock in their work-shops toga'd marble bodies upon which can be screwed with the least possible delay heads modelled from the sitters with the most scrupulous realism."[18]

The "face and head" sculpted separately from the body represents an interest in individual character and a resulting self-consciousness typical of a time in which the "intellectual cone" has expanded to its maximum.[19] The fact that these portrait-heads were "screwed with the least possible delay" upon stock, prefabricated bodies symbolizes the separation between intellect and emotion of such a time. This is, according to Yeats's system, the kind of time we live in, and it is precisely this self-division of the "best," who "lack all conviction," that prepares the way for the "passionate intensity" of the "worst." The ruling minds that should know, handle, and assimilate the passionate irrationality of the Primary or Objective cone are at such times abstracted and separated from it; it is left to its own, to beget lion-like figures in the desert and threaten the stability of civilization.

According to Yeats's view, Christ's coming itself was such an irruption from Spiritus Mundi into the classical world: "Odour of blood when Christ was slain / Made all Platonic tolerance vain / And vain all Doric Discipline."[20] Like the "rough beast" of "The Second Coming," Christ is associated with the Objective solar principle and initiates its expanding gyre. By the mid-point of the Christian era (marked at A.D. 1050 on his historical diagram), the cone whose point grows from the stable at Bethlehem has spiraled to its maximum expansion, while the principle symbolized by the "world-considering eyes" of those separated Roman heads has shrunk to its narrowest.[21] "The intellectual cone has so narrowed that secular intellect has gone, and the strong man rules with the aid of local custom; everywhere the supernatural is sudden, violent, and as dark to the intellect as a stroke or St. Vitus' dance."[22]

It appears that Yeats uses the Objective, or Primary, in several senses. President Wilson in the portrait by Sargent was Objective in the sense of being abstracted from emotion, professional, administrative. His eyes represented "the anxious study and slight deflection of external force" (*Auto.*, 175). Those Romans of the sculpted, separated heads were likewise concerned, with "their world-considering eyes," with "that which is external to the mind."[23] But the realism of an orderly material world ruled by the watchful administrative eye and the brute physical force and inexplicable, seizure-like supernaturalism of the feudal situation at A.D. 1050 have this in common: both are worlds of the maximum separation between the ordinary human consciousness and its collective sources in Anima Mundi. Objectivity, therefore, means two seemingly opposite things that are in fact closely related. The administrative practicality of President Wilson or Roman official, the watchful eyes with their hard-facts, time-space consideration, suggest a subservience to a physical and cultural world by a mind that is, while ruling over it, nevertheless split apart from that world and unable to assimilate it in deepest origin. In the medieval world the relation of physical violence and supernatural violence to the conscious mind is analogous; spiritual Objectivity, like physical Objectivity, affects the waking mind like an assault from without which it cannot comprehend: "Everywhere the supernatural is sudden, violent, and dark to the intellect as a stroke or St. Vitus' dance."

One of the central fascinations of Yeats's mature poetry is just this impingement of the irrational and supernatural upon the human consciousness, whether in historical or personal terms. The Annunciation poems—"The Second Coming," "Two Songs from a Play," and "Leda and the Swan"—are especially clear cases of the entry into human affairs of a powerful and turbulent mystery. Leda, after all, is raped; Zeus as the "feathered glory" of a swan is unarguably magnificent, and divine purpose, we suppose, must be enacted. Yet much of our sympathy is with the poor girl, so surprised and used, so terrified by "that white rush" whose divinity she can sense in the "strange heart beating where it lies" but perhaps never comprehend. The final emphasis of the sonnet is upon an ironic question: "Did she put on his knowledge with his power / Before the indifferent beak could let her drop?" How could she have, we muse, so "mastered by the brute blood of the air"? She is, after all, like us, a fallible human consciousness thinking itself complete within itself until assaulted by the collective, like the poet's own mind in "The Second Coming," penetrated and arrested by "a vast image out of *Spiritus Mundi*."

Whether in the time of Leda, therefore, or of the Virgin Mary, or of "The break-up of Charlemagne's Empire," whenever the two cones are at widest separation, life has an unconscious, automatic quality. It may be the automatism of a secular intellect that fails to realize its origins, or the impact of a spiritual Objectivity that leaves scant room for any human realization. Medieval Christian authority was for Yeats as imperious and as unconscious in its effect upon the individual as the divine swan was upon Leda. "The spiritual life is alone overflowing, its cone expanded, and yet this life—secular intellect extinguished—has little effect upon men's conduct, is perhaps a dream which passes beyond the reach of conscious mind but for some rare miracle or vision. I think of it as like that profound reverie of the somnambulist which may be accompanied by a sensuous dream—a Romanesque stream perhaps of bird and beast images—and yet neither affect the dream nor be affected by it."[24]

Yeats is a central Romantic heir, therefore, in the dichotomy of his vision, whereby conscious and unconscious forces are projected into the landscape. In his vision the life of the individual and of society are stationed precariously between a sterile separation from the collective source and a possession of the specifically human by the irrational. What remains before us is a further appreciation of the typical imagistic structures through which Yeats symbolized this confrontation between Apollonian consciousness and its Dionysiac antecedent.

Yeats, like the Romantics, apparently lived his symbols, becoming inspired by significant place. Wordsworth settled with Dorothy in Dove Cottage, on the shores of Lake Grasmere. Yeats, who married in 1917, purchased the year before "an old Norman tower at Ballylee near Lady Gregory's estate at Coole in Western Ireland."[25] Through this tower, in which he lived for extended periods following his marriage, Yeats achieved relatively late in his career a solidity of structure and image like that of Wordsworth's "Tintern Abbey" or Coleridge's "Frost at Midnight." The tower became his personal version of the great dome of "Byzantium," a structure of consciousness stationed next to the fertile and irrational waters of a stream, the "frog-spawn of a blind man's ditch" as in "A Dialogue of Self and Soul"—just as Saint Sophia's is balanced against "That dolphin-torn, that gong-tormented sea." Yeats's acquisition of the tower appears to be the mature fulfillment of the youthful impulse to "buy or hire," for a mystical society, the "Castle on the Rock" in Lough Kay, and the underlying motivation seems to be a sense that inspiration or revelation would flow from such a spot.

Yeats discussed the symbol of the tower in relation to "the sea, and rivers" in the early essay "The Philosophy of Shelley's Poetry," mentioning Prince Athanase's "lighted tower above the sea." Yeats recognized from early on that only through images like Jung's archetypes would he be able to escape subjective isolation. "It is only by ancient symbols, by symbols which have numberless meanings . . . , that any highly subjective art can escape from the barrenness and shallowness of a too conscious arrangement, into the abundance and depth of Nature" (*E. & I.*, 87). Romantic Nature prefigures mystical Anima Mundi, but the relationship of elements is the same. The Subjective artist in the tower transcends isolation by experiencing the continuity between self-enclosed ego and the collective source that foams at the doorstep, washing up universal symbols from the depth of a collective memory.

The great poems of the tower begin with "In Memory of Major Robert Gregory," which simultaneously celebrates the settling-in to housekeeping in Thor Ballylee by the poet and his wife and mourns the death of Lady Gregory's son. As the first poem in *The Wild Swans at Coole* (1919) to signalize inhabitancy of an ancient symbol, the poem is paradoxically practical, particular, and chastened by the recognition of mortality. The many friends of youth who come to mind are dead, and dead also, in his prime, is "Our Sidney and our perfect man," the epitome, as he is described, of Unity of Being. Just as Wordsworth at Tintern Abbey recognized not only the oceanic origin as symbolized by the "inland murmur" of streams but also his own partial separation from that source by time, so does Yeats experience his own connection with the immemorial experience of marriage, domesticity, and death—of time itself—as a fall, and use the tone of elegy to describe it. The supernaturalistic poems "Ego Dominus Tuus" and "The Phases of the Moon," outlining the mystical system of *A Vision* in verse, come later in the book and employ also the symbols of tower "where

Milton's Platonist / Sat late" ("The Phases of the Moon") beside stream with "rat or water-hen." Yet Yeats apparently wished to establish first that the tower-by-stream was an actual location as well as a complex symbol. Even as he encountered the amazing fact of automatic writing by his wife, expressive of the system or ritual order that he had so long sought, he recognized the limitations of age and responsibility, and made his peace with the possible and the real.[26] Magic and reality came together in the tower, and Yeats wanted Sturge Moore to draw his building "as a permanent symbol of my work plainly visible to the passer-by. As you know all my art theories depend upon just this—rooting of mythology in the earth."[27] Wordsworth would have agreed with such a thought.

The ideal that animated Yeats's psychic life for so many years was Maude Gonne, the personification of the supernatural beauty Yeats imagined in Helen of Troy, with whom he identified his Maude. Yeats's marriage signalized his acceptance of the fact that he was never to possess her. If "In Memory of Major Robert Gregory" is an elegy for the poet and his friends in the face of unfriendly time as well as for Lady Gregory's son, then "A Prayer for My Daughter" of *Michael Robartes and the Dancer* is a poem that substitutes for the Romantic and turbulent ideal of beauty represented by Maude Gonne a more humane and attainable pattern of feminine perfection. In altering this image at the center of the psyche's life (which Jung would call the anima), Yeats investigates and further defines that all-important relationship between consciousness of tower and unconsciousness of sea.

He recognizes in this poem the necessity of ceremony and tradition as mediating factors in the relation of both the individual and the culture to "the murderous innocence of the sea." Yeats in his mature poetry sails, not with Shelley off the surface of the earth, but to Byzantium—an ideal, admittedly, but one achieved in terms of concrete "hammered gold and gold enamelling." He enters into an eternity that is, like that of Keats's urn, an "artifice." It is as if Yeats, following an opposite path from Wordsworth's, had arrived at a similiar destination. Wordsworth began with nature and followed it to the supernatural, to the voice from Stonehenge in "Guilt and Sorrow" which seems that of the collective unconsciousness. Yeats began by seeking the supernatural, discovered his Anima Mundi, then localized it in nature, in specific places like those of "Frost at Midnight" and other Romantic meditations on the landscape. The poet's observing, verbally formulative mind occupies the tower; Anima Mundi is identified with nature, as represented by the stream below.

Like Coleridge with his son in "Frost at Midnight," the poet in "A Prayer for My Daughter" is awake late at night beside a sleeping infant, imagining fearfully and prayerfully the future his child will inherit. But in contrast to the calm in which Coleridge meditates, Yeats evokes at the outset a howling wind, rather like that which animates and yet troubles the conclusion of "Dejection: An Ode." Coleridge's wind is a sweeping of turbulent imagination that suggests war, telling of "the rushing of an host in rout." Yeats's wind in "A Prayer for My Daughter" has a similar meaning; it is a troubled breath come to the poet from the sea. He walks and prays, listening to the destructive wind,

> Imagining in excited reverie
> That the future years had come,
> Dancing to a frenzied drum,
> Out of the murderous innocence of the sea.

The poet fears history, and for his daughter as a part of the future. As we have seen from his symbols of Objectivity and Subjectivity, Yeats dreaded phases of civilization so dichotomized between the intellectual, imaginative lunar gyre and the powerful, passionate, and pragmatic solar gyre that the fully human compromise between personal consciousness and the collective origin was imperiled. Both the character of his daughter and the times she is born into are matters of deep concern, for Yeats fears a future dichotomized between irrational power and abstract intellect.

Specifically, he has in mind the example of Maude Gonne as one who has succumbed to disunity of being and participated in (and contributed to) the violence of the times. In "No Second Troy" years earlier, Yeats had identified Maude with Helen of Troy, and there admired her romantic arrogance, which would have "hurled the little streets upon the great"; he here suggests again the identi-fication, but with sorrow rather than admiration.

> Helen being chosen found life flat and dull
> And later had much trouble from a fool,
> While that great Queen, that rose out of the spray,
> Being fatherless could have her way
> Yet chose a bandy-legged smith for man.
> It's certain that fine women eat
> A crazy salad with their meat
> Whereby the Horn of Plenty is undone.

Maude is Helen and Helen is, symbolically, Venus, who was born from the sea. The birth of Venus from the waves dramatizes that penetration of the divine and timeless One into this world of time and disunity that we have seen in "The Second Coming" and in "Leda and the Swan." Yeats's perplexity is occasioned by the troubled fate of such quintessential gifts of beauty and fruitfulness as Maude, Helen, and Venus. He seems to have concluded that the world cannot bear too direct an infusion of this superhuman origin; the sea's essential quality is a "murderous innocence." Beauty that makes "a stranger's eye distraught" may be too intense, may make people forget the necessity of civility and of the human compro-mise—forget that "hearts are earned / By those that are not en-tirely beautiful."

Moreover, Maude, like Helen, was not only too beautiful, too redolent of her source, but had also succumbed to the abstract hatred of politics. Yeats wishes for his daughter a different fate: "An intellectual hatred is the worst, / So let her think opinions are accursed." The "loveliest woman born" out of the horn of plenty has been wasted on an unsatisfactory husband, like Venus with Vulcan. Yeats's vision of a proper future for his daughter, in con-trast to the fate of Helen-Maude, is a projection of the pattern he has achieved for his own life. He imagines his daughter settling with her bridegroom in a house "Where all's accustomed, cere-monious," so that she may live fruitfully within the limitations of a traditional role and a particular spot: "O may she live like some green laurel / Rooted in one dear perpetual place." Yeats himself has finally made his peace with the quest for visionary knowledge and supreme beauty in a marriage, to one less beautiful than Maude, and in the acceptance of the role of father and house-holder, grounding all his visions and researches in the stones of an ancient tower.

This tower in the beginning of the poem was his protection against the "haystack-and roof-levelling wind, / Bred on the Atlantic." The poet suggests that the collective source symbolized by the sea must be approached through a structure of consciousness that limits and orders its impact. The tower (an ancient fortification), as the residence for poet and father, is a physical embodiment of Shelley's "towers of thought's crowned powers," which Yeats had written of so many years earlier (*E. & I.*, 87). It is a form embodying the conscious personality. The tower is like man's warrior identity developed in time, a multilayered symbol reinforced in "A Dialogue of Self and Soul" by the samurai sword the poet holds within his study atop the winding stair. The sword is phallic, war-like, identified with day and physical generation, and reminds us of the heroic role of individual consciousness. Since the early poem "Cuchulain's Fight with the Sea" (1899), Yeats had incorporated into his work a pattern reminiscent of the young Wordsworth's dragon fight upon the lake in *The Prelude*. In his late play *On Baile's Strand* the same pattern is enacted. In "A Dialogue of Self and Soul" Yeats claims "as by a soldier's right / A charter to commit the crime once more." This "crime" is the fight with the waves, the phallic enactment of the ritual of generation, the blind, inevitable, mistaken drama of the individual consciousness in interaction with the collective.

It is as if the water of generation made one drunk: "A living man is blind and drinks his drop. / What matter if the ditches are impure?" Men swallow wine but also "the intoxicating cold drink of generation" ("The Philosophy of Shelley's Poetry," *E. & I.*, 83). Yeats's vision here, both of poetic consciousness and of its irrational source, is more guarded than that of the Romantics, and this sense of the blind, passionate destructiveness latent in the sea is what gives the tone of classical restraint to "A Prayer for My Daughter."

"A Prayer for My Daughter" presents us, then, with a model of two patterns in symbolic correlation. On the one hand it shows us the tower metaphorically next to the sea, as it stands in the howling sea wind. On the other the poem shows us a pattern of personality, of individual and social values, that will allow the poet's daughter to escape the fate of those who, like Maude, Helen, and Venus, are born too directly from the waves. The "custom and ceremony" of the poem's last stanza are necessary if the chaotic sea source is to be fruitful rather than destructive. Man walks a narrow strand between intellectual abstraction and mindless servitude to an irrational imperative. The only escape from the extremes posed by "The Second Coming" wherein the passionless "best" (like President Wilson in the portrait) "lack all conviction" and the worst are "full of passionate intensity" is in the fully human balance between the contending principles. For human personality and society, it is the acceptance of ancestral values, of the limitations of houses and their conventions, of rituals such as marriage, that help master aboriginal "arrogance and hatred." We can see how Yeats's conservative vision of society is related to the Romantic theme of individual poetic consciousness coming to terms with inspiration.

We have seen in the earlier Romantics that the poet, while accepting the compromise with chaotic unconsciousness (simultaneously the creation and the fall), also is tempted to reject it, to demand full access to the "immortal sea" and a return to paradise. Wordsworth on top of Mount Snowdon under the "full-orbed Moon" enjoys a vision so capacious that the total sky-dome reminds him not so much of the world of limited experience as of a "majestic intellect" (*Prel.* 14:67); such minds are "truly from the Deity" (112) and resemble perhaps more the Creator than the creation. Coleridge's prophetic spinner of visions in "Kubla Khan" and "The Ancient Mariner" seems likewise outside the human scale. Was Yeats, after all the supernaturalism of his earlier quest, entirely satisfied with the realities of tower, marriage, fatherhood? His relation to Anima Mundi through physical realities remains of crucial importance from the time of his marriage to the end of his career, and his role of warrior-like manhood in the ancient tower is worn proudly, like a badge. But the value Yeats placed upon limitation, tradition, and order was not a restriction that kept him from appreciating, responding to, and symbolizing the call of that which transcends human identity. It is more nearly accurate to say that his poems of the tower and its related symbols deal with the tension between the supernatural and the human, and offer a variety of attitudes toward us and our encounter with what is beyond.

"Byzantium" might be singled out as the poem by Yeats that most closely associates itself with the trans-human possibility for consciousness suggested by Wordsworth in *The Prelude*, book 14, and by Coleridge in "Kubla Khan." The "starlit or a moonlit dome" suggests a point of view outside human incarnation for, in respect to the symbolic phases, Yeats said, "There's no human life at the full or the dark" ("The Phases of the Moon"). The "Emperor's drunken soldiery," on the symbolic level, are mortal men in their warrior roles, blind, passionate, and associated with day, as the sword is in "A Dialogue of Self and Soul." They are "abed" by the second line of "Byzantium," that the poetic focus may be upon a consciousness superior to their "drunken" involvement in the "fury and the mire" of their own veins. The Emperor himself, the "great cathedral gong," and the "moonlit dome" of Saint Sophia's are images that cohere into the portrait of, to use Wordsworth's phrase, a "majestic intellect," which arches smoothly above the furious self-division of human incarnations in time.

Yeats's dual attitude toward this compromise—toward our mixture of consciousness and unconsciousness, spiritual wisdom and chaotic, warrior sexuality—manifests itself in the subtle irony whereby the dome, serene and whole in starlight or under the full moon, in phases beyond human life, "disdains / All that man is, / All mere complexities." The poet is scorning the very role he has earlier embraced in "A Dialogue of Self and Soul." But the motive is clear enough: artistic imagination needs a perspective that is larger, simpler, and more complete than that of warrior-man if it is to refine and simplify the mortal "ore" of its materials into the "hammered gold" of perfected form. Acceptance of marriage, social ritual, bodily sexuality, and a particular dwelling is one kind of ordering identity, which the poet has embraced. The mastery of the waters of the turbulent source by the forms of art is a different limitation, one not so obviously subject to human imperfection and time.

The middle three stanzas of "Byzantium" depict a process of refinement that is simultaneously an account of the soul's purification after death (unwinding the "winding path") and an account of an imagination with power analogous to the supernatural. The Emperor and his dome preside over the transformation of human experience into the perfected soul, giving the poet vision of "Breathless mouths" and causing him to "hail the superhuman." The poet is powerfully attracted to this world where the golden sculptures seem "More miracle than bird or handiwork"; that they are "by the moon embittered" must surely be the projection of his own dissatisfaction with mortality and change. He is tempted to identify directly with the Emperor's consciousness, which is as magical as that "pleasure-dome" decreed by another emperor, Kubla Khan, as "truly from the Deity" as that "ethereal vault" arcing over Snowdon (14:50).

To transcend the limiting act of creation that is a fall, the poet would become this emperor, whose mind is collective, the giant who subsumes all our individual experience, all the sounds of "drunken soldiery," into a single smooth dome illumined by the moon. Yeats here reveals his impatience toward the passionate half-knowledge associated with "mire and blood."

The peculiar paradox of this strand in "Byzantium" is that the order and sense of timelessness we ordinarily associate with the divine have to be reflected back upon it from the dome and statues of the human shore. The Emperor able to "decree" golden bird and dome would lack discrete identity without those individual artisans whose collective achievement forms the best emblem of his thought. The Emperor is an archetypal pattern, but the realization of his timelessness in time is a human function. "Eternity" as it has been defined by "Monuments of unageing intellect" ("Sailing to Byzantium") is indeed an "artifice": that higher consciousness created by intellectual structures in contact with their origin in the sea, a contact holding the extremes of Subjectivity and Objectivity in fruitful balance. As Blake said, "Eternity is in love with the productions of time."[28]

> Astraddle on the dolphin's mire and blood,
> Spirit after spirit! The smithies break the flood,
> The golden smithies of the Emperor!
> Marbles of the dancing floor
> Break bitter furies of complexity,
> Those images that yet
> Fresh images beget,
> That dolphin-torn, that gong-tormented sea.

The creators of those art objects that reflect the Emperor's consciousness, his "golden smithies," are said to "break the flood" almost as if they were stones or pilings set up in waves of the harbor. Then we read "break" in the sense of one's breaking a wild horse, or a code, as denoting mastery, making manageable and intelligible the wild and the unknown. "Marbles of the dancing floor" seem washed about by waves full of dolphins, as if the primal sea were impinging directly upon a ballroom's civilized floor and its statues.

Perhaps the Coleridge of "Kubla Khan" is closest to Yeats's mature vision, for the turbulent fountain and the "ancestral voices" that threaten war suggest a version of the sea source more like Yeats's "murderous innocence" than Wordsworth's "immortal" reservoir of souls. Coleridge's emphasis upon the exact five-mile "measure" of "walls and towers" and upon the "mingled measure" of the sound that is poetry in relation to those "caverns measureless to man" is also applicable to Yeats. In "The Statues," for example, Yeats extends the idea of artistic form as fruitful limitation upon the chaotic ocean origin, and he invokes numerical measure as a part of the artistic definition. In the poem's first stanza he sees Pythagoras as the planner of Greek sculpture, his "numbers" as an animating presence in "marble or in bronze," a paradoxical infusion of artistic vitality through an abstract measurement of proportion that "moved or seemed to move," and that had the power, even in the absence of the particular features of "character," to evoke passion in the young:

    boys and girls, pale from the imagined love
Of solitary beds, knew what they were,
That passion could bring character enough,
And pressed at midnight in some public place
Live lips upon a plummet-measured face.

The fusion of the conscious intellect's measuring, abstracting capability with preconscious sources produces powerful effects. Just as the "golden smithies" of "Byzantium" create works that evoke the Emperor's consciousness, so do these Greek sculptors succeed in giving concrete definition to some of the huge archetypes of Anima Mundi—as if the "rough beast" of "The Second Coming" had been rendered in stone. But here an element of greater humanity has been incorporated into these "Calculations that look but casual flesh," so that adolescents in their sexual awakening discover ideals that will direct their desire and influence their quests. Maude-Helen-Venus, born out of the spray, was such a model for Yeats, and Rossetti, William Morris, and other Pre-Raphaelite painters had embodied her for Yeats through their art.

    The measurement of the symbolic sea by art, therefore, has an enormous impact upon civilization. Something of the divine and timeless source seems embodied in these figures of marble and bronze that boys and girls are moved to embrace. Yet the formulation is also discrete, exact, "plummet-measured." Coleridgean "measure" is what enabled Western art and life to separate itself from the vague, unconscious immensity of Asia:

           the men
That with a mallet or a chisel modelled these
Calculations that look but casual flesh, put down
All Asiatic vague immensities,
And not the banks of oars that swam upon
The many-headed foam at Salamis.   ("The Statues")

That phrase "put down," like "break" in "Byzantium," has a fruitful ambiguity. The Greek sculptors were the heroes who "put down" (in the sense of defeated, put down the uprising of) those Asiatic hordes more properly than the Athenian Galleys at Salamis in 480 B.C. But "put down" also suggests such a formulation as "put down in words," a quality expressed rather than eliminated. This is exactly the second reading that Yeats's essential concept supports. The "many-headed foam" is a version of that tumultuous source whose waves flood the "dancing floor" in "Byzantium," and the "banks of oars" of the galleys upon it are enacting the heroic dragon fight, as when Wordsworth rowed the mountain lake (*Prel.* 1:357–400). The vessel of consciousness within the waves of unconsciousness suggests both the dominance of intellect and its contact with the primal, which is incorporated, expressed, "put down," in an heroic synthesis preserving both the hero's clarity and the dragon's immensity. The "measure" of the artist, therefore, rather than the warrior's sword stroke, is the preferable way of dealing with the Asiatic ocean of both "The Statues" and of "Kubla Khan."

This ocean is not only the reservoir of Coleridge's "ancestral voices" but also the source of a continuing influx of the "many-headed foam" into contemporary events. Yeats fears that the modern world has forgotten the Grecian art of mastering and giving form to this "innocence," which can be "murderous." "The Statues" ends on a note of dread and hope, as Yeats interprets the Easter Rebellion of 1916 in terms of an identification between Pearse, its leader, and the mythic Irish hero Cuchulain, who died while fighting with the sea.

> When Pearse summoned Cuchulain to his side,
> What stalked through the Post Office? What intellect,
> What calculation, number, measurement, replied?
> We Irish, born into that ancient sect
> But thrown upon this filthy modern tide
> And by its formless spawning fury wrecked,
> Climb to our proper dark, that we may trace
> The lineaments of a plummet-measured face.

Yeats allows himself an unusual rhetorical fullness as he modifies "filthy modern tide" with "formless spawning fury." The terms are familiar, as in the Byzantium poems. But the repugnance is unusual. The vessel of consciousness is "wrecked" in the formless unconsciousness of the present. Yeats's wish or demand that the Irish race return to a heroic, "plummet-measured" relation to its unconscious source is insistent, even desperate. Only the "face" of that larger being who stalks behind the scenes of trivial daily experience seems able to reunify action and "character" into heroic personality. Can we define any further the relation between this hero and ordinary awareness?

The "climb" of the Irish to "our proper dark" suggests a return to the archetype, and it is there, "The Statues" implies, that contemporary men may "trace / The lineaments of a plummet-measured face."

This figure owes something to the image of Saturn, fallen king of the Titan gods, in Keats's "Hyperion." Saturn has become in "The Fall of Hyperion" a vast statue that embodies an imperative: he symbolizes all that forces the poet-figure to ascend the mountain-like pyramid out of personalism into a tragic and objective art.[29] The statue of Saturn is an embodiment of an ancestral inheritance: the archetypal history of the fall of a grand progenitor (the primal ruling god) into division and time. As such he inspires the young poet to seek exactly what Yeats achieved in his lifelong quest for occult symbolism, the deliverance of a "highly subjective art" from "the barrenness and shallowness of a too conscious arrangement," into the "abundance" of nature and the "ancient symbols" (*E. & I.*, 87). Having climbed the great stone steps, Keats's poet discovers "A power within me of enormous ken, / To see as a god sees" ("The Fall of Hyperion," 1:303–4). What Keats intended him to "see" was the epic vision of the first "Hyperion," to reiterate in a subtler style that moment when the young Apollo feels

> Names, deeds, grey legends, dire events, rebellions,
> Majesties, sovran voices, agonies,
> Creations and destroyings, all at once
> Pour into the wide hollows of my brain.
>
> ("Hyperion," 3:114–17)

In tracing the "lineaments of a plummet-measured face," Yeats has achieved a similar ascent of vision into the impersonal, a similar identification with a heroic and tragic perspective. Yeats's conceptualization of history as a cycling process governed by the oppositely whirling gyres achieved a point of view like that represented by the statue of Saturn "huge of feature as a cloud" ("The Fall of Hyperion," 1:88). In the poem "The Gyres" Yeats identifies his historical diagram with the symbolic stone countenance: "The gyres! the gyres! Old Rocky Face, look forth." What "Old Rocky Face" sees is the Empedoclean flux of civilizations that might have broken the heart of the sensitive, subjective poet Yeats once was. "Rocky Face," however, looks on "in tragic joy." Like Keats's Apollo as transformed in "The Fall of Hyperion" by the statue of Saturn and what it represents, Yeats in "The Statues," "The Gyres," "Lapis Lazuli," and "Under Ben Bulben" of *Last Poems* has transfigured his vision. For the moment of the poem the poet is like a statue or "Rocky Face" able to see and symbolize things as they are with an impassive countenance. Like Keats in "The Fall of Hyperion," he ascends a symbolic mountain and identifies with a stone figure in order to see from a perspective outside time.

Jung's description of the collective unconscious as an "ocean of images or figures" is elaborated as the figure of a giant. If we were to personify it, Jung says,

> we might think of it as a collective human being combining the characteristics of both sexes, transcending youth and age, birth and death, and, from having at its command a human experience of one or two million years, practically immortal. If such a being existed, it would be exalted above all temporal change; the present would mean neither more nor less to it than any year in the hundredth millennium before Christ; it would be a dreamer of age-old dreams and, owing to its limitless experience, an incomparable prognosticator. It would have lived countless times over again the life of the individual, the family, the tribe, and the nation, and it would possess a living sense of the rhythm of growth, flowering, and decay.   (*C.W.* 8, par. 673)

Keats in "The Fall of Hyperion" steps away from his earlier narrative of a division between the gods and makes of it a myth of the dawn of time. The "old sanctuary" with "carved sides" and "roof august" (1:61–62) serves as a monument to the civil war that stands at the beginning. "Builded so high, it seem'd that filmed clouds / Might spread beneath" (63–64), this architecture has the dimensions and apparent antiquity of landscape. Both Gothic ruin and geologic record of "rocks toil'd hard in waves and winds" (69) seem transitory in comparison with this "eternal domed monument" (71) that is larger than eras and epochs because containing their distances. This mighty *house* is a collective consciousness vast enough to include also the collective unconsciousness: this *landscape*. The space enclosed seems a field ample enough for the enactment of all history. Keats's hall of "columns north and south, ending in mist / Of nothing" (84–85) and Yeats's soil in "Under Ben Bulben" where the gravediggers "thrust their buried men / Back in the human mind again" carry us finally beyond consciousness, time, and the adequacy of words. We are left with the symbols. Man-mountain. Eternal dome. Being, made of earth, who receives our individual identities, subsumes our moments. The final word on Romantic poetry of landscape may be Yeats's own epitaph, cut by "his command" on "limestone quarried near the spot." A grave like one of those in Gray's "Elegy Written in a Country Churchyard" seems to have spoken, to have told us of this return of the poet into the soil of his "rude forefathers." One body has disappeared into this earth that is memory, both mountain and man: the giant Ben Bulben.

5 Death and Rebirth in a Modern Landscape

In approaching Romantic landscape poetry in terms of a typical tension between conscious structure or figure and wild or unconscious moorland or sea, we are participating in a psychological interpretation that has already been made, in effect, by intellectual and artistic developments in our own century. Our time, after all, is that of the discovery of the unconscious. Henri Ellenberger, in the book from whose title this phrase comes, has traced the psychoanalytic movement from its origins in Romanticism.[1] Awareness of the doctrines of Freud, Jung, and their followers has permeated modern life and marked modern art and criticism. Maud Bodkin's *Archetypal Patterns in Poetry* represents a pioneering attempt to apply the concepts of C. G. Jung to the interpretation of poetry—an attempt that appears to have influenced the thinking of the modern American poet Theodore Roethke.[2] Our artistic inheritance is Dada, Surrealism, and Abstract Expressionism, movements wherein artists have sought deliberately to introduce change, illogic, and emotional association into their work, to free it from the dominance of the conscious will so that more primal powers may be manifest. The presence of African masks and various totemic deities in our galleries and as influences in the work of painters, sculptors, and other artists attests to our time's fascination with the primitive, the irrational, the unconscious.[3]

The theme of psychological death and rebirth in the context of a landscape imagery symbolizing access to the unconscious comes to an especially clear formulation in the work of Roethke. As a poet who imbibed the central Modernist influence (his work is clearly marked by both Yeats and Eliot) and who also returned

sympathetically to Romantic predecessors, Roethke is representative of the Romantic and postromantic themes we have traced as
they arise in a new but recognizable form in the period following
World War II—a time that saw a reaction to, and reformulation of,
the Modernist version of the poetic act.[4] We will find in Roethke an
explicit interest in the unconscious, as well as a pattern resembling
the Romantic resuscitation ritual, and the house and ship imagery
symbolizing consciousness in its interaction with the unconscious.

In an "Open Letter," published in 1950 with a selection of
poems from *The Lost Son and Other Poems*, Roethke acknowledges
the poet as "conscious instrument," as opposed to "some kind of
over-size aeolian harp upon which strange winds play uncouth
tunes," yet sees the poet's task as to "fish, patiently, in that dark
pond, the unconscious, or dive in, with or without pants on." The
rather playful tone of this beginning does not disguise the essential
seriousness of what Roethke is saying, for as he speaks of "The
Lost Son" sequence, something of the agony behind these poems
of psychic breakdown and regeneration becomes apparent: "Each
in a sense is a stage in a kind of struggle out of the slime; part of a
slow spiritual progress; an effort to be born, and later, to become
something more."[5] The psychic birth to which Roethke refers is a
form of that separation of individual consciousness from the unconsciousness of nature that we have identified as central Romantic motif.

Roethke sees the movement of these poems as cyclic, as hard-
won progressions founded upon a reimmersion of the adult
psyche in the primal, chaotic, unconscious world symbolized by
memories of his Michigan childhood and its landscape with
marshes, rivers, and ponds. "I believe that to go forward as a spiritual man it is necessary first to go back." Thus, as the poems dramatize, there is a regression amounting to breakdown, to a dissolution of the old restrictive consciousness, then an almost deathly
absorption in unconsciousness (symbolized by landscape) followed by a painful, difficult journey back into the conscious personality, as if the stages of evolution were being retraced in the life
of a single man: "Some of these pieces . . . begin in the mire, as if
man is no more than a shape writhing from the old rock." The
antiquity he feels in this psychic landscape suggests C. G. Jung's

concept of a collective unconscious: "Sometimes one gets the feeling that not even the animals have been there before; but the marsh, the mire, the void, is always there, immediate and terrifying."[6]

This muddy marsh before human history corresponds both to Wordsworth's oceanic reservoir and begetter of individual souls in the "Intimations" ode and to W. B. Yeats's "frog-spawn of a blind man's ditch" in "A Dialogue of Self and Soul." Roethke's source, like Yeats's, is presented so as to acknowledge the terror and misery associated with this primordial symbolic water, as well as its fertility. Thus, Roethke's image of the origin of consciousness resembles that of his much-admired W. B. Yeats more than that of Wordsworth. Roethke did, however, name the book of his following *The Lost Son* with a phrase from Wordsworth. "Praise to the end!" occurs in *The Prelude*, book 1, in a passage dealing with exactly this process of cyclical separation/return of a developing consciousness in respect to nature/unconsciousness, which Roethke treats in more explicitly psychological terms.[7]

Karl Malkoff points out that Maud Bodkin's *Archetypal Patterns in Poetry* (with its long exegesis of "The Ancient Mariner" in terms of the "rebirth archetype") was the "application of Jung's ideas to poetry with which Roethke was unquestionably familiar." In his analysis of two other short poems from *The Lost Son*, "Night Crow" and "River Incident," Malkoff establishes the connection between those "unconscious forces" within the mind, the psychic residue of ancestral experience (which Bodkin deals with as "archetypes") and the poetic method of Roethke. Like "Night Crow," he argues, the "atavistic imagery of 'River Incident' probes still further into the nature of the collective unconscious. The protagonist, with sea water in his veins, is taken back to his origins, to man's origins":

> . . . I knew I had been there before,
> In that cold, granitic slime,
> In the dark, in the rolling water.

The return to this "slime" and "water" is seen as the necessary regressive journey for the man who has encountered an obstacle "with which he cannot cope."[8]

Both his own experiences and intuitive inclinations and Maud Bodkin's Jungian analysis of "The Ancient Mariner" appear to have prepared Roethke to deal in poetry with "a state of introversion and regression, preceding a kind of rebirth." And Bodkin had made explicit for Roethke a connection between Jung's "unconscious contents . . . disfigured by the slime of the deep" and Coleridge's "slimy things" that lived within the shadow of the Ancient Mariner's becalmed vessel. Having adduced some of the many references to slimy yet glowing seas that J. L. Lowes found as sources for the poem in Coleridge's reading, Bodkin suggests the paradox that meaning and beauty were to be found in things initially repulsive and alien. "We begin to see what kind of symbolic value the imagination of Coleridge, ever seeking a language for something within, would feel in those shapes, slimy and miscreate in the stagnant water, that yet glowed with gemlike colour and strange fire." In psychological terms, the value of the slime of the unconscious is made clear when the more conscious self, forced by crisis, comes back to this primal origin and is fertilized, reborn through its contact. But such a return, such a "night journey," associated by Bodkin with Jonah's trip into the whale's belly, is dangerous and repugnant to the conscious personality.[9] Returns to the unconscious and its primal sea, therefore, are seen as episodes of death and rebirth.

In the beginning of "The Lost Son," Roethke makes explicit what has to be fished for with some ingenuity in "The Ancient Mariner": that the journey away from the world of the expected, into a different order, is psychic. There is an initial indication of death, a death that pulls the poet downward, into contact with underground spaces of the landscape.

> At Woodlawn I heard the dead cry:
> I was lulled by the slamming of iron,
> A slow drip over stones,
> Toads brooding wells.

The death was perhaps that of the poet's father, although we cannot know it at this point.[10] Here we feel primarily the sense of absorption into another level of being: somnolent, identified with subterranean "drip," close to the perspective of toads. "All the leaves stuck out their tongues" makes us sense that nature is vital yet taunting. Feeling himself incorporated into decay, the poet invites creatures of this minimal, unconscious level to aid him.

> I shook the softening chalk of my bones,
> Saying,
> Snail, snail, glister me forward,
> Bird, soft-sigh me home,
> Worm, be with me.
> This is my hard time.

The conscious self feels soiled, humiliated, useless, and has to call on elements of nature's unselfconscious process for models of how to adapt to the world of dissolution, of loss of the former identity.

The poet is becalmed, like the Ancient Mariner—in a fertile place but in a sterile condition.

> Fished in an old wound,
> The soft pond of repose;
> Nothing nibbled my line,
> Not even the minnows come.

The self-absorption is isolation.

> Sat in an empty house
> Watching shadows crawl,
> Scratching.
> There was one fly.

The house of consciousness is emptied of the old contents. Yet nothing else has taken the place of adult interaction. The protagonist must continue to question, to ask for direction. Finally "Dark hollows" and "The moon" reply, cryptically. Then "The salt said, look by the sea." He must abandon the world of conversation, of external events, for the regressive quest: "You will find no comfort here, / In the kingdom of bang and blab."

At this point the sequence of images seems to shift suddenly into childhood memory—a specific time and place as in the recollections of Wordsworth.

> Running lightly over spongy ground,
> Past the pasture of flat stones,
> The three elms,
> The sheep strewn on a field,
> Over a rickety bridge
> Toward the quick-water, wrinkling and rippling.

Here is motion rather than brooding stasis, and lightness rather than the downward, bone-softening heaviness of the beginning. Childhood offers an opening to the way back, then, a "bridge" from this sterile present to the "quick-water"—where *quick* suggests "alive" as well as "fast-moving." The search into the unconscious wears a healthier aspect as the poet becomes again his childhood self,

> Hunting along the river,
> Down among the rubbish, the bug-riddled foliage,
> By the muddy pond-edge, by the bog-holes,
> By the shrunken lake, hunting, in the heat of summer.

His instinctive boyhood activities provide a model for this return to primal origins now forced upon him by a crisis in adult life. Like Wordsworth in *The Prelude*, book 1, he finds in the native self, before the sophistications of conscious intellect, a pattern for a unified being that incorporates conscious and unconscious dimensions of personality without a disastrous conflict.

Though the model of a more unified psyche is available, however, certain earlier traumas have now to be relived before healing can occur. The phallic, underwater principle of sexuality and its connection with the unconscious is evoked through a kind of altered nursery rhyme.

> The shape of a rat?
>> It's bigger than that.
>> It's less than a leg
>> And more than a nose,
>> Just under the water
>> It usually goes.

Freudians may have their field day with the rat, leg, nose (and later eel and otter) images. But clearly this poet is aware of the symbolism and is dramatizing, through a half-playful, almost child-like voice, the uncomfortable attraction-repulsion surrounding that part of the boy's physical being whose roots are most obviously in the unconscious.

Sexual conflict continues into the present in part three of "The Lost Son," as "Dogs of the groin / Barked and howled." The poet feels an alienation so strong that weeds, snakes, cows, even briars "Said to me: Die." The central wounds, his father's early death and his own unresolved feelings about that matter, have now to be faced. "Rub me in father and mother," he asks, cold and alone, needing comfort like a child. But he feared his father. "Fear was my father, Father Fear." The following appears to be a dream version of his father's death from cancer during the poet's adolescence:

> What gliding shape
> Beckoning through halls,
> Stood poised on the stair,
> Fell dreamily down?

This primordial fall seems to unglue the very structure of matter.

> From the mouths of jugs
> Perched on many shelves,
> I saw substance flowing
> That cold morning.

This scene is set, no doubt, in the house of childhood, but it is also the house of consciousness, and that structure is dissolving as the dream ends—"As my own tongue kissed / My lips awake."

"The Lost Son" sequence was continued in *Praise to the End!* (Roethke's next volume), and a section from the poem entitled "Where Knock Is Open Wide" helps clarify the scene of fall and dissolution looked at above. Section four presents a memory of the father, beginning with a fishing trip.

> We went by the river.
> Water birds went ching. Went ching.

Stepped in wet. Over stones.
One, his nose had a frog,
But he slipped out.

The language here is more obviously representative of a child's
point of view. A crane, perhaps, has speared a frog with its beak
("One, his nose had a frog"). Memories of the father are no longer
fearful. He throws back a fish when the child is "sad" for it.

Then there is the lovely image of the florist-father as virtually
God-like sustainer of the garden-greenhouse.

He watered the roses.
His thumb had a rainbow.
The stems said, Thank you.
Dark came early.

His premature death, suggested in the last line above, leads to the
following mournful cry:

That was before. I fell! I fell!
The worm has moved away.
My tears are tired.

The fall of the father, then, leads to the fall of the son, and to a
mythic sense of fall so apocalyptic that the very structure of consciousness was partially dissolved.

According to our paradigm, individuation itself, the separation of consciousness from its source, as of the child from the
womb, is perceived as a fall. But in the case of Roethke (as well as
of Sylvia Plath), this archetypal sense of exile, on the child's part,
from the "watery cradle" of childhood was reinforced by the un-
timely death of a father.[11] "The Lost Son" and those related poems
represent Roethke's attempt to modify the finality of that fall by a
modern, psychological version of Wordsworth's return to the "immortal sea" of origin. For Roethke, a commitment to psychic turmoil, to the breaking down of the old self, was required.

In "The Lost Son," following the dream-vision of the falling
figure, ordinary psychic coherence (as well as the normal structure
of the landscape) appears to break down.

Is this the storm's heart? The ground is unstilling itself.
My veins are running nowhere. Do the bones cast out
   their fire?

. . . .

All the windows are burning! What's left of my life?

The narration of psychic process moves through an associative,
often obscure progression from image to image, phrase to phrase,
as fragments of nursery rhyme and nonsense are conjoined with
suggestions of boggy landscape and phallic animal life to suggest
with maximum directness the less structured perceptual flow of a
personality in turmoil, regressing toward childhood. But as "the
time-order is going," under "the lash of primordial milk," the protagonist begins to find a way back, through childhood and again
toward the present. He revisits the greenhouse of his florist-father,
remembering the coming of light and heat after the night. The
structure of consciousness is reaffirmed in this house of cypress
and glass, with the dirt and slime underfoot. Creation is reaffirmed, reiterated, as the father and order come after the night.

Once I stayed all night.
The light in the morning came slowly over the white
Snow.
There were many kinds of cool
Air.
Then came steam.

Pipe-knock.

Scurry of warm over small plants.
Ordnung! ordnung!
Papa is coming!

A fine haze moved off the leaves;
Frost melted on far panes;
The rose, the chrysanthemum turned toward the light.
Even the hushed forms, the bent yellowy weeds
Moved in a slow up-sway.

The poet is inviting us to view this scene through the child's eyes but also in mythic terms. As Roethke said of this passage, "With the coming of steam and 'papa'—the papa on earth and heaven are blended—there is the sense of motion in the greenhouse, my symbol for the whole of life, a womb, a heaven-on-earth." But it is a heaven approached through a kind of hell, a structure of consciousness made fertile again by reunion with the primal ooze of "that dark pond, the unconscious."[12]

Through images suggestive of the original act of creation and thus, by extension, of the conscious psyche's birth from the unconsciousness of nature, the artist revisits or relives the process of his own individuation at a quite early stage. Courage is needed to face the world before creation has finished, for chaos represents an unconscious and threatening condition. Yet here the rank vegetation and slime of the earlier sections are successfully incorporated within a more stable house of glass. Even the lowest "hushed forms" respond to the benign illumination, with an "up-sway" as if moving in water.

The symbolic separation of the conscious from the unconscious, seen by Jung in the creation story in Genesis, is to be found in the landscape structures of both Wordsworth and Roethke.[13] For Roethke it is the celebration of sunrise illuminating the greenhouse, assimilating the dark materials of ooze and slime into a single, unitary round, "A Womb, a heaven-on-earth." For Wordsworth, most centrally, it is the moon-illuminated sky above Mount Snowdon in *The Prelude*, book 14, into which lighted space, from

> A fixed, abysmal, gloomy, breathing-place—
> Mounted the roar of waters, torrents, streams
> Innumerable, roaring with one voice
> Heard over earth and sea, and in that hour,
> For so it seems, felt by the starry heavens.   (58–62)

These are triumphant reconciliations of the dualities of consciousness and unconsciousness, of human psyche and the objective landscape. These are assertions of a vital correspondence between an inner structure and an outer world of experience into which we are able to project the ordering and unifying ability of imagination. Such moments transcend alienation and say, in effect, that the poet is immersed in a collective origin where nature and the deep psyche are continuous and now claims the right to interact with the landscape on a level of reidentification yet creative freedom. The resuscitation ritual, in bringing the poet's psyche back to life, makes nature live again for the senses, as fertile source of those symbols that allow artistic expression.

Thus, the regressive journey back into the minimal, the inarticulate, has ended in a return to the greenhouse-consciousness by a poet now possessed of a new body of imagery, a new language. Those minimal, unconscious things—stems rooting, shoots "Lolling obscenely from mildewed crates" ("Root Cellar"), even "bacterial creepers" in wounds ("The Minimal"), have been incorporated into a more unified consciousness and given names and meanings in the total drama of the psyche, which now claims nature as a part of itself, as its source. A very similar claim for nature as origin of the psyche's vitality, and of symbolic language, is urged by Wordsworth in the Snowdon scene we have looked at above. Those "higher minds" who are properly attuned to nature "build up greatest things / From least suggestions." They inhabit "a world of life," and, while not "enthralled" (or enslaved) by "sensible impressions," are nevertheless "by their quickening impulse made more prompt / To hold fit converse with the spiritual world" (*Prel.* 14:101–8).

Robert Pinsky argues that the Romantic impulse toward loss of self in the landscape, as seen in Keats's "Ode to a Nightingale," continued into the twentieth century, has made the poem pursue "the condition of a thing." Roethke is singled out as the contemporary poet who has carried furthest this "attempt to get back to the plainest roots of the situation."[14] Certainly Roethke's vocabulary of lowly particulars seems to assemble things into poems, yet the poems would not affect us as they do had these particulars no symbolic power. Pinsky wishes to reemphasize the necessarily abstract quality of language, to point out the illusion involved in words as objects. Yet words do evoke objects, and the discovery or dramatization of an intelligible correspondence between objects and psychic states creates a fresh artistic excitement. Eliot has said that the "only way of expressing emotion in the form of art is by finding an 'objective correlative'; in other words, a set of objects, a situation, a chain of events which shall be the formula of that *particular* emotion."[15] His own life-measuring "coffee spoons" in "Prufrock," the butterfly upon the pin, as well as the "white hair of the waves," are all objective correlatives.

The question, of course, is how the object comes to be correlated with the emotion. A name such as Lazarus, traditionally associated with resurrection, is one sort of symbol—a symbol, we might say, out of civilization's collective consciousness. Eliot, and to a lesser (but still important) extent, Sylvia Plath, depend upon these symbols. Another category of symbols was first brought into importance by the Romantics: images drawn from direct observation of nature, from personal experience and the immediate environment. Such symbols depend upon interrelationships in the developing context of the poem—that is to say, upon the total structure of landscape imagery and upon the reactions of the observer. As we have seen, a typical division or tension separates images of the observing self from that which the self observes, and which it more and more closely approaches as the poetic action progresses. As Coleridge said, "In looking at objects of Nature . . . I seem rather to be seeking, as it were *asking* for, a symbolical language for something within me that already and for ever exists, than observing anything new."[16] The drama of the Romantic self's approach to the not-self of nature depends upon just this obscure intuition that the self and the not-self, at some deep enough level, are coextensive and correspond.

The drama in one sense is that of the creation of language—thus the fascination of Adam's naming of the animals in Genesis, and, more generally, of the creation story as a whole. The drama is also that of escape from isolation, transcendence of the psyche/world, mind/matter separation made threatening by the development of science and philosophy. Roethke, like the Romantics, attempts to get back to "the plainest roots of the situation" precisely because he feels those roots in danger. Sterile consciousness threatens to enclose him, along with the many other "duplicate gray standard faces" ("Dolor"). But the experience of return to the minimal, the memory of response from mere things remains, perhaps as memory from childhood. So the drama unfolds again, the civilized man shucking off his inhibiting garments of convention and learned mind/world separation.

> Must pull off clothes
> To jerk like a frog
> On belly and nose
> From the sucking bog.   ("The Shape of the Fire")

When light comes to the greenhouse in "The Lost Son," we feel the freshness of creation having begun over again, of consciousness having risen into the light directly from its sources, and still in contact with them.

The question of archetypes is central, of course, and not finally answerable. Yet we can assert that certain situations, divisions, tensions, and contrasting types of structures are traceable from Romanticism. This scenario of individuation, this coming into light from the dark, this identification of the separateness of the self beside the all-embracing sea, or in relation to the "muddy pond-edge," is inevitable in landscape poetry deriving from Wordsworth and Coleridge, The self realizes its separateness and expressive autonomy in relation to the environment with which it formerly identified, and which it still carries within itself in the unconscious, just as we carry a residuum of ancient sea water in the salt of our blood. The language with which the new self is born is partly that of the biological facts of its condition of life and history, and partly that of the innate patterns of its development. Thus, for Roethke, objects such as stems, roots, and bacteria are caught up into a "situation, a chain of events"—which is consciousness' dissolution or loss of identity, followed by reindividuation—and thus correlated with emotion. There is nostalgia/disgust for the slime of this biological origin, and exhilaration/elegiac regret at the reseparation into freedom, autonomy, and limitation. Part of eternal, mindless nature falls into the freedom to realize itself, to act and to die. The garden of Genesis is the scene of the oldest drama.

Pinsky's evaluation of the Romantic impulse toward unconsciousness, as seen also in Roethke, is not quite fair because it fails to comprehend just how closely the mind of the poet is related to this landscape that calls him to itself. Keats feels not merely aesthetic charm and the hope of escape from personal cares in the bird's timeless song, he also feels the nostalgia of having formerly belonged to this "warm South," this Provençal landscape of collective song and underground wine. But he is committed, as we all are, to the "alien corn" of our individual adult lives. In *A Study in the Process of Individuation,* Jung describes a "fantasy-image" of one of his patients, who imagined herself "with the lower half of her body in the earth, stuck fast in a block of rock." Just as for Wordsworth, the scene of this psychic birth is beside the ocean: "The region round about was a beach strewn with boulders. In the background was the sea." With the help of the good doctor himself, in his guise as sorcerer, the stone is burst open and she is able to step free (C. W. 9, par. 525). Keats has had to be both sorcerer and figure released, and his return at the end of "Ode to a Nightingale" leaves him partly undecided between vision and dream, waking and sleep. From the perspective of the collective sea, ordinary reality may be the illusion from which we awake in vision and in death.

What disturbs Pinsky in Roethke's poetry is probably the relative absence of that more rational, abstracting consciousness that he feels should be acknowledged as a legitimate and inevitable part of the poetic act. Roethke's triumph as poet of the primal does tend to leave him perhaps too continuously in the realm of sense perception and visceral intuition, with too little of the specifically human wisdom we find in the Eliot of *Four Quartets* or in Auden or in Yeats. But we must also remember that intellectual self-consciousness has become, in our time, a potential imprisonment, a bell jar or bottle enclosing the ship of the psyche.[17] Roethke exercised his particular genius in escaping this trap by presiding over the destruction of something in himself. Having fled from abstraction to childhood and the particular, he must assert his ultimate values through symbols rather than concepts. It is therefore particularly interesting to see how, in Wordsworth's terms, he uses the "least suggestions," the "sensible impressions" of lowly organic life, "to hold fit converse with the spiritual world."

The cyclic struggle "out of the slime," the "effort to be born, and later, to become something more," of "The Lost Son," is repeated over and over in the poems that continued that sequence into Roethke's next book, *Praise to the End!*[18] We need not follow this movement in its repetitive detail and variation. Yet the poem that ends *The Lost Son* and so served as the original conclusion to development presents images that deserve our attention. The boat, a vehicle for psychic voyaging upon the "enchaféd flood" of the Romantics that became Roethke's own greenhouse-ship of "Big Wind," appears in the second stanza of "The Shape of the Fire."

> Water recedes to the crying of spiders.
> An old scow bumps over black rocks.
> A cracked pod calls.

The recession of water suggests psychic sterility, the "crying of spiders" psychological torment and perhaps personal neurosis. The psychic ship is aground, an "old scow." The sounds convey effort, heaviness, drought. The association of a "cracked pod" with this vessel more becalmed than the Ancient Mariner's implies that out of its wreck may come the kernel of a rebirth, just as a pod must crack open to release its seed.[19]

But the immediate context of rebirth is the suffering of dissolution. "What more will the bones allow?" the poet cries out. "These flowers are all fangs"—his central image of the spirituality in physical things has become venomously threatening. The agony is partly that of chaos. A few stanzas on we meet "Him with the platitudes and rubber doughnuts, / Melting at the knees, a varicose horror." This figure may be recalled from the mental institution where Roethke underwent treatment during his psychic collapse, but it is also, we suspect, a potential image of the self for this poet who stands appalled by the "melting" he must undergo. And the agony is also the threat that the human dimension, the sense of spirituality and sacredness, may be wholly lost in this descent into the primordial slime of the unconscious. "Where's the eye?" he asks, questioning a more conscious sensory function. "The eye's in the sty," he replies. The human identity may be lost entirely.

Who, careless, slips
In coiling ooze
Is trapped to the lips,
Leaves more than shoes;

Must pull off clothes
To jerk like a frog
On belly and nose
From the sucking bog.

Yet in the triumphant sections four and five, Roethke trans-
mutes the base metal of sensuality and unconsciousness into a
kind of spiritual gold. Water is the central image, as it unob-
trusively pervades memory from childhood—in particular, the
shoreline world of herons and "little crabs" in "silvery craters."
The climactic image in section five is of a Wordsworthian moment
of transcendance (like the boat-rowing episode in *The Prelude*,
1:357–400) wherein the physical, unconscious water shines with a
numinous presence.

To stare into the after-light, the glitter left on the lake's
    surface,
When the sun has fallen behind a wooded island;
To follow the drips sliding from a lifted oar,
Held up, while the rower breathes, and the small boat drifts
    quietly shoreward;
To know that light falls and fills, often without our knowing,
As an opaque vase fills to the brim from a quick pouring,
Fills and trembles at the edge yet does not flow over,
Still holding and feeding the stem of the contained flower.

Here the water is purified, and spiritualized by light. The psyche as
"old scow" in the beginning has been transformed into a "small
boat" that moves now without conscious effort, supported by the
light-filled lake, just as a rose is sustained in its vase by water filled
even above the brim. A beautiful balance is suggested by the boat's
drifting quietly with lifted oars, and by the water above the edge of
the vase that "does not flow over." The boat and the rose are images of the ego, now in contact with the source of fertility.

Harmony between opposed dimensions of personality, like that created by God with the separation of light and land (the "wooded island") from darkness and water (the lake) produces a Yeatsian Unity of Being, and the ooze or slime of earlier sections of "The Lost Son" sequence has been transformed, as by the moon's effects upon "the rotting sea" in "The Ancient Mariner." Spiritual value is thus symbolically represented as the harmonizing reconciliation between the limitlessness of "the whole air" and water (part five), versus the small boat that drifts in this surround; between the unconscious childhood when "Death was not," when the poet "lived in a simple drowse" (part four), and the mature perspective of this memory; between water and the light of this present intelligence. The boat of ego, like a rose in a vase, drifts on the surface between above and below, waking and sleep, where the unconsciousness of nature touches articulating consciousness and language.

CONCLUSION

Roethke's poetic heirs, such as Sylvia Plath (who seems to have learned her death/rebirth pattern largely from him), his student James Wright, Robert Bly, James Dickey, Margaret Atwood, and many others would probably agree with him that in the act of creation some "ghost comes out of the unconscious mind / To grope" the sill of consciousness ("The Dying Man"). In fact, the intention of probing this subterranean world through imagery of water, stones, and other geological and biological forms has become so pervasive as to constitute one of the poetic commonplaces of our time. In an essay entitled "Stone Soup: Contemporary Poetry and the Obsessive Image" David Walker has commented on the legacy of work such as Bly's 1962 *Silence in the Snowy Fields*, wherein the prevalence of the image of stones is bound up with "attention to the subconscious sources of darkness and dream." Articulating craftsmanship seems to Walker frequently surrendered in the effort to "find an entrance to the mysterious life" symbolized so often by stones.[1] This recent version of the relation between the self and the object is, of course, simply another form of the Romantic dynamic between observer and landscape (and the projected conscious and unconscious dimensions of personality) that we have traced. More than the later poets he influenced, Roethke grounded his quest into the unconscious in the work of the Romantics and of their great Modernist successors, especially Yeats and Eliot. Following his *The Far Field* of 1964, however, poetry of the 1960s and 1970s seemed too often marked by an impulse toward disavowal of the past, in conjunction with an attempt to explore the "deep image" through the verbal flux of a "new surrealism."[2]

Recognition of the Romantic ancestry of our contemporary bent toward exploration of the landscape of the unconscious should prove valuable in several respects. The knowledge that post-Modernist poets who disdained the past were in an inchoate way repeating that past should help explain how historically based Roethke is more complete than his successors. And our analysis of the Romantic dialectic between consciousness and its landscape opposite should help us appreciate the necessity of a two-term poetic—one that maintains the conscious personality and its measured (and therefore limiting) window or sill, even in the presence of most primal *sea, earth, stone,* or *water,* and the associational simplicities they imply.

The present seems a propitious moment for a reevaluation of the poetic premises of our time in relation to Romantic precedent. From this distance the tendencies of the period following World War II stand clearer, and Wordsworth and the other English Romantics seem more than ever important models for a psychological poetry wherein significance arises directly out of events apprehended in their immediacy. Modernist abstraction as centered on the individual psyche could hardly go further than the dissolutions written of by Roethke and Plath, wherein the breakdown of language's normal sequence replicated the mirror of mind in fragments. Though Abstract Expressionist painting could dispense with representational outline and still embody artistic personality in its own act, through the signatures of brushstrokes, poetry without coherent narrative was in danger of being unable to present significant events.

Sometime after World War II, helped on by the example of William Carlos Williams, poets seem to have become newly aware that the unconscious was to be made conscious and its imperatives realized, not through self-analyses, but through intuitive acts. The great need was for sufficient psychic wholeness that life and art could continue. The mind had to remain rooted in the body. The unborn meanings were to be brought into being through participation in the natural patterns of behavior—marriage, professional decisions, farming, hunting, healing, making, begetting—rather than through analytic preying upon the intuitive underpinnings of existence. And nobody in literary history had dramatized symbolic acts with mind and body alive together so well as Wordsworth. In his poetry, physical events focus whole constellations of psychic and metaphysical meanings.

The necessity was to live in the world, to take hold again of hammer or Indian pony or canoe paddle or flesh of a lover and experience a meaningful transaction. This realization is in part the bond in common among poets so diverse as Robert Lowell, James Dickey, Robert Bly, James Wright, and Margaret Atwood. Acts were the conduit between the unrealizable world of unconscious nature and the specifically human ego that must define itself in deeds and words. Poets must be the metal between charged atmosphere of intellect and old earth into which the current of meaning is grounded.

The Western involvement with reason and instinct, analysis and intuitive vision, left brain and right brain, has been far more complex and profound than can be represented adequately by a poetry ignorant of that past and unable any longer to marshal consciousness' articulating structures of form and convention. If the Romantic chorusing of ancestral voices is, as we have argued, in the direct line of descent for the poetry of our time, then we should expect future poets of this cumulative landscape to feel influence (perhaps as creative anxiety) from at least some members of their more distant family tree.

NOTES

INTRODUCTION

1. See Hugh Honour, *Romanticism* (New York: Harper & Row, 1979), 25–35; Alfred Einstein, *Music in the Romantic Era* (New York: W. W. Norton, 1947).

2. Michael Riffaterre, *Semiotics of Poetry* (Bloomington: Indiana University Press, 1978), 3.

3. Jacques Derrida, *Of Grammatology*, trans. Gayatri C. Spivak (Baltimore: Johns Hopkins University Press, 1976), 33, 34, 135.

4. Ibid., 135, 225, 261, 262.

5. Ibid., 50, 61, 267.

6. New York: Oxford University Press, 1977, pp. 40, 41, 44.

7. Ibid., 46, 44, 43.

8. See the Preface, *Psychoanalysis and the Question of the Text*, ed. Geoffrey H. Hartman (Baltimore: Johns Hopkins University Press, 1978).

9. For Coleridge's use of *unconscious*, see Humphrey House, *Coleridge* (London: Rupert Hart-Davis, 1967), 142–55. I will particularize Wordsworth's usage in chapter 1.

10. Henri F. Ellenberger, *The Discovery of the Unconscious* (New York: Basic Books, 1970), 204, 205; James Rather, *The Dream of Self-Destruction: Wagner's Ring and the Modern World* (Baton Rouge: Louisiana State University Press, 1979), 110–18.

11. Rather, 66, 110.

12. *Mysteries of Identity*, 87.

13. Bloom begins his "The Internalization of Quest-Romance," the initial essay in *Romanticism and Consciousness*, ed. Harold Bloom (New York: W. W. Norton, 1970), with several references to Freud. His *The Anxiety of Influence* (New York: Oxford University Press, 1973) applies a decidedly Freudian model to the analysis of a range of Romantic and modern poetry. Hartman's *Saving the Text* (Baltimore: Johns Hopkins University Press, 1981) wrestles with the problematic relationship between more recent French psychoanalytic and linguistic insight and the literary text.

14. Trans. Joan Riviere (London: Hogarth, 1947), pp. 20, 24, 21.

15. Trans. C. J. M. Hubback (London: Hogarth, 1948), 21, 75, 44.

16. *Natural Supernaturalism* (New York: W. W. Norton, 1971), 151, 204–21.

17. New York: McGraw-Hill, 1967, p. 19.

18. *The Origins and History of Consciousness* (New York: Pantheon, 1954), 6, 8, 14, 40.

19. *C. W.* 8, par. 750, 339, 754, 339.

20. Boston: Houghton Mifflin, 1977, pp. 119, 140, 223–313.

21. Ibid., 320.

22. *The Naked Ape*, 65.

23. "Freud and the Poetic Sublime," *Freud: A Collection of Critical Essays*, ed. Perry Meisel (Englewood Cliffs, N.J.: Prentice-Hall, 1981), 213.

24. Meisel, "Introduction: Freud as Literature," 27.

25. Quoted by Irving Sandler, *The Triumph of American Painting* (New York: Harper & Row, 1970), 206.

26. Bloom speaks of Freud's "enabling fictions." *Freud*, ed. Meisel, 229.

27. *The Complete Psychological Works of Sigmund Freud*, trans. James Strachey and Anna Freud, 24 vols. (London: Hogarth, 1961), 14:228, 230, 231.

28. *Of Grammatology*, 266.

29. Ibid., 150–57.

30. *Mysteries of Identity*, 6.

31. Ibid., 109.

32. Attributed by Meisel to Kenneth Burke. *Freud*, 21.

33. Trans. James Strachey (New York: W. W. Norton, 1962), 11.

34. *The Birth of Tragedy*, trans. Francis Golffing (New York: Doubleday, 1956), 22.

35. Jaynes, *Origin of Consciousness*, 320, 60.

36. *The Enchafèd Flood: The Romantic Iconography of the Sea* (New York: Random House, 1950), 7, 13, 12, 8, 10.

37. Ibid., 12.

38. Trans. Golffing, 38, 39, 41.

39. See *Beyond the Pleasure Principle*, 19.

40. The manuscript is labeled W and dates from February of 1804. See *The Prelude 1799, 1805, 1850*, pp. 496–99.

41. "Home at Grasmere" was printed as a volume in 1888, by William Knight in his *Life of William Wordsworth* in 1889, and not again until 1949 in *P.W.* 5: appendix.

42. See Rather, *The Dream of Self-Destruction*, 102.

43. *The Living Dead* (Durham, N.C.: Duke University Press, 1981), 3–29.

44. Bloom says in "The Internalization of Quest Romance" that "The Romantic poet turned away, not from society to nature, but from nature to

what was more integral than nature, within himself." *Romanticism and Consciousness*, 15. Yet while making the quest internal, Bloom refuses to grant the poet any objective substratum of psyche analogous to nature (17f). Hartman's essay in this same volume, "The Romance of Nature and the Negative Way," argues that Wordsworth's essential discovery in *The Prelude* was of the primacy of imagination over nature.

45. *Freud*, ed. Meisel, 217, 216.

46. *The Anxiety of Influence*, 66.

47. *Freud*, ed. Meisel, 30.

48. *The Prose Works of William Wordsworth*, ed. W. J. B. Owen and Jane Worthington Smyser, 3 vols. (Oxford: Clarendon, 1974), 1:139.

49. Freud's analysis of suicide in "Mourning and Melancholia" argues that "the ego can kill itself only when . . . it can treat itself as an object, when it is able to launch against itself the animosity relating to an object—that primordial reaction on the part of the ego to all objects in the outer world." *Collected Papers*, trans. Joan Riviere, 4 vols. (London: Hogarth, 1948), 4:163. Poets and critics in our strange century have directed dehumanizing analyses against literature, against their own impulses, and against the ego itself. The connection between the self's analytic, objective treatment of its deepest concerns and suicide is suggestive. The writer would more reasonably turn the analytic knife against dehumanizing events and conditions in the outer world than against the literary psyche.

50. *Gothic Architecture and Scholasticism* (Cleveland: World, 1970).

1   *Cosmos from Chaos:*
     The Story of Individuation

1. Robert A. Aubin's *Topographical Poetry in XVIII-Century England* (New York: Modern Language Association of America, 1936) surveys the origins and growth of a new poetic genre. Descriptions of named localities in verse became increasingly popular, paralleling the many reprintings of Denham's "Cooper's Hill," the first version of which dates from 1642. "Windsor Forest," *The Poems of Alexander Pope*, ed. John Butt (New Haven: Yale University Press, 1963).

2. *Paradise Lost and Selected Poetry and Prose*, ed. Northrop Frye (New York: Holt, Rinehart, 1951).

3. Trans. Willard R. Trask (New York: Harcourt, Brace, 1959), 78, 79.

4. P.W. 5: 35–40.

5. See Mark Reed, *Wordsworth: The Chronology of the Early Years* (Cambridge, Mass.: Harvard University Press, 1967); Mary Moorman, *William Wordsworth*, 2 vols. (Oxford: Clarendon, 1957, 1965), 1:339–42, 369–70; *Poems of S.T.C.*

6. New York, 1954, pp. 6, 8, 14.

7. Ed. Herbert G. May and Bruce Metzger (New York: Oxford University Press, 1962), 1.

8. Ibid.

9. *Defending Ancient Springs* (London: Oxford University Press, 1967), 90, 97, 92, 90, 91.

10. "A Defence of Poetry," *Shelley's Poetry and Prose*, ed. Donald H. Reiman and Sharon B. Powers (New York: W. W. Norton, 1977), 503–4.

11. *William Blake: Jerusalem, Selected Poems and Prose*, ed. Hazard Adams (New York: Holt, Rinehart, 1970), plates 3–20.

12. Friedrich von Schiller, *Naive and Sentimental Poetry* and *On the Sublime*, trans. Julius A. Elias (New York, Frederick Ungar, 1980), 116.

13. *The Origins and History of Consciousness*, 15. The child, like Wordsworth's Lucy, reliving this archetypal separation from the unconscious paradise of nature, feels its individuality endangered by the vastness of its uroboric mother. The individual ego "feels itself a tiny, defenseless speck, enveloped and helplessly dependent, a little island floating on the vast expanse of the primal ocean" (40). Lucy Gray's drowning is an excellent representation of the danger of uroboric reabsorption.

14. Neumann, 16.

15. *Prel.*, 498. The vision, by moonlight, is of a horse immobile against the sky, "Like an amphibious work of Nature's hand, / A borderer dwelling betwixt life and death, / A living statue or a statued life."

16. *Prel.*, fragment from Ms.JJ, p. 493.

17. Neumann describes the archetypal dragon fight as a contest between the masculine spirituality of the developing ego and "the despotic rule of the unconscious" (161).

18. In his *Memories, Dreams, Reflections* Jung recounts a dream wherein he found himself walking into a wind-blown fog while cupping a light precariously in his hands. Looking back, he saw the black figure of a giant, which he realized was his own shadow projected onto the mist. He interpreted the light as his consciousness and his going forward with it as his necessary progression into an adult role in its social context. His shadow symbolized the unconscious dimension of personality with its own primal wisdom, a part of himself that would always be there, gigantic, natural, but a part with which he could not directly identify if the individual life was to be maintained. The shadow was too large for comfort and frightened him like Wordsworth's vision of a striding mountain. Aniela Jaffé, ed. (New York: Random House, 1965), 88.

19. *Romanticism Reconsidered*, ed. Northrop Frye (New York: Columbia University Press, 1963), 14, 16, 17, 19.

20. Ibid., 7.

21. Ibid., 21, 22.

22. Friedrich Nietzsche, *The Birth of Tragedy and the Genealogy of Morals*, trans. Francis Golffing (New York: Doubleday, 1956), 22.

23. For the chronology of the two-book and five-book versions of *The Prelude*, see *The Prelude 1799, 1805, 1850*, pp. 512–20.

24. *Prel.*, Ms. fragment (496).

25. *Prel.* 1799, First Part, 130, 196–98.

26. *Eliade*, 78, 79. A personal experience of Jung's in Africa provided a parallel realization that the human consciousness contributes, in a sense, to the creation of the world. On a visit to Nairobi he looked across a vast savanna filled with "slow rivers" of grazing animals: "This was the stillness of the eternal beginning, the world as it had always been, in the state of non-being; for until then no one had been present to know that it was this world." The realization came to him that man's conscious perception of nature's unconsciousness constitutes a completing, creative act, and that in such creative consciousness man is sharing in the work of the creator. He saw that "man is indispensable for the completion of creation; that, in fact, he himself is the second creator of the world, who alone has given to the world its objective existence." *Memories, Dreams, Reflections*, 255, 256.

27. *Romanticism and Consciousness*, ed. Harold Bloom (New York: W. W. Norton, 1970), 56.

28. Geoffrey H. Hartman, *Wordsworth's Poetry 1787–1814* (New Haven: Yale University Press, 1971), 63.

29. Ibid., 60, 67, 38, 39, 67, 49.

30. Ibid., 46, 60, 61, 41.

31. Ibid., 47.

32. Ibid., xx.

33. *Romanticism Reconsidered*, 8.

34. "Intentional Structure of the Romantic Image," 76, 77.

35. "The Internalization of Quest-Romance," 9, 10, 12.

36. From *On Dramatic Art and Literature, Romantic Criticism 1800–1850*, ed. R. A. Foakes (Columbia, S.C.: University of South Carolina Press, 1970), 59.

37. *Prel.*, 496–99.

38. *Romanticism Reconsidered*, 14.

39. Ed. May, 9.

40. *Inflation* is a term used by Jungian analysts to indicate an identification of the conscious ego with its unconscious source, the Self. Such identification is the natural condition of infancy but dangerous later on: "In earliest infancy, no ego or consciousness exists. All is in the unconscious. The latent ego is in complete identification with the Self. The Self is born, but the ego is made; and in the beginning all is Self. This state is described by Neumann as the Uroboros (the tail-eating serpent). Since the Self is the center and totality of being, the ego totally identified with the Self experiences itself as a deity"—Edward F. Edinger, *Ego and Archetype* (New York: G. P. Putnam's Sons, 1972), 7. Such identification later in life, if

continued too long, can lead to disaster. Ixion on his fiery wheel is interpreted as the ego wrongly fixed to the circle of the Self; the ego is tortured until it is "able to separate from the Self and to see its instinctual energy as a suprapersonal dynamism" (31). In returning to the childhood materials of *The Prelude*, Wordsworth probably predisposed himself to a reidentification with the Self, which comes to a climax in Ms.W. He then used the myth of the fall as a way of separating ego from Self. Other Romantic poets were not so successful in dealing with the phenomenon of inflation.

2   Guilty Reason and the Curse of the Unconscious

1. When Coleridge visited William and Dorothy Wordsworth at Racedown in June of 1797, he was read a poem then entitled "The Ruined Cottage," and so impressed by it that he induced Dorothy to copy almost forty lines of the conclusion in his letter to a friend. The manuscripts dating before his visit appear to have included or to have implied the major events of Margaret's story, while lacking the expanded version of the narrator's character to be found in the manuscript of March 1798. In July 1797 Coleridge assisted the Wordsworths in their move to Alfoxden, within walking distance of his cottage at Nether Stowey. Here the real cooperative interchange between Wordsworth and Coleridge began. In November 1797 Dorothy wrote of a walking trip during which the two poets were "laying the plan of a ballad." This became "The Ancient Mariner," which was worked on during the winter of 1797 and finished in its first form in late March 1798. An expanded version of "The Ruined Cottage" focusing attention on the character of the pedlar was also complete by March of 1798, and the addendum written onto this Mss.B develops the early-life experiences of the poem's narrator and points the way toward the early composition of *The Prelude* in 1799. See *The Ruined Cottage* and *The Pedlar*, ed. James Butler (Ithaca, N.Y.: Cornell University Press, 1979), 3–22; *Collected Letters of Samuel Taylor Coleridge*, ed. E. L. Griggs, 4 vols. (Oxford: Clarendon, 1956), 1:325, 327, 330, 334; *Letters of William and Dorothy Wordsworth: The Early Years, 1787–1805*, ed. Ernest De Selincourt, 2d ed., rev. Chester L. Shaver (Oxford: Clarendon, 1967), 194.

2. *P.W.* 1: 374. De Selincourt records the following comment, attributed by Baron Field to Wordsworth: "I gave him the subject of his *Three Graves:* but he made it too shocking and painful, and not sufficiently sweetened by any healing views." See also Mary Moorman, *Wordsworth* (Oxford: Clarendon, 1957), 1:388n: "Parts I and II [of 'The Three Graves'], by Wordsworth, were printed from a manuscript copy in Coleridge's hand in Coleridge's *Poems*, 1893, and were thought to be by him until the discovery of the MS."

3. See Henri F. Ellenberger, *The Discovery of the Unconscious* (New York: Basic Books, 1970), 445–48. Freud apparently not only studied psychosomatic symptoms in others but suffered them himself, during the period of "creative illness" (449) that led, through suffering and self-analysis, to the central tenets of his theory in *The Interpretation of Dreams*. Similarly, Wordsworth seems to have been creatively ill until the completion of "The Ruined Cottage." See especially Moorman, *Wordsworth*, 1:286, 287.

4. See *The Ruined Cottage*, ed. Butler, transcriptions of "Ruined Cottage" Ms.A (1797), pp. 85–87, "Incipient Madness," p. 468.

5. Moorman, *Wordsworth*, 1:178–201.

6. *Letters: The Early Years*, 162.

7. If, as Butler argues (9), the "Incipient Madness" fragment represents a development of rejected lines from the 1797 Ms.A rather than an earlier attempt in the "Ruined Cottage" direction, still "Incipient Madness" clearly represents a first-person version of a disordered process of imagination very similar to that which is objectively dramatized in the decline of Margaret. We are forced to suspect a transference of the poet's mental process into his heroine, whether the expression of that process from his own point of view preceded or followed first composition toward "The Ruined Cottage." The debate over the relative priority of Ms.A and "Incipient Madness," which Butler acknowledges in a note on p. 9, is evidence of the close relationship of these important early expressions of negative imagination.

8. Quotations from "The Ruined Cottage" (unless otherwise specified) are drawn from the reading text of the 1798 Ms.B provided by Butler. l.l. 490–93.

9. Ms.D (1799), 312–29.

10. *Memories, Dreams, Reflections*, ed. Aniela Jaffé (New York: Random House, 1965), 158–59.

11. In *Aion: Phenomenology of the Self*, Jung discusses the "lower level of personality" associated with the Shadow. "On this lower level with its uncontrolled or scarcely controlled emotions one behaves more or less like a primitive, who is not only the passive victim of his affects but also singularly incapable of moral judgment." The Shadow is a portion of the *"personality as a total phenomenon"* extending beyond the ego into unconscious reaches that "cannot be grasped cognitively." The Gothic underground appears to symbolize these recesses of dark possibility. C. W. 9, pt. ii, pars. 15, 8, 7.

12. The heroine of *The Mysteries of Udolpho* considers her situation "in the wild and solitary mountains of a foreign country, in the castle, and the power of a man, to whom, only a few preceding months, she was an entire stranger; who had already exercised an usurped authority over her, and whose character she now regarded, with a degree of terror, apparently justified by the fears of others. She knew, that he had invention

equal . . . to the execution of any project, and she greatly feared he had a heart too void of feeling to oppose the perpetration of whatever his interest might suggest. She had long observed the unhappiness of Madame Montoni, and had often been witness to the stern and contemptuous behavior she received from her husband." Horace Walpole, *The Castle of Otranto,* Ann Radcliffe, *The Mysteries of Udolpho,* Jane Austen, *Northanger Abbey,* ed. Andrew Wright (New York: Holt, Rinehart, 1963), 210.

13. The emotional, irrational, and therefore wretched nature of Swift's Yahoos hardly needs comment. In Pope, we think of images such as the ineffectual Sylphs of "The Rape of the Lock," as well as Sporus in the "Epistle to Dr. Arbuthnot," who is alternately "painted Child of Dirt that stinks and stings" (310) and an inconsequential version of Satan, "at the ear of *Eve,* familiar toad" (310). *Poems of Pope,* ed. Butt.

14. Text of the first quarto edition (1751), as presented in *Eighteenth-Century English Literature,* ed. Geoffrey Tillotson (New York: Harcourt, Brace, 1969).

15. *Rimbaud: Complete Works, Selected Letters,* trans. Wallace Fowlie (Chicago: University of Chicago Press, 1966), 302.

16. *Shelley's Poetry and Prose,* ed. Donald H. Reiman (New York: W. W. Norton, 1977).

17. *Poems of Tennyson,* ed. Jerome H. Buckley (Cambridge, Mass.: Houghton Mifflin, 1958).

18. A letter by Coleridge written in the spring of 1797 contains an early draft of "This Lime-Tree Bower My Prison," together with a note wherein the poet describes himself as a Berkeleian. *Letters,* ed. Griggs, 1:335.

19. *Biographia Literaria,* ed. J. Shawcross, 2 vols.(London: Oxford University Press, 1907), 1:76.

20. Ibid., 81.

21. De Selincourt notes the resemblance between Wordsworth, as suffering from "the combined effects upon him of the French Revolution and Godwinism," and the young man described in the prefatory essay to *The Borderers* who "has deeply imbibed a spirit of enterprise in a tumultuous age" and who therefore "goes into the world and is betrayed into a great crime." *P.W.* 1:344, 345.

22. New York: Macmillan, 1960, pp. 73, 79, 74, 65.

23. "Cartesian dualism breaks man up into two complete substances, joined to one another none knows how: on the one hand, the body which is only geometrical extension; on the other, the soul which is only thought—an angel inhabiting a machine and directing it by means of the pineal gland." Jacques Maritain, *The Dream of Descartes* (Port Washington, N.Y.: Kennikat, 1944), 179. Quoted by Allen Tate, "The Angelic Imagination," *The Man of Letters in the Modern World* (New York: Scribner's, 1955), 122.

24. *The Notebooks of Samuel Taylor Coleridge*, ed. Kathleen Coburn, 4 vols. (New York: Pantheon Books, 1957), 1: entry 1770.

25. *Memories, Dreams, Reflections*, 160.

26. Moorman, *Wordsworth*, 1:209, 211.

27. The journey on foot across Salisbury Plain in the late summer of 1793 was apparently one of the most evocative episodes of Wordsworth's poetic career. Not only did the various Salisbury Plain poems originate in this experience, later characterized as seeing "Our dim ancestral Past in vision clear" (*Prel.* 13:320), but the continuation of the journey up the river Wye led to the first visit to Tintern Abbey, preparatory to the famous return five years later, and to the encounter with the little girl described in "We Are Seven." *P.W.* 1:360; Moorman, *Wordsworth*, 1:237.

28. Moorman, *Wordsworth*, 1:235.

29. The evolution of "Salisbury Plain" of 1793–95 through "Adventures on Salisbury Plain" of 1795–99 to "Guilt and Sorrow; or, Incidents Upon Salisbury Plain," published in 1842, is traced, with reading texts and transcriptions, in *The Salisbury Plain Poems of William Wordsworth*, ed. Stephen Gill (Ithaca, N.Y.: Cornell University Press, 1975). References to the text of 1793–94.

30. Moorman, *Wordsworth*, 1:339, 401–2.

31. John Locke, *An Essay Concerning Human Understanding*, ed. A. C. Fraser, 2 vols. (Oxford: Clarendon, 1894), 1:174, 175.

32. Betty J. Dobbs, in *The Foundations of Newton's Alchemy* (Cambridge: Cambridge University Press, 1975), argues that Newton's alchemical studies influenced his mature conception of gravitational force away from pure mechanism: "The universe lived again as Newton's thoughts swung on toward the *Principia* in the 1640's, for forces and active principles were everywhere. Not only was there the attractive force of gravity binding the planets and the stars into a vibrant whole, there was also activity in the substructure of matter. Gone, to Newton's mind, were the inert particles of Cartesian matter resting quiescently together between impacts" (212). E. A. Burtt, in *The Metaphysical Foundations of Modern Science* (New York: Doubleday, 1954), resolves the paradox that the Newton of such speculations should have been regarded as a chief source of the mechanistic vision of the cosmos. Burtt shows how "the bulk of his scientific followers" could "blindly ignore the master's own words," in order to move from the proposition that *"bodies are masses*, to the assumption that *bodies are nothing but masses."* "Thus Newton, quite in opposition to certain presumptions fundamental in his own thinking, appeared to succeeding generations in the light of a hearty upholder of the full mechanical conception of physical nature" (253, 244).

33. The circle and the ocean are central among the symbols for the uroboros as Neumann describes them: "One symbol of original perfection is the circle." "This round and this existence in the round, existence in the

uroboros, is the symbolic self-representation of the dawn state, showing the infancy both of mankind and of the child." This is the "time before the birth of the ego, the time of unconscious envelopment, of swimming in the ocean of the unborn." *The Origins and History of Consciousness*, 8, 11, 12. It is remarkable that Wordsworth combines, in the phrase "round ocean" ("Tintern Abbey") these two central symbols.

34. According to Jung, the primitive "lives in such 'participation mystique' with his world, as Lévey-Bruhl calls its, that there is nothing like that absolute distinction between subject and object which exists in our minds. What happens outside also happens in him, and what happens in him also happens outside." *C.W.* 8, par. 329.

35. "Genesis represents the act of becoming conscious as a taboo infringement, as though knowledge meant that a sacrosanct barrier had been impiously overstepped. I think that Genesis is right in so far as every step toward greater consciousness is a kind of Promethean guilt: through knowledge, the gods are as it were robbed of their fire, that is, something that was the property of the unconscious powers is torn out of its natural context and subordinated to the whims of the conscious mind." *C.W.* 7, par. 243n.

3   Symbols of Dichotomy and the Failure of Resuscitation

1. *Poems of Tennyson*, ed. Jerome H. Buckley (Cambridge, Mass.: Houghton Mifflin, 1958); *Poetry and Criticism of Matthew Arnold*, ed. A. Dwight Culler (Cambridge, Mass.: Houghton Mifflin, 1961). See Robert Langbaum's treatment of Arnold in *The Mysteries of Identity* (New York: Oxford University Press, 1977), 51–82.

2. *Poems and Prose of Gerard Manley Hopkins*, ed. W. H. Gardner (London: Penguin, 1953).

3. Shelley's *Poetry and Prose*, ed. Donald H. Reiman (New York: W. W. Norton, 1977).

4. *Blake: Selected Poems and Prose*, ed. Hazard Adams (New York: Holt, Rinehart, 1970), pl. 16.

5. *Poems and Prose of Hopkins*, ed. Gardner, xxv.

6. *Selected Poems of Thomas Hardy*, ed. John Crowe Ransom (New York: Macmillan, 1966).

7. From "The Metaphysical Poets," *Selected Essays* (New York: Harcourt, Brace, 1950), 247.

8. The nightingales of "Sweeney Among the Nightingales" and of *The Waste Land*, ll. 100–103, and the "Whining of a mandoline" (*Waste Land*, l. 261) are particularly ironic reminders of Romantic inspiration through bird and harp. T. S. Eliot, *The Complete Poems and Plays* (New York: Harcourt, Brace, 1952).

9. *Selected Essays*, 247.

10. New York: Doubleday, 1957, pp. 42–51.

11. Weston, 123, 120, 41, 119.

12. Eliot's notes to *The Waste Land* mention at the outset *From Ritual to Romance* and *The Golden Bough. Complete Poems*, 50.

13. "Leaving the bubbling beverage to cool, / Fresca slips softly to the needful stool, / Where the pathetic tale of Richardson / Eases her labour till the deed is done." *The Waste Land: A Facsimile and Transcript of the Original Drafts*, ed. Valerie Eliot (New York: Harcourt, Brace, 1971), 39.

14. C. K. Stead emphasizes the self-divided literary personality of Eliot: "*The Waste Land* has to be seen, not as the work of an anti-Romantic, but as a poem whose antecedents are unmistakably Romantic; . . . a great deal of Eliot's criticism, particularly as it bears upon the important question of poetic composition, is likewise Romantic, despite its eye-catching anti-Romantic declarations and neo-classical catch-phrases. Eliot wore the ribbons of one party while in the secrecy of the polling booth compulsively voting for the other." "Eliot, Arnold, and the English Poetic Tradition," *The Literary Criticism of T. S. Eliot*, ed. David Newton-De Molina (London: Athlone, 1977), 200.

15. *The Waste Land*, ed. Valerie Eliot, 55 57.

16. London: Faber & Faber, 1934, pp. 68, 69, 156, 155.

17. See T. S. Matthews, *Great Tom* (New York: Harper & Row, 1974), 158, 159.

18. *To Criticize the Critic* (New York: Farrar, Straus & Giroux, 1965), 28, 41.

19. Ibid., 32, 38, 39, 40.

20. Baudelaire: *A Collection of Critical Essays*, ed. Henri Peyre (Englewood Cliffs, N.J.: Prentice-Hall, 1962), 12.

21. *Selected Essays*, 7, 8.

22. See "The Philosophy of Composition," *Selected Writings of Edgar Allan Poe*, ed. Edward H. Davidson (Cambridge, Mass.: Houghton Mifflin, 1956), 454.

23. "The Fall of the House of Usher," *Selected Writings of Poe*, 99, 102.

24. *Selected Writings of Poe*, 144.

25. *To Criticize the Critic*, 30.

26. Ibid., 41.

27. Hugh Kearney, *Science and Change 1500–1700* (New York: McGraw-Hill, 1971), 63–64.

28. Alfred North Whitehead, *Science and the Modern World* (New York: Macmillan, 1925), 48.

29. E. A. Burtt, *The Metaphysical Foundations of Modern Science* (New York: Doubleday, 1954), 98, 99.

30. *Science and the Modern World*, 54.

31. Kearney, *Science and Change*, 156–58.

32. Pp. 93, 95.

33. Kearney, *Science and Change*, 64.

34. *The Selected Poems of Ezra Pound* (New York: New Directions, 1957).

35. "East Coker," pt. 4, *Complete Poems*.

36. John Russell, *The World of Matisse 1869–1954* (New York: Time-Life, 1974), 56.

4   *Romantic Duality and Unity of Being*

1. *Poems of W.B.Y.*; *Auto.*, 175; *A Vision* (New York: Macmillan, 1971), 277.

2. *Auto.*, 71, 88, 111, 116, 117, 118.

3. "The Song of the Happy Shepherd," *Poems of W.B.Y.*

4. *Auto.*, 116–17, 108, 112, 143, 153, 157.

5. James Olney, "The Esoteric Flower: Yeats and Jung," *Yeats and the Occult*, ed. G. M. Harper (Toronto: Macmillan of Canada, 1975), 36.

6. *Auto.*, 119, 157–58; *E. & I.*, 45, 46.

7. *A Vision*, 142.

8. Ibid., 279.

9. Morris seems the prototype of the "fat / Dreamer of the Middle Ages" of the late poem "The Statues."

10. Olney, in *Yeats and the Occult*, 36.

11. "Expostulation and Reply," *P.W.* 4.

12. *A Vision*, 71, 72, 74, 187.

13. Ibid., 69.

14. Ed. John Shawcross, 2 vols. (London: Oxford University Press, 1907), 2:14.

15. *A Vision*, 73.

16. See "On Baile's Strand," *Plays in Prose and Verse* (London: Macmillan, 1931), 156–57.

17. "Two Songs from a Play," *Poems of W.B.Y.*

18. *A Vision*, 276, 277.

19. Ibid., 283.

20. "Two Songs from a Play," *Poems of W.B.Y.*

21. *A Vision*, 266, 277.

22. Ibid., 283.

23. Ibid., 73.

24. Ibid., 283.

25. Richard Ellmann, *The Identity of Yeats* (New York: Oxford University Press, 1964), 147.

26. Ibid., 151.

27. Ibid., 147.

28. "The Marriage of Heaven and Hell," *William Blake*, ed. Hazard Adams (New York: Holt, Rinehart, 1970), pl. 7.

29. See "The Fall of Hyperion: A Dream," esp. canto 1, ll. 81–215, *John Keats: Selected Poems and Letters*, ed. Douglas Bush (Cambridge, Mass.: Houghton Mifflin, 1959). Saturn's statue looms over the altar mountain-like, a human-featured projection of the landscape.

5   *Death and Rebirth*
     in a Modern Landscape

1. Henri F. Ellenberger, *The Discovery of the Unconscious: The History and Evolution of Dynamic Psychiatry* (New York: Basic Books, 1970).

2. *Archetypal Patterns in Poetry: Psychological Studies of Imagination* (London: Oxford University Press, 1951). For Bodkin's influence on Roethke, see Karl Malkoff, *Theodore Roethke: An Introduction to the Poetry* (New York: Columbia University Press, 1966), 52–60.

3. The current *Encyclopaedia Britannica*, for example, speaks without preamble of "the liberating influence of the Surrealist doctrine that art springs from the spontaneous expression of the unconscious mind" in a brief article on the sculptor David Smith. The pervasive influence of tribal art on Modernist painting and sculpture was documented by the 1984 "Primitivism" exhibition at the Museum of Modern Art. See *"Primitivism" in 20th Century Art*, ed. William Rubin, 2 vols. (New York: The Museum of Modern Art, 1984).

4. The sequence "The Dying Man" of *Words for the Wind* (1958) is dedicated to Yeats and marked by his metric and tone. The Eliot of *Four Quartets* sounds in Roethke's *North American Sequence* (1964), most noticeably in "The Rose."

5. John Ciardi, ed., *Mid-Century American Poets* (New York: Twayne, 1950), 67, 68.

6. Ibid., 69.

7. *Prel.* 1:350. Roethke's *Praise to the End!* appeared in 1951.

8. *Theodore Roethke*, 59, 60.

9. *Archetypal Patterns in Poetry*, 73, 52, 43, 53.

10. Malkoff, *Theodore Roethke*, 85. *The Collected Poems of Theodore Roethke* (New York: Doubleday, 1975).

11. Sylvia Plath, "Ocean 1212-W," *Johnny Panic and the Bible of Dreams* (New York: Harper & Row, 1980), 22.

12. *Mid-Century American Poets*, 69, 67.

13. C. G. Jung, *Psyche and Symbol*, ed. Violet S. de Laszlo (Garden City, N.Y.: Doubleday, 1958), 131.

14. *The Situation of Poetry* (Princeton, N.J.: Princeton University Press, 1976), 58, 53.

15. "Hamlet and His Problems," *Selected Essays* (New York: Harcourt, Brace, 1950), 124–25.

16. *Anima Poetae*, ed. E. H. Coleridge (New York: Houghton Mifflin, 1895), 115.

17. I have in mind here Sylvia Plath's novel *The Bell Jar* (New York: Harper & Row, 1971), as well as the conclusion of her essay "Ocean 1212-W" (see above), which describes her sense of fall-like separation from the things of the world. Her childhood years by the sea, after her father's death, "sealed themselves off like a ship in a bottle" (p. 26).

18. *Mid-Century American Poets*, 68.

19. Roethke's poem "Big Wind" of *The Lost Son and Other Poems* uses a fierce storm as image suggesting a chaotic sea, so that this glass house, Roethke's favorite consciousness symbol, is converted metaphorically into a ship at sea. The "old rose-house, / . . . hove into the teeth of it, / The core and pith of that ugly storm, / Ploughing with her stiff prow. . . ." Thus the potential identity between Coleridge's pleasure dome and his Ancient Mariner's sailing vessel is underlined by a twentieth-century American admirer.

CONCLUSION

1. *A Field Guide to Contemporary Poetry and Poetics*, ed. Stuart Friebert and David Young (New York: Longman, 1980), 148, 149.

2. Ibid., 149.

INDEX